Global
and
Local Polemics of Development

VOLUME II

Sustainable Development and Inclusive Growth: Histories, Institutions, Ideologies and Praxes

By the same Author

— Development Ethics

About the Editor

Dr. Prasenjit Maiti (1971-) is presently an Assistant Professor at the Public Systems Management and Human Resource Management Departments of the Indian Institute of Social Welfare and Business Management, Kolkata. He has written three books and several papers on the problems of governance and development. He was invited to the University of Southern Denmark as a Guest Professor in 2007. Dr. Maiti has also worked as a Consultant on different projects funded by the World Bank, Asian Development Bank and the Department for International Development, United Kingdom.

Global and Local Polemics of Development

VOLUME–II

Sustainable Development and Inclusive Growth: Histories, Institutions, Ideologies and Praxes

Edited by
DR. PRASENJIT MAITI

CONCEPT PUBLISHING COMPANY PVT. LTD.,
NEW DELHI-110059

ISBN-13: 978-81-8069-661-9 (set)
ISBN-13: 978-81-8069-662-6 (Vol. I)
ISBN-13: 978-81-8069-663-3 (Vol. II)

First Published 2010

Published and Printed by:

Concept
Since 1974

Concept Publishing Company Pvt. Ltd.
Regd. Office:
A/15-16, Commercial Block, Mohan Garden
New Delhi-110059 (India)
Phones : 25351460, 25351794, *Fax* : 091-11-25357109
Email : publishing@conceptpub.com,
Website: www.conceptpub.com

Editorial Office:
H-13, Bali Nagar, New Delhi-110 015, India.

Cataloging in Publication Data--*Courtesy*: D.K. Agencies (P) Ltd. <docinfo@dkagencies.com>

Global and local polemics of development / edited by Prasenjit Maiti.
2 v. cm.
Contributed articles.
Includes bibliographical references and index.
Contents: v. 1. Disquieting divides : politics of the self and the other -- v. 2. Sustainable development and inclusive growth : histories, institutions, ideologies and praxes.
ISBN 13: 9788180696619 (set)
ISBN 13: 9788180696626 (v. 1)
ISBN 13: 9788180696633 (v. 2)

1. Globalization--Economic aspects--India. 2. Globalization--Economic aspects-- Developing countries. 3. India--Economic policy. 4. Developing countries-- Economic policy. 5. Sustainable development--India. 6. Sustainable development--Developing countries. 7. Rural development--India. 8. Rural development-- Developing countries. I. Maiti, Prasenjit, 1971-

DDC 338.954 22

Preface and Acknowledgements

This Volume on Sustainable Development and Inclusive Growth is an edited anthology where contributors from diverse backgrounds and professional disciplines have united in order to share their multi-cultural experiences and research insights to add both academic value and practitioner worldviews to the ongoing debates on the best practices of sustainable development strategies worldwide.

This multi-volume book series is a global project that seeks to make available a common platform to academicians, researchers, practitioners and activists alike so that they may in turn document their pluralist voices and specific choices of sustainable development interventions and initiatives based on their own local endeavours underpinned by global compulsions.

As the Editor of this book project I must admit that my initial motivation to plan and execute such an academic exercise was catalyzed during my visit to the Danish Institute of Rural Research and Development (IFUL) under the University of Southern Denmark in Esbjerg as a Guest Professor in 2007. I am grateful to Professor Flemming Just of IFUL and his colleagues who had inspired me considerably to edit this Volume.

It was at IFUL that I first hit upon the idea of designing a book series that would suitably try to incorporate lessons learnt and research methodologies of sustainable development projects (among other related issues and concerns such as the history, institutional arrangements, case studies, land reforms, decentralized governance, community mobilization, gender empowerment, indigenous technologies, multi-stakeholder dialogues and success stories) both from the North and South.

Sustainable development is an important concern at the policy and praxes levels, as this issue leads to related concerns like political decentralization, good environmental governance, human ecology, legal reforms, institutional rethinking, fiscal readjustments, eminent domain and the overall ethics of development. Sustainable development strategies and practices have recently emerged in the context of the Millennium Development Goals as a *problematique* of Neo-Liberal and Neo-Institutional Globalization that may be ideally negotiated in terms of locally workable strategies.

Participatory development strategies can be supported by an entire array of methodological tools like Focus Group Discussions, Gender Interviews, Community Meetings, Logical Framework Analyses and Risks Assessment. Resource Mapping, for instance, is an imperative requirement for Sustainable Development Projects. Micro-planning at the grassroots must inform the aims and aspirations of the concerned stakeholders. Management of sustainable development is nearly always intrinsic to local-level realities. So it is critical to be attuned to the local insights for sustainable development projects to emerge as exemplars at the global level. This leads to our global approach as a combination of the global and the local.

Sustainable development and management indicators can be both quantitative and qualitative in nature in order to provide primary inputs to monitor different projects, evaluate progress of project implementation and guide the stakeholders to sustain the benefits of these projects. Such indicators may also evaluate the impacts of these projects on the quality of life of the stakeholders before and after implementation, and also examine the increased level of community participation and awareness-generation *vis-à-vis* project interventions.

Sustainable development plans must also strategize and implement both qualitative and quantitative methods in order to examine the ground realities and design physical interventions for different identified projects. Such interventions should generally be participatory and qualitatively differ from the conventional top-down approaches that involve measurement of project performance against pre-set indicators by using standardized procedures and tools.

Participatory development may be defined as an interactive process during the passage of which the concerned stakeholders gain access to effective decision-making either directly or *via* institutionalized dynamics. This helps to identify the needs and perceptions of the primary stakeholders, sustains project benefits even after withdrawal of the implementing agencies, monitors physical progress, streamlines civil societal institutional arrangements and develops a sense of ownership among community members *vis-à-vis* their collective assets.

Problems of sustainable development and inclusive growth may be identified by deploying participatory processes. The problems identified should be converted into need-based statements. This exercise requires prioritization of development projects. The achievements of sustainable development projects usually depend on how project beneficiaries react to the resources created, managed and/or sustained by the project initiatives.

Management of inclusive growth is generally an arrangement of value-specific interventions where progress indicates contrasting world-views, where new actors help evolve different modes of production and where dynamic stakeholder interfaces result in participatory mechanisms. Sustainable development so tends to emerge as an ongoing process that tries to resolve (with uneven success) the tension of priorities between the Centre and periphery.

I am grateful to the Publisher who has steadfastly supported my idea of editing this book project. Special thanks are due to Dr. Gunnar Lind Haase Svendsen of IFUL with whom I share common research interests and inclinations in the social sciences. I am also much beholden to the contributors of this Volume who kindly responded to my Call for Papers in a prompt manner. I am certain that their valuable papers would duly receive scholarly attention and academic recognition world wide.

August 2008 **Prasenjit Maiti**

Contents

Contributors

Dr. Prasenjit Maiti <pmaiti@vsnl.com> is a political sociologist. He taught at the Department of Political Science of the University of Burdwan during 1995-2002 before joining the Development Sector in 2003. He was on secondment as a Doctoral Fellow at the Institute of Federalism of the University of Fribourg, Switzerland in 1999. Dr Maiti also worked for the Forum of Federations, a Non-Government Organization based at Ottawa, Canada in 2003. He was invited as a Guest Professor to the Danish Institute of Rural Research and Development (IFUL) under the University of Southern Denmark at Esbjerg in 2007.

Abu Sayed <sayedurp@yahoo.com> is an urban planner and working in one of the local government organizations in Bangladesh. His major field of interest is focused on rural transportation and development.

Ali Abdel Aziz Salih <hadiasib@yahoo.com> is an agricultural economist. Dr Salih taught at the Department of Agricultural Economics under the Faculty of Agriculture at the University of Khartoum, Sudan during 1993-2007. He obtained his PhD from Purdue University in Agricultural Economics. His areas of research interest are focused on rural and agricultural development, food security, poverty and trade.

Anil K. Rajvanshi <anilrajvanshi@gmail.com> has been the Director of the Nimbkar Agricultural Research Institute at Phaltan, Maharashtra, India since 1981. Dr Rajvanshi has concentrated his efforts for the last 25 years on how to use modern science and technology to achieve environmentally sound rural development.

Binay Kumar Sahay <sahaybinay@yahoo.co.in> is a Field Specialist (Social Development) with the Gramin Vikas Trust in Ranchi, Jharkhand, India. He completed his post-graduation from Xavier Institute of Rural Development, Ranchi and a Short course in Social Development from Wye College, University of London, UK. He has been engaged in the field of rural development, especially for improvement of the livelihood of the tribal poor of Jharkhand, West Bengal and Orissa in Eastern India.

Gert Tinggaard Svendsen <gts@ps.au.dk> is Professor of Public Policy, Department of Political Science, University of Aarhus, Denmark. Dr Svendsen has been the Director of the Danish Social Capital Project (SoCap) since 2002. Among his research interests are environmental regulation, social capital and political economy. He is the author of four books and numerous articles in leading international journals.

Gunnar Lind Haase Svendsen <glhs@sam.sdu.dk> is an anthropologist and cultural historian. He has been working with the concept of social capital since 1999, both theoretically and empirically. He has mainly used the social capital approach in studies of Danish civic movements since 1800, in particular the cooperative movement, as well as in fieldwork studies. He is Associate Professor at the Danish Institute of Rural Research and Development, University of Southern Denmark. MA in Social Anthropology in 1996, PhD (History) in 2004. Member of the Danish Social Capital Project. Author of The Creation and Destruction of Social Capital: Entrepreneurship, Co-operative Movements and Institutions (Edward Elgar 2004) (co-author: Gert T. Svendsen), 3 books in Danish, 10 scientific articles in international peer-reviewed journals and numerous articles in Danish journals within history, sociology and economics. He is also the editor of a forthcoming *Handbook of Social Capital* (Edward Elgar 2007) (co-editor: Gert T. Svendsen).

Khan Rubayet Rahaman <krrporag@gmail.com> is an urban planner and now teaching as an Assistant Professor in urban and rural planning discipline in Khulna University, Bangladesh. Dr Khan has a wide experience in doing research in urban and rural issues for the last 10 years. He has completed his Doctorate Degree from the University of Tokyo, Japan in 2006 and his masters from the Royal Institute of Technology (KTH),

Stockholm, Sweden in 2002. Dr Khan is now conducting several projects focusing the issues of rural development in Bangladesh.

Krishnan Manikandan <krish_drmani@rediffmail.com> is working as a Lecturer in Economics in Gandhigram Rural University, Gandhigram. Prior to this he worked as Lecturer in Economics in Arignar Anna Government Arts College, Karaikal of Pondicherry UT. He has five years of teaching experience and fifteen years of research experience. He has published three books and many research articles. He has served in different capacities in development projects in Gandhigram Rural University, NGOs and funding agencies. He also provides consultancy services to NGOs and funding agencies. He has evaluated many development projects of Government and NGOs. He has rich extension experience in the fields of rural development such as agriculture, participatory development, watershed development, water and sanitation, joint forest management, child development and elderly care. He has conducted several training progrmmes for community members and development professionals.

Md. Zakir Hossain <zakir9913@yahoo.com> is an urban planner and teaches in the Urban and Rural Planning discipline, Khulna University, Bangladesh. Zakir has a wide range of knowledge in rural planning and governance issues in Bangladesh.

M. Shivamurthy <murthy_sandhya@yahoo.com> is a Professor in the Department of Agricultural Extension, University of Agricultural Sciences (Bangalore, India). He teaches courses in Agricultural Extension, Rural Development and Women Education and conducts research in the areas of Technology Transfer and Assessment of Technologies. He has focused on developing strategies in rainfed areas for sustainable agriculture, particularly in dryland horticulture. He has a special interest in farm extension and designing farm development plans.

Nirankar Srivastav <nirankarsrivastav@yahoo.com> is a Professor in the Department of Economics, North-Eastern Hill University at Shillong (Meghalaya, India). He did his Ph.D. from IIT Kanpur and taught at the Rohailkhand and Kanpur Universities before joining NEHU. He was awarded a Post-Doctoral Fellowship at the Massey University, New Zealand. Dr Srivastav has published three books and several research papers in the various journals and books. Currently he is Dean,

School of Economics, Management and Information Sciences at NEHU, Shillong.

Raga M. Elzaki <ragaelzaki@yahoo.co.uk> is an economist. She jointed to the Department of Agricultural Economics and Rural Development at University of Gezira, Sudan since 1994 to date. She study her Ph.D in University of Khartoum supported by DAAD (Germany). She attended various international workshops and conferences and presented some papers. Dr Elzaki has published two papers on the livestock economic issues for the poor tenants in Sudan. She is the main author of the research entitled: "Poverty among Social Groups, Effects on Farming Systems and Resources Allocation: The Case Study of Rural Sudan". Supported by the ERF, Egypt (June 2007). She is the main leader of the ongoing project "Livelihood Risk Determinant facing Female Headed Households and Role of the Livestock in Poverty Eradication in Western Sudan".

R. Chinnadurai <drrchinnadurai@yahoo.com> has completed graduation in Development Administration, Post Graduation in Rural Development, M.Phil in Micro Level Planning and Ph.D in Regional Planning from Gandhigram Rural Institute (Deemed University), Tamil Nadu. He worked as Guest Lecturer at Rural Technology Centre (RTC) in Gandhigram University for two years. Then, he worked as Assistant Professor and Administrator in "the Institute of Rural Studies and Administration" for more than 3 years (IRSA) at Guntur, A P. At present the author has been working from the last 3 years as "Assistant Professor" in the Centre for Planning, Monitoring and Evaluation, in the National Institute of Rural Development, (Ministry of Rural Development Government of India) Rajendranagar, Hyderabad. He has several articles published in the national and international journals, books and also participated and presented several papers in the national and international seminars. He has also editor-cum-author of one book and co-author of one book. He has also conducted several nationwide field-based research on various topics in the field of Rural Development.

R. Mani is currently working as a Senior Lecturer in Rural Reconstruction in the Department of Gandhian Thought and Peace Science in Gandhigram Rural University. He has also worked in different capacities in NGOs. He has done many evaluation studies of Watershed Development Programmes of Government and NGOs. He has twelve years of research experience besides a rich teaching experience to his credit. He has written three books and published more than fifteen research articles in reputed journals. He is guiding three research scholars for Ph.D. and he has guided ten M.Phil. dissertations. He possesses rich extension experience by carrying out programmes such as Participatory Learning and Action, providing Urban Amenities in Rural Areas, National Service Scheme and Watershed Development.

R.B. Patil <patilrb2001@yahoo.com> is a Professor in the Department of Sociology, Shivaji University, Kolhapur (Maharashtra, India). Dr Patil has presented papers in National and International Seminars and Conferences. He has also carried out a UGC Major Research Project. He is the co-editor of *Problems and Prospects of Development in Rural India* (Mittal, 1994), *Sociology of Environment* (Rawat, 1998), and *Environmental Movements in India* (Rawat, 2005).

Sadik Hasan <sadik_hasan@yahoo.com> is an Assistant Professor of Public Administration at the University of Chittagong, Bangladesh. He received the Master of Public Administration (MPA) from the University of Baltimore, Maryland, USA in 2000 and the Master of Social Science (MSS) in Public Administration from the University of Dhaka, Bangladesh with honors in 1994. His teaching and research focuses on e-governance initiatives in developing countries, local government, leadership styles, use of ICT in public administration and micro-credit.

Shams Eldein H. Ahmed <shamshahmed@yahoo.com> is attached to the faculty of veterinary medicine and animal production of the University of Sudan as an Assistant Professor since 2000. He also taught at the Department of Basic Science, University of Sudan. He studied for his PhD at the University of Khartoum during 1997-2000. He researches on poverty eradication by livestock rearing in Sudan. He has contributed to various poverty eradication projects.

Shankar Chatterjee <shankar_nird@yahoo.com> has been working as Senior Assistant Professor in National Institute of Rural Development (NIRD), Hyderabad. Before joining NIRD he worked as Assistant Professor in degree colleges in Assam and Tripura. Dr Chatterjee served in Eritrea (NE Africa) as Associate Professor for 2 years. He also visited Iran at the invitation of Government of Iran as Resource Person. He has already published 5 books on rural development (Three individually and two as co-author). He has published more than 120 articles in National and International Journals.

S. Sathiya Babu is a sociologist. He has obtained his Ph.D. from Gandhigram Rural University. He is currently working as the Project Manager in the Tsunami Rehabilitation Project implemented by Help Age India in Cuddalore. Earlier, he served as a development professional under UNDP in Thailand, Philippines and Sri Lanka. He has also served in NGOs in different capacities. As a development professional, he has designed and implemented several innovative programmes for the betterment of rural people including the ESHG dealt in the paper. He is a master trainer in various areas of rural development.

Tapomoy Deb <tdeb1969@rediffmail.com> is a management teacher. He holds M. Phil. (Management), MBA (HR), MSW (PM&IR), PGDHRD, DLL & B. Sc (Hons) Physics. He is Guest Faculty to a number of reputed management institutes in Delhi such as Rukmini Devi Institute of Advanced Studies, Skyline Business School, Jamia Millia Islamia, etc. He has authored four MBA textbooks on Human Resource Management, Human Resource Development, Training and Development and Strategic Talent Management besides four derivative books. His latest book is on Performance Management (forthcoming, 2008, with Oxford University Press).

1

Sustainable Development for the Rural Poor

ANIL K. RAJVANSHI[1]

Introduction

There are 3 billion people in the world who earn less than $2/day. With increased access to TV and other mass media, they aspire to an "affluent life style" which is mostly dictated and defined by the Western media. As we all know, this life style is unsustainable yet it provides the role model and living standard towards which the developing world aspires. However, for the world's sustainability this life style has to change. Becoming spiritual will help us do that.

Spirituality is the state of mind that helps us to understand that Truth is beyond the barriers of worldliness, caste, creed, race or geographical boundaries. Spirituality connects us to Universal Consciousness and gives a certain perspective in and towards life. As a person progresses on the path of spirituality, his or her priorities in life change. The focus of life shifts more towards getting personal happiness through mental peace and less on material needs and desires and hence more towards sustainability.

Spirituality also helps us become more secure. Increased internal security helps in reducing greed. When each one of us becomes less greedy, then the world will become more sustainable. Sustainability should, therefore, be practiced by each of us in our daily life. We cannot impose it in a democratic society. However, we need to talk, cajole, educate and generate awareness in young people in different fora, schools and colleges. It is a long process but it will have its effect. All of us have to be actively involved in this process, especially because of the tremendous onslaught by big companies, corporations and advertising media on people's sensibilities, exhorting them to buy more and more goods, to drive bigger cars, to consume more of the earth's resources.

The 3 billion poor nevertheless cannot wait for the rest of the world to become spiritual and use fewer resources. They need the basic necessities of life right now and want to improve their life style. Thus, greed reduction in the West and technology development for poors should take place simultaneously.

What Needs to be Done?

Development and deployment of technologies specifically designed for the 2-3 billion rural poors can help improve their lifestyles and livelihoods, while bringing them in mainstream development process. Technology intervention will also help in rural employment generation. Thus the North, from where most of the new technologies originate, should encourage rural technology development and its availability on very soft terms for *e.g.*, make freely available drug recipes, charge very little for technologies, etc.

Most of the technology efforts in the past for providing basic facilities to rural areas have been based on a "tinkering" approach, meaning a small adjustment here and there, and using "low" or appropriate technology. This approach, which has been used by aid agencies, normally resulted in incremental changes like development of improved cook-stoves or better bullock carts. Tinkering, however, has barely made a dent in the quality of life of poor people. And often, the introduction of these technologies brought other problems such as increased workloads for women.

I believe that sophisticated—or "high" —technology is needed to convert efficiently the locally available resources and materials into useful products. This is the hallmark of evolution where natural systems evolve into very efficient materials and energy converters. In this process, size reduction and sophistication of system takes place. Some of our designs and technologies are following the size reduction route, for example, computer chips, cellphones, power plants, etc. Technology developers should follow this strategy in developing rural technologies. In fact, much more sophisticated thought and high technology is required for solving rural problems since the materials and energy resources available in these areas are fewer and often only available in "dilute forms". The strategy of high technology could be used in poor areas of the world to allow maximum energy and materials to be extracted for useful end products.

Strategy for Sustainable Development

Three technology areas need to be given priority for rural areas:

1. Provision of clean cooking fuel and stoves.
2. Provision of adequate lighting.
3. Availability of clean drinking water.

Cooking and lighting constitute 75 per cent of total energy used by rural households. Together with the provision of clean water, the total energy used from locally available renewable resources like biomass becomes quite large. I believe that by using technology to improve the availability of above three items—clean cooking fuel, lighting, and clean water—to rural areas, a quantum jump improvement in the quality of life for the poor would be achieved.

The engine of rural development has to be fueled by locally produced energy. Thus efficient biomass, solar and wind technologies need to be developed. Since they are low-grade energies, very efficient energy converters are needed to provide useful end products. Emerging high technology areas like biotechnology and nanotechnology can provide solutions.

For example, liquid and gaseous fuels from biomass can provide clean cooking fuel. High technology biogas digesters running on locally available biomass and in conjunction with space age storage materials to store this gas can revolutionize the cooking energy industry in rural areas. These storage materials are similar to what is being used for hydrogen storage for fuel cells and other applications.

Similarly ethanol, bio-diesel and pyrolysis oil from locally available biomass resources can provide clean cooking fuel. NARI has developed a high tech stove running on low concentration ethanol/water (50% and above) mixture. This safe mixture can be easily distilled in rural areas and can provide clean cooking fuel. Breeding techniques for crops and using genetically modified bacteria for fermentation can further help in increasing the yields of these fuels from the biomass resources so that less land is utilized for energy producing crops. Liquid fuel production from biomass will also help create rural wealth and employment through the creation of possibilities.

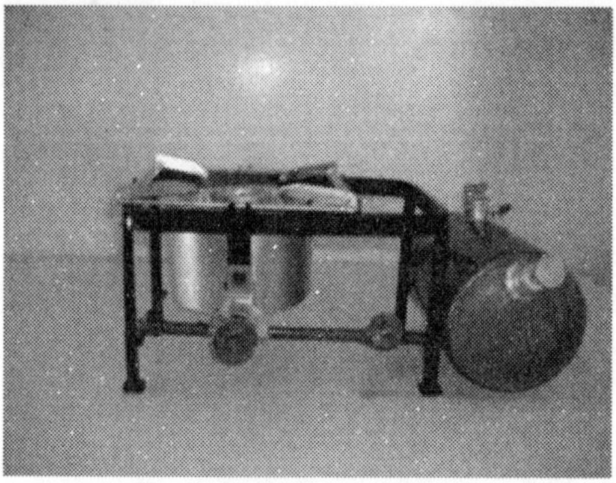

NARI Ethanol Stove

The strategy for rural lighting should be based on renewable liquid fuels and small-scale electricity producers. Nanotechnology can help in producing better mantles for biodiesel or alcohol lamps. These mantles can glow and produce light efficiently at lower flame temperatures thereby effecting energy savings. Similarly, nanotechnology can also help in providing more durable and unbreakable mantle materials. Our institute has developed a very efficient multifuel lantern called Noorie, which produces light equivalent to that from a 100-watt bulb. This lantern runs on kerosene, diesel and with slight modifications on ethanol. With efficient and durable mantles these lanterns can provide very good light for rural households.

Recent developments in materials technology has also made it possible to produce very efficient small steam engines for power generation. Similarly small scale (~ 100 kW) gas turbines, fuel cell plants, etc. running on renewables can be used for powering light sources in rural areas. Nanoengines producing 10-20 W of power and running on ethanol or methanol can power LED lamps for lighting thereby bypassing the need for bulky storage batteries. Nanotechnology may also help to produce cheap and efficient photovoltaic (PV) systems for rural areas.

Noorie Lantern with Cooking Arrangement

In the field of clean water production, nanoparticles based filters are helping to purify water. For rural areas, a micro-utility which can produce both power (~ 100-500 kW) and clean water would be a great boon. This utility company can produce power through renewables and the heat from flue gases can be used to produce clean water either through distillation or simply through boiling it. This will help in increasing tremendously the power plant efficiency. The utility can also access water resource by rainwater harvesting techniques.

Conclusions

The outlined strategy can help improve the quality of life of rural poor. It will have other benefits :

1. The use of renewables will help in improving local and ultimately global environment.
2. Fossil fuels will be conserved. These can then be used as raw material for chemicals and value-added products. Using less fossil fuels might help reduce world conflict since the pressure on fossil fuels from emerging economics like India and China could be lessened. It is, therefore, in the interest of the North to provide the latest energy technologies to developing world at very soft terms.
3. Electricity and liquid fuel production from biomass would increase rural wealth and generate employment.

Preliminary economic analysis shows that in India alone this could be a $ 6 billion/year industry.

4. New technologies will create huge market for technology providers.
5. Providing clean fuels, light, and clean water will help bring the 3 billion people into the mainstream of progress.

To my mind the highest spiritual work for mankind is to help poor people improve their quality of life. As engineers and scientists we can do it by providing right-sized technologies at the right "price" to the poor. It is a doable goal. What is needed is the direction and will of leaders both in North and South to make the life of poor people better.

Finally, it should be pointed out that rural population of the world is much more spiritual than most of us in this room. They have the great strength of being satisfied with few material comforts. Thus I believe that the provision of high technology for meeting the basic needs of rural poors together with their spiritual strength may provide a new model of sustainable development and in the process may teach the North a lesson or two in sustainability.

NOTE

1. Invited talk given in the forum "Spirit and Sustainability" at ISES Solar World Congress 2005, Orlando, Florida, USA. August 8-12, 2005.

REFERENCES

Anil K. Rajvanshi, "*Rocket Science for Rural Development*". NARI website.

Anil K. Rajvanshi, "*Nature Conservation + Spirituality = Sustainability*", ISES 2005 Proceedings.

Anil K. Rajvanshi, "*Rediscovering Fire in 21st Century*", Sci. Dev. Net article, May 2005.

Spiritual writings of Anil K Rajvanshi. *http://education.vsnl.com/nimbkar/spiritual.html*

2

Strategy for Sustainable Rural Livelihoods: An Experience from EIRFP

BINAY KUMAR SAHAY

Introduction

The eastern plateau is one of the poorest regions in India, with a population of 30 million. Annual rainfall is 1,200-1,400 mm but erratic with 80-85 per cent falling during the monsoon (June-September). Drought spells are common even during the monsoon. Soils are shallow and acidic with poor fertility and low water-holding capacity. The average land-holdings are 1-2 hectares with few irrigation facilities. The land-holding is also declining due to rapid population growth.

Scheduled Tribes are the dominant inhabitants of the eastern plateau and the majority of them produce food for subsistence, but it is usually insufficient to meet their needs. In other words, the majority of the tribal habitants of eastern India are living in a situation of "hunger", a symptom of poverty. The causes of poverty among tribal communities include illness, social and economic exclusion, lack of voice, powerlessness, lack of representation, inadequate income and growth of human resources. In other words, food insecurity is the principal cause of hunger among these tribal poor people, or we can say that poor people cannot find the means of getting enough food, either through growing or buying it, especially during periods of hunger.

Strategy against "Hunger"

Strategies against poverty or the elimination of hunger are in response to a deepening understanding of its complexity. In the 1950s and 1960s, many viewed large investments in physical assets and infrastructure as a primary means of development. From the 1970s onward, awareness grew that physical assets are not enough and as important are health and education. The years of the 1980s saw another shift and poverty reduction was seen as a two-part strategy: promotion of labour-intensive growth through economic openness and investment in infrastructure, and providing basic service to poor people in health and education. Gradually in the 1990s, governance and institutions moved towards centre stage. These emphasized strategies for attacking poverty through promoting opportunities, facilitating empowerment, enhancing security and institutions, by ensuring participation of marginalized communities.

The concept of participation has been a part of an emancipatory discourse and practice in most of the developmental programmes for the last decade. Advocates of these concepts have claimed that they allow the representation of the most marginalized groups—women and poor people.

EIRFP – Project Context, Strategy and Objectives

The Eastern India Rainfed Farming Project (EIRFP) is located in the eastern plateau region of India, which covers a part of nine districts of three States: Jharkhand, Orissa and West Bengal. It was conceived in 1994-95 with the support of KRIBHCO[1], the Government of India and the Department for International Development (DFID) of the UK, and is now managed by the Gramin Vikas Trust[2].

The operational area of the project is Ranchi, Hazaribagh and Palamau districts of Jharkhand; Purulia, Birbhum and Midnapore districts of West Bengal; and Keonjhar and Dhenkenal districts of Orissa. These districts are amongst the poorest in these States and are managed at State level by GVT State Offices in Ranchi, Baripada and Purulia for Jharkhand, Orissa and West Bengal respectively. The Project Management Unit (PMU), situated at Ranchi (Jharkhand), is managing the project in all three States. The project received relatively intensive support from a team of consultants from the UK and DFID. The PMU is headed by a

Project Manager and has a team of technical and social science specialists who support Community Organizers placed in the field for the facilitation and implementation of work at village and cluster levels The project is working in 252 core villages grouped in 60 clusters. The Community Organizers are from agriculture, forestry, livestock, aquaculture and social science backgrounds, most with post-graduate qualifications in rural development. They are posted on to a cluster and 40 per cent are women.

The EIRFP is oriented toward its goal of improving the livelihoods of poor men and women of the eastern plateau using participatory approaches. It envisages participation, poverty and gender issues for the sustainable improvement of livelihoods in these areas.

RNR To Sustainable Livelihoods

EIRFP began its life in all three States as a "Participatory RNR[3] Management Project". It is a process project and facilitates a participatory planning process for the development of a village. In principle, local problems are identified and prioritized by villagers and they identify development options for implementation with the facilitation of project staff. The programme activities cover a range of farming system components, *e.g.,* crops, agro-forestry, wasteland development, soil and water conservation, aquaculture, livestock development and irrigation.

The Community Organizers are the key functionaries under the project and usually facilitate community members in the development of a plan of their village through natural resources management and institutional development. A *jankar*[4] (See Box 2.1) system has been evolved under the project for empowering the community and transferring and adopting technologies for improvement of sustainable livelihoods of deprived and marginalized people. They facilitate the process for the identification and selection of motivated men and women with interest in working for the benefit of a community or group. The project provides a series of training programmes and exposure visits in different areas of their interest and develops expertise and skills to make available it in and around villages and avoid dependency on outsiders for their development. A number of *jankars* in areas

Box 2.1: Role of Jankar

- Motivate the community to understand the needs for development;
- Initiate vision development of community to sustainable livelihoods development;
- Facilitate the community to participate in the process, *i.e.*, planning, implementation, monitoring and evaluation of the activity or programme;
- Adoption of suitable technologies by the community;
- Empowerment of the community and distribution of their roles and responsibilities in the development process;
- Linkage with GOs, NGOs and others for development and institution-building; and
- Dissemination of project approach to surrounding areas to achieve the wider goal.

Source: Empowering Community for Sustainable Livelihoods through Jankar System: An Experience from EIRFP by B.K. Sahay — *Kurukshetra* (India): A Journal Published by Department of Rural Development – Feb. 2002

of crops, trees, aquaculture and Soil and Water Conservation (SWC) have been identified and trained to facilitate and support the community within their villages.

In terms of the general approach, EIRFP has developed from a "provider" project of RNR technical know-how and financial support, to an enabler project which encourages villagers to autonomously address a wide range of livelihoods constraints. With the facilitation of the project, villagers have undertaken different farm and non-farm activities such as crops, trees, watershed management, livestock development and different income-generation activities. They have further scaled up the activities to increase their income and ensure their food security. The technology transfer has been made through training and exposure of the community and strengthening of the *jankar* system in each village. A series of community and *jankar* training has been organized for this purpose in and outside villages.

Over the years, it has kept these emphases but has changed in many respects—as the project reflected and learnt from its experiences in the field. The RNR focus remains because natural resources remain a main source of livelihood for people in the project area, but it is not the only source. For example, even poor and landless people are mainly dependent on the village for fuel wood and fodder requirements, but have to rely upon their own wage labour for other requirements. The project has, therefore, had to develop a differentiated approach based on existing livelihoods strategies. It also seeks to get villagers themselves to address poverty in both social and economic dimensions—in particular the social exclusion and disempowerment of women. The work with people classified as BLAD[5] and women's empowerment are indicators of this change.

Gradually the project has realized that poverty among tribal poor people is strongly associated with lack of assets, or inability to use the assets for productive purposes. The assets in this context include human, social, natural, physical and financial capital (Careny, 1998). The project's participatory process leads to increased opportunities available to individuals, groups and communities for improvement and scaling up of assets for the sustainable improvement of their livelihoods.

Evolution of "Asset Based" Livelihoods Improvement Strategy

In the beginning, because of its priority, due importance was given under EIRFP to RNR issues using a participatory approach. With the facilitation of the project, villagers have undertaken different farm and non-farm activities to reduce the poverty or hunger situation. Gradually the project envisaged an holistic approach for sustainable improvement of livelihoods by mobilizing the existing five capitals (Tomar *et al.*, 2001) in and around villages. A brief description of project interventions centred on the existing capital for sustainable improvement of livelihoods is presented below.

(a) *Social Capital*

Social capital includes members of groups, castes, networking, relationships with institution, and access to wider institutions of society through which people pursuer their livelihoods. While working with tribal and marginalized sections of the community, project realized that a different set of coping strategies is required to get their participation. The project believed that, "Community participation in a development programme is not only ensuring the involvement of people in rendering financial assistance, giving one's own labour, or resource mobilization. In a true sense, participation of people can only be considered if they also have a role in the formulation, implementation, monitoring and evaluation of a programme."

The project places a strong emphasis on people's participation in planning, implementation, monitoring and evaluation of the activities using six steps under a participatory approach (Box 2.2).

Box 2.2: Participatory Approach to Development

Six Steps

- Rapport Building,
- Analysis of livelihoods and existing resources,
- Group Formation,
- Group Planning,
- Participatory Impact Monitoring, and
- Participatory Impact Evaluation.

Refer Flow Chart for Process of GVT under Participatory Approach.

To bring marginalized sections of the community—especially tribal groups and women into the mainstream of development—the project envisaged = creating an environment and level of understanding among the community to get their participation. The project has engaged Community Organizers to initiate the step of rapport-building. A strategy has been adopted for rapport-building and to ensure participation, *e.g.*, door to door visits, organizing meetings, distribution of vegetable seeds to enter into the kitchens of women.

Participatory Rural Appraisal (PRA) based on the five capitals of a sustainable livelihood has been used to analyse livelihoods (Sahay, 2003, Understanding) and to make the community realize about existing assets in and around the villages and further plan accordingly for the sustainable improvement of livelihoods.

The "group focus strategy" (Box 2.3) of the project provides social recognition, status and security, especially to the poorest, most marginalized and vulnerable groups including women, and minimizes gender discrimination and encourages them to get involved in the decision-making process.

Box 2.3: Group Focus Strategy – "Why"

- To get a common understanding of villagers problems and solve them,
- To make collective planning possible,
- To provide a mechanism for implementing activities which will create new assets or allow for better use of existing ones,
- To allow a sense of collective responsibilities and system of accountability to be set-up, and
- To provide a mechanism for sustainable livelihoods improvement.

Formation of groups, starting of income-generation activities by women's group, cash payments in hand to women under the SWC, are a few example under EIRFP centred on steps of a participatory approach to strengthen social capital. The strength of social capital is also reflected in the case study presented in Box 2.4.

Box 2.4: Shifting towards a Better Livelihood (A Case Study of a BLAD Household)

A little support can help overcome hurdles—no one realizes this more than Ravati Mahato of Khanasdih, Kaipara, West Bengal. A widow with leprosy—and with a marriageable daughter—she was discarded by society and left to struggle for her survival. It was at this juncture when EIRFP came forward and identified her as a BLAD household. Through a rapport-building process, EIRFP facilitated her to develop a strategy to fight the situation. She was given two goats with help from the project and two more goats were provided through a group fund by villagers who understood their community's social responsibilities. On realizing the urgent needs of fulfilling day-to-day requirements, additional support was given to Ravati in the form of short-term paddy dehusking activities that assured her regular income.

It is a different story now. The dehusking activity not only helped her survive, but she has built up a bank balance of Rs 2,000. She now has ten goats and established a business with access to the wider market. On the top of all this, she has been able to arrange her daughter's marriage. And she has been recognized by society.(*Sahay, 2003 " Poverty Ranking Tools....."*)

To avoid dependency, the project envisaged a participatory monitoring and evaluation system and involved the community and *jankars* in the process. The Strength, Weakness, Opportunity and Threat (SWOT) and Livelihood Asset Status Tracking (LAST) are tools used to strengthen the process.

(b) *Human Capital*

Skills, abilities, knowledge, willingness to work, entrepreneurship, good health and awareness are important assets for individuals or communities to improve their livelihoods. Enhancement of skills and capacity of men and women is one of the important interventions under the project. The community has been exposed and trained to develop an understanding on different aspects including the importance of a group and its management and about different technologies for adoption. The *jankar* system is the most suitable example of project initiation for the development of human assets (Box 2.5).

Box 2.5: Benefits of *Jankar* System

- Motivation of community becomes easier,
- Technology can easily be transferred to the community for its adoption,
- Confidence development among the group members to make their own plan and implement it effectively,
- The skill and capacity development among *jankars* reduces dependency,
- Helps to sustain activities and groups,
- Empowerment of women and deprived sections of the community for their active participation in decision-making,
- Dissemination becomes cost effective and sustainable, and
- Leads to integrated RNR development and improvement of livelihoods (*Sahay, 2002, Empowering…*).

An average of five *jankars* have been trained in one group and after five years of their functioning some have been identified as dissemination *jankars* to disseminate the process in surrounding villages. The project has initiated the process to link *jankars* with government programmes to get financial support to these self-motivated and trained *jankars* to ensure the sustainability of the system. The project has developed around 1,500 men and women *jankars*. Women *jankars* are working on a par with men *jankars* and are self-motivated and working without financial support from the project. Now the trained *Jankars* are being absorbed by NGOs, GOs and PRIs* to provide technical support for the implementation of their developmental programmes more effectively.

(c) *Financial Capital*

Financial assets available to people, *e.g.,* savings, credit and regular remittances, provide them with different livelihood options. The intervention under EIRFP includes facilitation of the member of groups for their contribution and generation of group funds to provide improved security and access to the credit at their door. With the facilitation of *jankars*, 1,498 groups have been formed, some exclusively men or women, and some mixed. They have generated a total of Rs. 23,307,903 in group funds. Group details are presented in Table 2.1.

Table 2.1: State-wise Group Details under EIRFP

States Covered	*Type of Groups*				*Group Fund (Rs.)*
	Male	*Female*	*Mixed*	*Total*	
Orissa	221	241	61	523	2,250,421
West Bengal	301	265	28	594	8,586,220
Jharkhand	205	133	43	381	9,258,199
Total	**727**	**639**	**132**	**1498**	**23,307,903**

The groups contribute part of their earnings from activities undertaken to the group fund, which has provided working capital to diversify their activities and scale up. Marginalized groups, including women, have easy access to credit to meet urgent subsistence, medical or emergency needs, and even some working capital to create productive assets for them. The facilitation and empowerment further leads to access to government programmes and financial institutions to play a wider role in their livelihoods improvement.

* PRIs—Panchayati Raj Institutions—a local level people's institution.

(d) *Natural Capital*

Natural resources—land, water, forest and the environment—are a gift of nature to humans to make them useful for their livelihoods. The project facilitated communities to undertake different farm and non-farm activities which have extended entitlement, even for marginalized sections of community, both men and women, as a productive asset directly or through sharing arrangement. The groups and *jankars* play a vital role in development of natural resources using their skill and financial strength for its optimum utilization through crops, trees and aquaculture activities based on these natural resources. It also leads to management of common property, *e.g.,* forest, land, water resources and wasteland, through collective effort. There is evidence of a 72 per cent increase in area through SWC measures and a 54 per cent increase in productivity and increase in gross cropped area with the introduction of High Yielding Varieties (HYV) cropped seed and its adoption. Sixty per cent of the wasteland area has been covered by agro-forestry. A number of households have also adopted different income generation activities. Group members have further diversified their farm-based activities to non-farm based activities to meet their requirements during hunger periods. Social, human and financial capital play a vital role in this direction and create an opportunity for using existing natural resources in and around the village to meet subsistence requirements during hunger situations.

(e) *Physical Capital*

Physical capital includes basic infrastructure and the production equipment and means which enable people to pursue their livelihoods. Collective action leads to development of physical assets as per the needs of a community, either through linkages with Government or with the support of people to get long-term benefit. Examples adopted in EIRFP villages include construction of community halls, link roads, renovation and excavation of ponds, installation of hand and irrigation pumps.

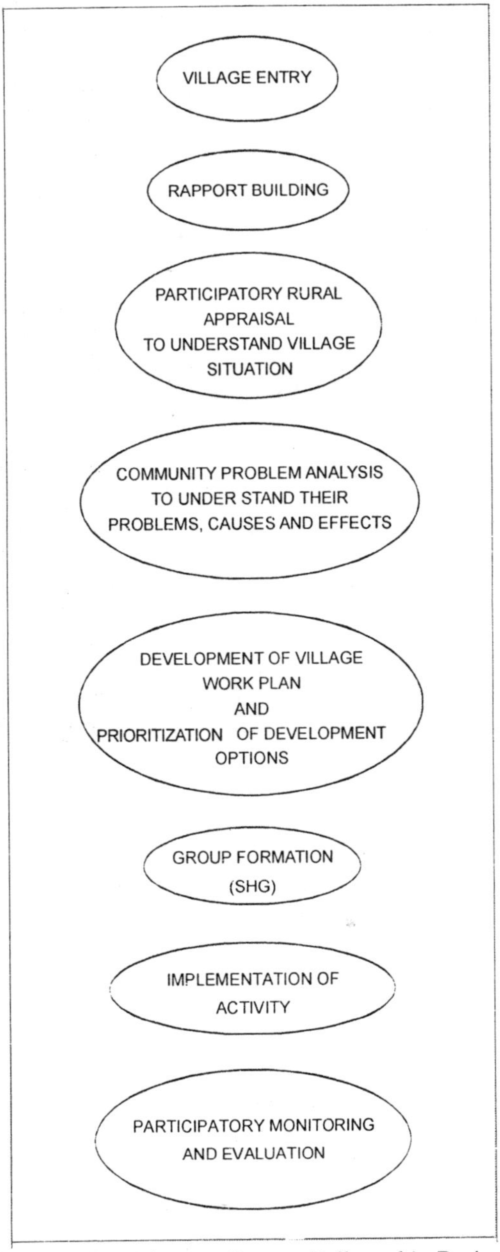

Flow Chart 2.1: Participatory Process Followed in Project Villages

Box 2.6: Project Interventions and Impact on Different Capital

Asset/Capital	*Objective*	*Types of Interventions*	*Outcomes/Impact*
1. Social Capital	More Supportive Social Environment	▪ Rapport building and realization of existing capital with in village. ▪ Identification and facilitation of the deprived including BLAD. ▪ Facilitation for collective action/group effort. ▪ Group formation and its strengthening. ▪ Promotion of male, female and mixed group. ▪ Gender Sensitization. ▪ Facilitation to the women for women liking activities for their participation in decision making. ▪ Payment in hand against SWC works. ▪ Promotion of activities for inclusion of BLAD.	▪ 53 per cent members of groups are from deficit category and 47 per cent women are the members of group formed and 72 per cent groups have strong saving and credit system. ▪ Work plan for village developed. ▪ Women are empowered and 47% are trained as *jankar* and working as par men. ▪ 79 per cent group members are participating in decision-making process and development of village work plan.
2. Human Capital	Awareness, skill, capacity-building and transfer of technology for sustainable livelihoods.	▪ A series of infield training and exposure organized on different components. ▪ Identification of *jankar* on different components their skill upgradation on different components. ▪ Need-based training and scaling up of the activities and its diversification. ▪ Training of community, *jankar* on groups, its management and monitoring and evaluation of activities.	▪ Introduction and adoption of *jankar* system. ▪ Formation, development and strengthening of groups. ▪ Dissemination of process and approaches by dissemination *jankar*. ▪ Recognition and hiring of service of *jankar* by different organisation including PRI/Govt. ▪ Increase in technical know-how. ▪ More communication. ▪ Higher degree of awareness among the members. ▪ Increase in confidence. ▪ More children attending School.

(*Contd.*)

Box 2.6—Contd.

Asset/Capital	*Objective*	*Types of Interventions*	*Outcomes/Impact*
3. Financial Capital	Access to Financial Resources	▪ Facilitation for small saving in-group funds. ▪ Group fund development and its management. ▪ Linkages with financial institution and Government programmes.	▪ Rise in thrift habit. ▪ Rise in source of loan ▪ Group fund generated ▪ Improved security to the deprived ▪ Credit at door.
4. Natural Capital	Access to and Better Management of Natural Resources.	▪ Non-farm and farm activities undertaken by groups based on existing natural resources in and around the villages. ▪ Management of common property i.e. forest, land, water resources, wasteland etc. through collective effort. ▪ Introduction of technology for its adoption to improve agricultural services.	▪ 72 per cent increase in area through SWC measure. ▪ 54 per cent increase in productivity and increase in gross cropped area with the introduction of HYV cropped seed and its adoption. ▪ 60 per cent of the waste land area has been covered by agro-forestry.
5. Physical Capital	Access to Facilities and Infrastructure.	▪ Introduction of improved tools as per requirements. ▪ Creation of infrastructure as per need of community with participation of group's members. ▪ Linking the groups with Government programmes for improved infrastructure.	▪ More well/hand pumps for drinking purpose created. ▪ Increase in irrigation facilities in and around the village. ▪ Improved housing condition of the deprived community in the villages.

Box 2.7: Transforming Livelihoods of Poors for Achieving Sustainability

CASE [I]

Rajhar is one of the village adopted by EIRFP—a tribal dominated village situated in Hazaribagh district of Jharkhand—spell a remote, poorest, traditional and habitant of Mahato and ST community with poor infrastructure facility in the village. The livelihoods of these tribes depends upon the forest and mono-cropping practice.

One of the group "Krishi Club" of Rajhar cluster was identified by EIRFP for pilot project to promote micro-finance/micro enterprise, leads the group to undertake a poultry activity on their upgradation of skill on poultry farming. The project facilitated the group for linkage with Block and Bank. After getting assurance from a Bank, the group constructed a poultry house by using their contribution in cash and labour and further got a loan of Rs. 50,000 to start a poultry business and are running successfully after repayment of Bank loan out of the income from it.

Now the poultry business has become a primary source of income and it leads to undertake various other activities like paddy dehusking, goatary, mate making, sattu making etc. in groups. The skill and capacity of the member have improved accordingly and are now playing key role on transforming their livelihoods for sustainable development.

CASE [II]

Construction of a check dam in Muretha village of Bagda cluster is another example of creating income generation opportunity by EIRFP through effective use of natural resource. The Muretha village is predominated by scheduled caste. The topography of village is highly undulated with sandy soil. One perennial *nala* exist in the village rarely used for irrigation purpose. The livelihoods of the families in surrounding village were dependent on mono-cropping.

Consequently the villagers decided for the construction of a check dam on the *nala* so that they can make an effective use of it. An intensive plan was developed by villagers with the support of project staff to develop the area on watershed basis. The construction of check dam completed in 1999 and 45 ha. land has been treated by field bund with the support of project.The project has also provided support in installation of lift irrigation to optimized the benefits.

(Contd.)

Box 2.7—Contd.

The scenario has been now completely changed. The group members are taking various crops covering 70 acres on individual/community basis and are practicing double crops including the marketable vegetable for cash generation.

Thus the participatory process adopted by the project leads a step forward for transformation of the livelihoods even of the deprived men and women.

Source: GVT NEWs April–June 2002.

6. Impact of Interventions under EIRFP

The EIRFP envisaged an holistic approach to ensure sustainable improvement in livelihoods, especially in marginalized section of the community. The processes adopted have their epicentre in social and human capitals to achieve their goal. The project has used capital-based PRA for helping the community realize about existing assets in and around the villages and also to facilitate the community in well-being ranking (Sahay, 2003, Tools....) in BLAD, deficit, self-sufficient and surplus category, and to ensure the participation of target groups in the process of development. Strengthening of social and human capital leads toward generation of financial capital through small savings within the group. The upgrading of skills through training, exposure and the introduction of technology facilitate group members in judicious use of existing natural resource such as land, water and forest to ensure food security. The impact of project interventions is being reflected in case studies presented below:

Empowerment and participation in decision-making processes has also ensured creation of infrastructure by establishing long-term linkages with Government programmes. Gradually the effort leads toward institutional sustainability with more knowledge, capacity, confidence, greater skill, financial support and further greater access to Government programmes. The initiative has also been taken to replicate the learning to other organizations, NGOs, GOs, PRIs and FIs to ensure its sustainability.

EIRFP has also taken an initiative to quantify the achievements of project interventions. It has evolved a "LAST"[6] tool to measure the degree of improvement made in livelihoods components. The LAST tool has been developed using a participatory process and is based on the criteria of the five capitals. The findings are measured on a matrix scale indicating degree of improvement made in a limited time span. The results (Box 2.8) show that effort in community involvement and social issues seem to have a direct impact on livelihoods. In five-year intervals of project interventions, social and human capital has been increased by 114 per cent and 83 per cent, whereas financial and natural capital have grown by 77 per cent and 69 per cent. The results also reflected a shift of deficit to self-sufficient by 23 per cent, 96 per cent of vulnerable—BLAD shows some improvement of which 71 per cent have moved to the next category.

Box 2.8: Livelihoods in Project (Overall Avg.)

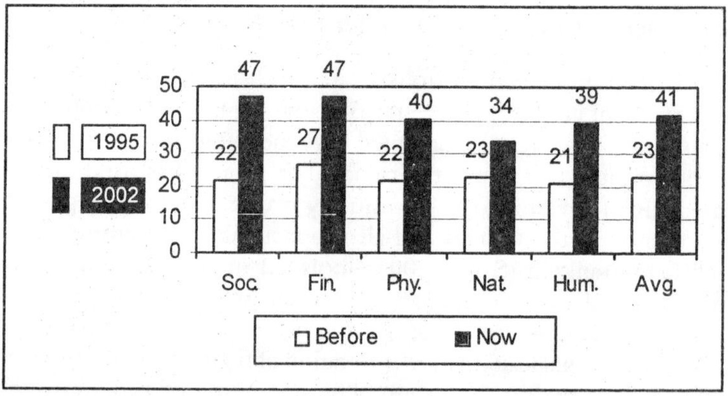

The emerging organizational structure of the project in the form of the Gramin Vikas Trust—a combination of Government system and flexibility in work as an NGO—for the management of EIRFP, shows the process using a participatory approach and the *jankar* system are playing vital roles under the project for sustainable improvement in livelihoods.

Conclusions

The livelihood profile of the different economic categories identified by the project through poverty ranking show that each of these categories has a different set of coping strategies to deal with the situation of scarcity and distress. Very poor or lower deficit households migrate over a long period of time or are engaged in low return activities such as head loading and sale of fuel-wood.

People in the BLAD category in particular live under conditions of malnourishment and distress. These households do not get access to easy loans for consumption purposes to deal with the distress situations.

The project realized that poverty is strongly associated with lack of assets or inability to use assets for productive purposes and scaling up. The project strategy encouraged the community in their realization of the existing five capitals for the improvement of their livelihoods. The improvement in social and human capital increased the opportunities available for the sustainable improvement in livelihoods. This has been reflected through qualitative indicators of change such as empowerment processes, social recognition, confidence among deprived sections and women, scaling up of different capital, capacity and dealing with outside resources, over the quantitative targets leading toward sustainable improvement of livelihoods.

NOTES

1. KRIBHCO – Krishak Bharati Cooperative Limited, a cooperative under the Ministry of Fertilizer, Government of India.
2. Gramin Vikas Trust (GVT) – An organisation established and supported by KRIBHCO, GOI and DFID.
3. RNR is Renewable Natural Resources.
4. A *jankar* is a para-professional, a female or male member of the community, who serves as an internal catalyst, information bank, service provider, trainer, disseminator and innovator (Source: *Kurukshetra* (India), 2002).
5. BLAD – Between Life and Death category of household, *i.e.,* widow, handicapped, socially or mentally handicapped.
6. LAST: Livelihoods Asset Status Tracking.

REFERENCES

Carney, Diana, 1998, Sustainable Rural Livelihood: What Contribution can We Make? London, U.K: Department for International Development.

Tomar, V.S.; Gangwar, J.S. and Sahay, B.K., 2001, Evolution of Sustainable Livelihood Strategy for Poor Men and Women: Experiences of EIRFP. Copenhagan, Denmark: www.anthrobase.com.

Sahay, Binay Kumar, Feb 2002, Empowering the Community through *Jankar* System: An Experience from EIRFP, New Delhi, *Kurukshetra* (India).

Sahay, Binay, October-December 2003, Poverty Ranking Tools—Experience of EIRFP in Addressing Poverty, Bangkok, Thailand, *Stream* Journal. www.streaminitiative.org.

Sahay, Binay, October-December 2003, Understanding of Assets-Based Livelihoods through Participatory Rural Appraisal to Eliminate Hunger, Bangkok, Thailand, *Stream* Journal. www.streaminitiative.org.

Abbreviations

BLAD	: Between Life and Death
DFID	: Department for International Development
EIRFP	: Eastern India Rainfed Farming Project
Fls	: Financial Institutions
GVT	: Gamin Vikas Trust
Gos	: Government
HYV	: High Yielding Varieties
KRIBHCO	: Krishak Bharati Cooperatives Limited
LAST	: Livelihood Asset Tracking
NGO	: Non Governmental Organization
PRA	: Participatory Rural Appraisal
PMU	: Project Management Unit
PRI	: Panchayat Raj Institution
RNR	: Renewal Natural Resource
SHG	: Self Help Group
SWC	: Soil and Water Conservation
SWOT	: Strength Weakness Opportunity and Threat
UK	: United Kingdom

3

The Kick-Starter: Entrepreneurship and Social Capital in the Danish Cooperative Movement

GUNNAR LIND HAASE SVENDSEN
and GERT TINGGAARD SVENDSEN

I

Introduction

The question addressed in this article is *whether entrepreneurship in the Danish Cooperative Movement fostered social capital.* Answering this question is important because we argue that entrepreneurs facilitate the creation of a very important production factor, social capital, which is crucial for understanding the welfare state, collective action problems and voluntary co-operative movements in Scandinavia. Social capital is broadly defined as the ability to co-operate and it is often measured using a wide range of trust indicators (Svendsen and Svendsen, 2003).[1]

Explaining the Flight of the Bumblebee

Denmark and the other Scandinavian universal welfare states are not only among the richest countries in the world. They also have the highest social capital levels (Svendsen and Svendsen, 2006). At the same time, the Nordic welfare systems seem very fragile because there are rich possibilities for citizens to free-ride, *e.g.* by avoiding work and thereby paying no taxes, while still consuming a lot of expensive welfare services. Therefore, for economists the Nordic welfare states are nearly as puzzling as the flight of the bumblebee is to entomologists. Is it possible to explain how a Nordic bumblebee such as the Danish one actually flies? What does the bee run on? What is the fuel?

We suggest that the roots of the Danish welfare society may be found in the social capital-building generated by major rural civic movements during the nineteenth century. Social capital-building by energetic social entrepreneurs within *the Danish Cooperative Movement* may go a long way toward explaining 'the flight of the bumblebee'.

This argument is supported by the fact that the exemplary Danish co-operative movement is the strongest voluntary co-operative movement in the world, matched only by Poland in the nineteenth century and Iceland after World War II.

The well-documented development of the voluntary Danish co-operative movement enables us to trace a number of crucial factors that determine the creation or destruction of social capital. Our focus on entrepreneurship and rural communities raises general questions for the future of Western democracies as more and more rural areas undergo the kinds of transformations that have occurred in Denmark in recent years. The implications of this cross-disciplinary investigation, ranging from political economy, to sociology, history and anthropology, are of general interest to social scientists.

Theoretical Framework: Bridging and Bonding Social Capital

Various social capital studies have already been undertaken (for overviews, see Boix and Posner 1998; Portes 1998; Woolcock 1998; Sobel 2002). We have chosen Robert D. Putnam's (2000) recent book *Bowling Alone* as our main inspiration. Our contribution profits in many ways from Putnam's study. Most significantly, we have adopted his notions of 'bridging' and 'bonding' social capital—*i.e.,* inclusive and exclusive types of social capital—the key concepts in this chapter. So when we speak of building positive or beneficial social capital we mean 'bridging' social capital, which Putnam defines as open networks that are 'outward looking and encompass people across diverse social cleavages' (*Ibid.*, 22).[2]

When we speak of destruction of social capital, we refer to bridging social capital giving way to 'bonding' social capital, which is monopolistic-like and 'inward looking' networks that 'tend to reenforce exclusive identities and homogeneous groups' (*Ibid.*). We shall show that such processes lead ultimately to what economists call 'negative externalities', or to what sociologist Enzo Mingione (1991) termed 'fragmented societies'. We shall also show that bridging social capital compels personal contact and acts as a 'lubricator' for co-operation, whereas bonding social capital makes for distance between people and, consequently, acts as a 'superglue', increasing distrust and thereby transaction costs.

Whereas Putnam's quest in *Bowling Alone* by primarily using statistics was to operationalize, quantify and thereby measure a shrinking stock of bridging social capital in the United States since the mid 1960s, our method is somewhat different. Rather than relying completely on statistical material, we shall demonstrate how (bridging) social capital is built and destroyed by people *in situ*—both historically and in contemporary society (Svendsen, 2006). In other words, we want to show how bridging social capital is built and how it is transformed into bonding social capital.

At the micro level, we are interested in entrepreneurship that facilitates voluntary collective action and the creation of inclusive types of social capital. It is a crucial factor that these entrepreneurs are motivated not only by economic, but also by social incentives. This mix of economic and non-economic incentives forms the basis for the accumulation of social capital. We hope that this new view on entrepreneurship and the creation of social capital will contribute to the current academic and political discussions on group action and human behaviour.

Contribution

We propose that the presence of a social 'glue' in the form of bridging social capital—defined as regular face-to-face, co-operative relations across social boundaries—may explain the paradox of collective good provision (See Coleman, 1988a; Bourdieu, 1986; Putnam, 1993a, 2000). The question of how social capital is created/destroyed has yet to be answered in the literature. In the following, we point to three crucial conditions for building strongly inclusive bridging social capital: (1) organizational principles, (2) regular face-to-face contact in small groups, and (3) local meeting places. This leads to a 'self-starter model', suggesting that bridging social capital may be built locally as an outcome of organizational innovations ('rules of the game') that may fertilize the soil for social entrepreneurship, which may again give impetus to collective action in a positive circle.

In the specific case of Denmark, we also contribute by analyzing the roles of leading entrepreneurs and decision-makers in the co-operative movement. Here we clearly demonstrate that the positive externality of bridging social capital is not taken into account when private economic decisions in the market are made such as further centralization of production. Because the economic value of social capital linked to local production has hitherto been ignored in private market decisions, politicians must intervene from a societal perspective and provide more support for local production to prevent too much market centralization, for example. The dominance of economic efficiency and 'hard' data in the public debate is also reflected by the fact that those opposing the closure of local co-operative associations were unable to vocalize their opposition due to the so-called 'theory effect' (Bourdieu, 1977: 178; 1990: 134)—they simply did not know the theory of social capital and consequently lost this symbolic struggle to the central leadership, who were well versed in traditional economic theories.

Outline

Thus, in order to analyze whether entrepreneurship in the Danish Co-operative Movement fostered social capital, Section 2 begins by defining the theoretical background of social capital and entrepreneurship. Section 3 turns to the empirical evidence and asks whether bridging social capital really is a production factor and why entrepreneurs voluntarily provide it in practice. We answer this question by focusing on the presence of entrepreneurship in Denmark as an explanatory variable for the occurrence of co-operative movements and the subsequent creation of bridging social capital. Finally, Section 4 concludes the article, proposing an overall explanatory model for entrepreneurship and the creation of bridging social capital.

II

Social Capital

Opportunism

The most important impact of the type and extent of shared norms on the strategies available to individuals has to do with the level of opportunistic behaviour that appropriators can expect from other appropriators (Ostrom, 1990: 36). Ostrom here uses Williamson's (1975) definition of opportunism, namely 'self-interest with guile', and continues:

> In a setting in which few individuals share norms about the impropriety of breaking promises, refusing to do one's share, shirking, or taking other opportunistic actions, each appropriator must expect all other appropriators to act opportunistically whenever they have the chance. In such a setting it is difficult to develop stable, long term commitments. Expensive monitoring and sanctioning mechanisms may be needed. (Ostrom, 1990: 36).

However, we shall argue that building trust in smaller groups facilitates the removal of opportunism because of the option of social sanctioning, thus leading to a higher level of aggregate economic growth. This idea is derived from the work of Ostrom and Swedberg. Ostrom (1990, 35) writes:

> Norms of behaviour reflect valuations that individuals place on actions or strategies in and of themselves, not as they are connected to immediate consequences. When an individual has strongly internalized a norm related to keeping promises, for example, the individual suffers shame and guilt when a personal promise is broken. If the norm is shared with others, the individual is also subject to considerable *social censure* for taking an action considered to be wrong by others. (Our italics).

Other social scientists have since taken up Ostrom's idea and the sanctioning of undesirable individual behaviour. A representative example is provided by Swedberg, who defined a social structure as a recurrent and patterned interaction between agents maintained through sanctions (Swedberg, 1994).

The implication is in our social capital approach that if group members trust one another and can sanction defectors, this group may achieve more economic growth compared to other groups without such internal trust because more transactions may take place at a lower cost and the predictability of behaviour increases, thereby eliminating the necessity to monitor and enforce most transactions formally. Trust lubricates society, as Putnam puts it (Putnam, 1993b)—which was also realized by early authors such as David Hume (1739) and Adam Smith (1776). One may, therefore, suggest that social capital is a new production factor in that it saves transaction costs in society, thus allowing more voluntary transactions to take place.

For example, it may be argued that voluntary organization among farmers lowers transaction costs by opening up for numerous informal transactions that are not formally sanctioned. It is not necessary to monitor and enforce all the transactions.

This positive externality pursuant to the presence of social capital is presumably created in small-group activities involving regular face-to-face interaction. An externality occurs when an agent (Be it a firm or a household) does not bear all the consequences of its actions and imposes an external benefit (or cost) on some other agent *outside the market system* (Tietenberg, 2002: 67).

For example, as we argue in Section 3, small-scale dairy production may stimulate local networking and social capital-building, thus providing the basis for more overall economic growth in society. Here we assume that increased small-scale production imposes an external benefit on society so that too little production of this kind will take place in a market economy without political intervention.

Bowling Alone

Putnam's first book about social capital, *Making Democracy Work* from 1993, is a comparative study of social capital in Northern and Southern Italy. Social capital is measured as traditions of civic engagement (In the form of voter participation, newspaper reading and number of civic associations). He concludes that the two regions for historical reasons have evolved in diametrically opposite directions. Northern Italy has relatively more associational life than Southern Italy and has, therefore, accumulated more wealth (Putnam, 1993a: 37).

Since his survey in Italy, Putnam has focused on his own country, the United States. Here the presumed erosion of social capital due to decreasing associational activity from 1969 until today caught his interest (Putnam, 1996, 2000). Putnam finds that the main eroding factor is television, which jeopardizes the large stock of social capital created during 'the long civic generation', the civil rights movements of the 1960s. Time that could have been spent on social activities is now spent watching TV. Thus, Putnam concludes, the rise of television has meant the privatization of leisure time:

> Television is . . . the only leisure activity that seems to inhibit participation outside the home. TV watching comes at the expense of nearly every social activity outside the home, especially social gatherings and informal conversations . . . [Television privatizes our leisure time. (Putnam, 1996: 47-8).

The idea about erosion of the American stock of social capital is the main theme in Putnam's latest book *Bowling Alone* from 2000. Indeed, one may perceive the book as an impressive collection of statistical evidence verified by numerous cases. This 'degradation of our public life' is reflected in a significant decline in political participation, church attendance, union work, frequency of informal social relations, voluntary engagement in cultural life, and so on (Putnam, 2000: 403). Putnam has furthermore incorporated the criticisms raised in the journal *American Prospect*, which led to his two articles 'Bowling Alone' (1995) and 'The strange disappearance of civic America' (1996). As one reviewer writes, Putnam has given an 'antitank gun of an argument, relentlessly researched and heavily armoured against academic counterassault' (Nyhan, 2000).

In his chapter on 'The dark side of social capital' in *Bowling Alone*, Putnam questions the one-sided focus on positive social capital (See especially Portes and Landolt, 1996 and Portes, 2000 for a critique). Here he recognizes that social capital is often created in opposition to something or somebody else (Putnam, 2000: 361). In other words, negative social capital of an excluding nature may arise in the form of excessive 'bonding social capital', as found within, for example, certain religious networks: '[P]roselytizing religions are better at creating bonding social capital than bridging social capital, and tolerance of unbelievers is not a virtue notably associated with fundamentalism' (*Ibid.*, 410).

The opposite of 'bonding social capital' is, therefore, 'bridging social capital'. What does Putnam mean by this expression? Simply that through a new political structure based on decentralization of political power and flexibility in the labour market, one must create fertile *conditions* for the creation of social capital. The bridging consists in moving beyond 'our social and political and professional identities to connect with people unlike ourselves' (*Ibid.*, 411). In other words, Putnam asks Americans from all societal sectors to create fertile soil for giving people the opportunity to meet one another in person. According to Putnam, only by doing so can the American stock of social capital be restored (*Ibid.*, 412).

III

Social Entrepreneurship and Social Capital-Building within the Danish Co-operative Movement

Bridging Social Capital

During the nineteenth century, a broad tradition of civic organization was established in the Danish rural districts. From the beginning of the century, this organization was led by energetic entrepreneurs and institutionalized in the form of associations, so numerous in the last part of the century that the period was known as *Foreningstiden*, 'the era of associations'.

As argued in Section II, bridging social capital is derived from regular face-to-face co-operative relations among larger groups in local areas as the outcome of close human relations based on balanced reciprocity—something that is clearly facilitated by decentralization. We argue that it is precisely such relations rooted in civic traditions—dating back to the civic society that emerged in the late eighteenth century—that were developed in rural Denmark during the second part of the nineteenth century. Furthermore, we argue that open and widespread co-operation is advanced by formulating formal 'rules of the game' that can be sanctioned effectively. This suggestion seems to be confirmed by empirical evidence from entrepreneurial activity in rural Denmark, 1800-1900. During this period, written rules in the form of the formal founding charters of co-operative associations enhanced informal co-operation among farmers and gave rise to stocks of beneficial social capital of an inclusive nature, what we term bridging social capital. As an outcome of this process, entrepreneurs voluntarily organized larger groups that provided collective goods locally, thus contributing to economic growth in rural areas that had hitherto been poor.

Furthermore, we argue that it was the formal organizational structure of these associations in the form of written rules of the game that, acting as a 'self-starter', led to extended networks and ultimately to beneficial capital-building. Right up to the 1960s, this process again gave rise to generations of entrepreneurs establishing and maintaining 'networks of associations at local, regional and national levels. In this way, once established and institutionalized on the basis of certain organizational principles that ensured predictability and the possibility of sanctions, bridging social capital was rapidly accumulated in all Danish rural districts, fostering local entrepreneurs who would guarantee group action and the provision of collective goods.

An understanding of the growth of new and more recent forms of bridging social capital is found in the massive wave of sports facility procurement in Denmark that followed the general increase in leisure time. The implications for volunteerism and public support are discussed in this perspective.

The Co-operative Movement

Around 1750, feudal Denmark was marked by economic stagnation due to serious shortcomings in the overall political-economic system. Therefore, and inspired by the new liberal ideas of Enlightenment in Western Europe, the Danish monarch and his officials began to search for new alternative ways of enhancing economic growth.

As a direct result, land reforms with wide-ranging consequences for political, institutional and physical organization were set in motion in the last decades of the eighteenth century, motivating and, in part, also forcing peasants to buy their own land. This necessitated the abolition of the Adscript of June 1788, severing the formerly strong and unequal economic ties between feudal landlords and peasants. In this way, the central administration tried to create strong incentives for ordinary peasants to increase personal profits to the general benefit of the Danish state. Thus, the purpose of this law, which introduced what turned out to be an extremely successful economic strategy, was summarized as the consolidation of the 'general prosperity' of the state by securing the 'rights of our dear and faithful subjects belonging to the peasantry in particular their personal freedom' (Law of Abolition of the Adscript of June 1788, in Hansgaard 1981: 194). Characteristically, on a famous monument—the so-called 'Monument of Freedom' (Frihedsstøtten) which was raised in Copenhagen about ten years later to celebrate the abolition and, more fundamentally, the transition from feudalism to liberalism and capitalism—it was written that the main purpose of the abolition had been to ensure the 'freedom of citizens', the 'thirst for knowledge', and 'desire of diligence' (Feldbæk 1988: 12-13).

However, such new liberal and physiocratic ideas not only reached the monarch and his closest advisors; they were also adopted by other sectors of the more educated population in the major towns and cities. As a consequence, the 'thirst for knowledge' was aroused, leading to the establishment of a large number of so-called clubs at the end of the century, particularly in Copenhagen. In these clubs—the model was imported from England—the Danish intelligentsia could discuss the new revolutionary ideas, undisturbed and in pleasant surroundings.

A contemporary author and historian of literature, Rasmus Nyerup, wrote in 1800:

> These clubs have brought about a major change in social intercourse in particular among the middle classes . . . These are closed societies having their own laws and arrangements, which, for a fixed yearly subscription from each member, rent out rooms, provide for reading and billiard tables, arrange concerts, balls and assemblies, and where a man, no matter which evening he chooses, can always be certain to meet acquaintances. (Nyerup, cited in Balle-Petersen 1976: 46, our translation).

All this new civic enthusiasm, which was formerly totally forbidden by Danish monarchs, led to the formation of a gradually more extended 'net of communication' (Leisner, 1988: 37), mainly comprising learned scholars who belonged to an ever more powerful citizenry. These new networks spread rapidly during the 1790s and, due to newly established non-government-controlled scientific, reading and philanthropic societies, scientific journals and so on, they were able to disseminate the ideas of the Enlightenment of Western Europe to a large part of the Danish population. Thus, largely exclusive networks in the clubs seemed to be transformed into strongly inclusive networks at the meso and macro levels, leading to open democratic debate, mutual confidence between groups, civic traditions and, in the long term, to political and economic conditions that promoted the accumulation of beneficial bridging social capital.

Thus, in the first part of the nineteenth century, the English-inspired clubs—as what we have here termed 'social platforms' for the accumulation of a primarily mild and non-aggressive form of bonding social capital—gradually died out, leaving room for the establishment of a multitude of voluntary associations within a still growing and ever more viable civic society (Svendsen and Svendsen, 2004).

Because of major innovations in organization, association building rapidly increased and culminated in the establishment of a Danish co-operative movement from the mid-1860s and on. Association-building hereby turned into social capital-building, fostering entrepreneurship and the provision of collective goods. Thus, bridging social capital, possibly *the* most crucial production factor, led to improved material as well as non-material living conditions in the countryside. These collective, that is, *non-excludable*, goods were provided by local activist entrepreneurs (*ildsjæle*), whose personal, economic net gains were clearly negative compared to the amount of time and energy they spent and, especially, the benefits they provided to their communities in the form of strengthened shared norms and, ultimately, enhanced economic growth. This is in accordance with James Coleman, who talks about 'underinvestment in social capital' because 'the actor or actors who generate social capital ordinarily capture only a small part of its benefits' (1988a: 119; See also 1988b: 389, 1990: 317ff.).

The gradual eradication of feudalism by land reforms by about 1800 led to the creation of a whole new class of family farmers who owned their own land. The struggle for a better life in the countryside appeared to stagnate under an economic crisis in the 1870s. International grain prices slumped, and the small corn-producing Danish farmers in particular found themselves in a hopeless economic situation (Bjørn 1982: 17-19).

Generally, the shift to exporting secondary agricultural produce instead of grain to satisfy the new demands of the world market led to an increase in the production of animal produce. But in 1879 Germany imposed a duty on all livestock coming from Denmark and cattle export was halved the following year (*Ibid.*: 48). The loss of the German market gave rise to the so-called 'home dairies' where neighbours collaborated in the production of butter.

As a counter-reaction, the early philanthropic associations described earlier were to form the basis of a regular co-operative movement in Danish agriculture—a movement that evolved quickly during the second half of the nineteenth century. In this period, the farmers established a multitude of co-operative associations ranging from co-operative wholesale societies from 1866, to co-operative dairies from 1882, co-operative fodder and fertilizer purchasing associations from 1883, and co-operative meat packing plants from 1887.

The decisive innovation consisted in the specific organizational structure of these associations that strongly promoted inclusive co-operative networks—and thus accumulation of beneficial social capital. As we shall see, from the very beginning this organizational structure was institutionalized in the standard founding charters of the co-operative association.

The idea originated in England. In 1844 in Rochdale near Manchester, a group of weavers founded the first co-operative wholesale society in the world, that is to say, a sales and wholesale company owned by the members themselves. Nearly 20 years later, two friends in the village of Møgeltønder in southern Jutland—F.F. Ulrik, a doctor, and H.C. Sonne, a vicar—discussed the Rochdale principles. Ulrik had been familiar with these ideas for some time and he now evoked passionate interest from Sonne (Ravnholt 1943: 30). These philanthropically minded men were in various ways trying to alleviate the conditions of the poorest among the population by establishing a wide range of charitable organizations and institutions in the area (Dollerup 1966: 34ff).

However, after the defeat by Prussia in 1864 and the subsequent loss of southern Jutland, Ulrik and Sonne, both ardent patriots, were forced to leave the region, but they continued their entrepreneurial activities in close co-operation with kindred spirits. So, in Copenhagen Ulrik set up a building association for shipyard workers in 1865, while Sonne established the first Danish wholesale society in the small borough of Thisted in 1866 .

The great success of this first wholesale society in Denmark was due to Sonne's vast insight into the original organizational principles used in the English co-operative wholesale movement—knowledge he had obtained in part during several study tours, and in part by reading all the English literature about the subject he could lay his hands on. All this is documented in a book he wrote in 1867, the year after he had founded his wholesale society (See also Dollerup 1966: 50). Drawing on the experiences of the wholesale society in Thisted, he propagated the 'laws from Rochdale', that is, the founding charter he had successfully implemented in a Danish local community (Sonne, 1867: 4ff.). Thus, inspired by key principles such as allocation of profits according to the purchases made by each member (§2 and §6), shared economic responsibility (§3), open membership (§4) and democratic decision-making (§5), the *purpose* of the wholesale society in Thisted (§1) was 'in perfect accordance with the Rochdale laws to establish a foundation by subscriptions voluntarily paid by the members, in order to allow them to purchase more profitably the necessities of life' (*ibid*., 5). However, this programme expressed only the 'means' whereby one could achieve the 'true' objective (*ibid*.). Sonne continues:

> If this is overlooked, our attention is easily attracted to the economic and purely material side and we lose sight of the true depth and great significance; no, the goal is to elevate what in the civic sense is the lower ranking, dependent and pressured segment of the population to a higher moral, intellectual and social level and thereby to a more honourable place in society. (Ibid.: 5; our translation).

If the founding statutes did not fully realize his idealist goals—at least not in Sonne's lifetime—they nevertheless offered an organizational structure that would increase the material welfare of the poor majority of the population, not least in the countryside, where the farmers followed Sonne's advice and formed their own wholesale societies to protect themselves from economic exploitation. Thus, and especially from the mid-1880s, the number of wholesale associations increased rapidly to about 850 by the turn of the century and—quite a remarkable feat in an international context—the vast majority were established in local rural communities.

However, and even more importantly, the founding charter of Sonne's co-operative wholesale society was to be widely applied within the agricultural sector, introducing important formal institutions in the form of self-enforced written rules of the game that strongly enhanced co-operation and the accumulation of bridging social capital among farmers. In the following, we shall look more closely at the sector within the co-operative movement that had the strongest socio-economic impact on farmers' everyday lives: the co-operative dairy movement.

The Dairy Sector

The co-operative movement achieved one of its most admirable ambitions with the establishment of numerous dairy co-operatives in the last two decades of the nineteenth century. Like the wholesale co-operatives, an important explanation of the success of the co-operative dairies was the organizational charters, written rules of the game. These formal rules came to constitute legally binding promises that facilitated co-operation between farmers and small holders, a co-operation that had hitherto been utterly inconceivable. In addition, the written rules made it possible to sanction any member who tried to cheat. Thus, network-based co-operation of an inclusive nature was promoted in the economic sphere, and it led to the accumulation of productive, bridging social capital.

Not surprisingly, it was particularly in the co-operative dairy movement from 1882 that the co-operative organization formulated by Sonne in 1867 (*andelskontrakten*) was further elaborated, juristically as well as in practice, to fit the norms and culture of the rural population. It was in the village of Hjedding in Jutland that a group of entrepreneurial farmers founded the first co-operative dairy. In his memoirs, dating from 1901, one of the main promoters of the project, farmer Niels Kristensen, writes about the initial discussions:

> During the negotiations, a general sentiment evolved expressing a preference for collecting milk instead of the butter . . . To be able to prepare the milk in one place, it was necessary to build a dairy. This, however, gave rise to another problem, since some of the farmers had no wish

> to build a dairy with others, while they agreed to selling their milk to the dairy. Thus, without anybody realizing, the negotiations moved in the direction of the realization of what was later to become a widespread and magnificent co-operative ideal: that everybody who joined the dairy should be allocated profits on the basis of the amount of milk he delivered. (Kristensen cited in Manøe Hansen, 1972: 13, our translation).

Immediately after this meeting, some of the farmers collaborated in writing the charter of the association. Overall, their articles reflect all the ideas of Sonne and the English wholesale society movement, stressing principles such as allocation of profits in proportion to the amount of milk delivered by each member, shared economic responsibility, open membership and, not least, democratic decision-making, which was further specified as 'one man, one vote' at the annual general assembly, where all major decisions regarding the dairy were to be taken (For further details, See Svendsen and Svendsen 2000: 76). Over the next two months, the dairy in Hjedding was built under the leadership of the committee members themselves (Kristensen, cited in Manøe Hansen 1972: 16-17), and production began in June 1882.

Less than 10 years later, the 'Hjedding model' had spread to all corners of the country. According to the figures, the economic success is evident. In 1890, one-third of all farmers delivered milk to one of the approximately 700 co-operative dairies. Consequently, Danish butter exports increased from 12.5 million kilograms in 1880 to about 90 million by the beginning of the new century, while milk exports increased from 200 litres to about 600,000 litres in the same period (Bjørn 1982: 21, 552, 561).

This development took place *in spite* of the Government. Until the end of the decade, the government—conservative and anti-socialist—did nothing to encourage the foundation of co-operative dairies. In fact, both the state and the agricultural organizations were often 'downright negative' in their relations to the dairies (*ibid.*, 80). But the movement was beyond their control. The rural population joined voluntarily and the number of co-operative dairies increased rapidly. People put up their own money as start capital, raised loans from their own local financial institutes, asked for and paid for technical advice, and so on. In short, they acted independently of the state, using their own resources. (*Ibid.*, 119).

These resources, scarce though they were in the countryside at the beginning of the 1880s, were made available because of mutual confidence and mutual trust between the members of each local society. To know one another well was clearly a precondition if people were to join in a shared economic venture, especially such a risky one:

> Because the number of participants of a co-operative dairy was limited by the small size of the local area, one may presume that these people knew one another very well, and the joint and several liability, therefore, seems to have been the appropriate way to resolve common, economic tasks. (*Ibid*., 96, our translation).

This phenomenon is reflected in Coleman's term 'closure'. This means beneficial social capital-building is facilitated if most people know one another in a neighbourhood, including parents who know their children's friends as well as *their* parents. Such chains of 'I know X, who knows Y, who knows Z … who knows me' enhance social control, make for rapid spread of information, generalized trust (*I* trust her, because *you* trust her, and I trust *you*) and similar collective goods. People who meet regularly face to face will most probably find each other trustworthy.

But why did all these generally trustworthy farmers engage in such activities? What purposes and interests did they share? And what common benefits did they achieve?

In addition to people knowing and trusting each other, another precondition for the success of a co-operative dairy was a common economic interest as described in the four standard paragraphs of the charter of such an organization (See Rørdam 1983: 27-34).

First, the idea of open membership was to invite everybody to join the local co-operative dairy (*andelsmejeri*), regardless of political/religious conviction or economic ability. An important outcome of the 'we welcome all' strategy was that the local *andelsmejeri* acted as a social meeting place or, in our terminology, a 'platform' securing a mix of different groups.

Second, this inclusiveness was supplemented and reinforced by democratic decision-making. Everybody, high and low, was equal.

Third, people shared economic responsibility for their dairy, supplied start capital, and all were liable for loans for buildings, equipment and so on. Thus, people were jointly and severally liable for the risks of loss and were, therefore, forced to co-operate in spite of political, religious or social conflicts—a crucial factor (Compare Bjørn, 1982: 95-6).

Fourth, profit was not shared in the socialist manner: each member was paid in proportion to the amount of milk delivered over a certain period of time. In other words, each member harvested the fruits of his/her labour. This satisfied farmers with large holdings and encouraged them to accept that voting within the co-operative association was on a one-man one-vote basis and not according to how many heads of cattle each farmer owned.

In this way the democratic, socio-economic elements—at that time interpreted by some as 'socialist influence'—were outweighed by the profit-making part of the whole business. The members actually earned money ! Rationalizations and, due to social capital, the maximum utilization of new technologies (Physical capital) and professionalization (Human capital) increased total profits from 20 to 25 per cent on average compared to the home dairies (*ibid*., 116).

Remarkably, these rules of the game, adapted to and embedded in a specific culture, seem to increase the profits turned by physical, human and social capitals, share many similarities with the work of Ostrom and her findings on social capital and collective action (See Ostrom 1992, 1994; Ostrom *et al*., 1994).

Citing a famous passage from Coleman's works, which echoes Durkheim's key notion of the collective being more than the sum of its parts, Ostrom (1994 : 528) sees social capital as a new production factor that enables people through joint effort to achieve something that in the absence of social capital would not be possible or that they would have been unable to achieve on their own. Thus, applying the case study of self-organized common-pool irrigation resources among farmers, she shows that regular face-to-face communication, common economic interests, social control, efficient sanctioning of free riders, and trust are fundamental elements in a viable, long term 'contract' among groups of farmers (*ibid*., 532ff). Self-enforced rules promoting strategies of inclusion, that is, clearly stated rules known and openly discussed in the public sphere and deeply embedded in reciprocity and common norms, seem to trigger (or 'self-start') the building of beneficial bridging social capital.

Therefore, following Ostrom, investment in formal institutions means investment in an organizational framework that fosters stocks of bridging social capital—a capital that is just as important as investments in physical capital, in some cases even *more* important (as many developmental projects in third-world countries clearly reveal). Ostrom goes on to conclude that 'if external agents of change do not take into account the delicate balance of interests [Among farmers] embedded in social capital, when investments in physical capital are undertaken efforts to improve productivity can have the opposite effect' (*ibid.*, 559). Again, this warns us to not underestimate the importance of the production factor *social capital* even though we cannot see it, touch it, or measure it in the same strict, classical economic way as we can more traditional forms of capital.

Entrepreneurship

The success of the co-operative dairies is grounded in the formal organizational structure behind the co-operation, that is, in the founding charter of the model dairy of Hjedding. As we shall see below, this long term, reciprocity-based 'co-operative charter' (*andelskontrakten*) formed the organizational framework that helped foster durable informal institutions in the form of bridging social capital. *Andelskontrakten* served to mediate between conflicting groups, thus ensuring a predictable and stable pattern of human interaction. However, founded on informal reciprocal relations—essentially, *unwritten* rules of the game—there was also room for spontaneity in the form of rational or, more precisely, *raissonable* socio-economic strategies among actors.

First, across the country, the contract (*andelskontrakten*) involved an extraordinary compromise between two conflicting groups: the well-to-do farmers and the small-holders. This compromise was based on their common economic interests institutionalized in the socio-economic principles of the co-operative association. In this way, the contract facilitated the formation of positive social capital (of an inclusive nature) or, in Putnam's formulation, *bridging social capital* encompassing 'people across diverse social cleavages'—an invisible, intangible, but nonetheless extremely important form of capital which, in the long run, enhanced economic growth in rural Denmark.

Using the Hjedding model as a concrete tool, two groups—the well-to-do farmers and the small-holders—now began to co-operate on equal terms. The Hjedding model made such 'impossible' co-operation possible by stressing the shared economic interests of all who farmed the land. So we understand why §1 of the founding charter from Hjedding underlined this shared interest by focusing on cash payment to the members in proportion to the amount of milk delivered by each farm over a certain period:

> The profit obtained from sale [of cheese and butter] is distributed among the members in proportion to the amount of milk each has delivered, minus the running expenses of the dairy. The profit from the sale of butter is distributed monthly, whereas the profit from the sale of cheese is distributed once a year. Every day, buttermilk and whey is delivered back to the members, in proportion to the amount of milk each member has delivered. (§1 of the founding statutes of Hjedding, Manøe Hansen 1972 : 33, our translation).

This paragraph satisfied the well-to-do farmers. Moreover, to satisfy the small-holders as well, the statutes ensured democratic decision-making (§12). The farmers voted 'according to heads and not according to cows' (with the exception of 10-15 per cent of all co-operative dairies where they voted 'according to cows and not according to heads', compare Bjørn 1982: 95). Everybody, high or low on the socio-economic ladder, was equal.

Written rules fostered the formation of bridging social capital. This meant clear rules of the game, which served to formalize co-operation, including the possibility of sanctioning members who violated the rules agreed upon by all (§ 9). Thus, any farmer who diluted the milk with water, used the wrong fodder for his cows, or in any other way tried to cheat the others, risked exclusion:

> The milk must be delivered to the dairy in a pure and unadulterated condition. Milk from sick cows must not be delivered . . . If it can be documented that the milk delivered by a supplier has been adulterated, either by the addition of water or other mixtures, or if foamy milk is delivered, if the milk of sick cows has been added, or if the pails are dirty—in such cases, the supplier is excluded from the association and will be fined an amount of [etc.]. (Manøe Hansen 1972 : 34, our translation).

Second, as farmers became accustomed to following a set of clear, written rules of the game, the formalized framework for co-operation became 'naturalized', that is, diffused into informal exchanges as well. Thus, co-operating according to the rules of the game, implying collective good provision, became a natural way of acting, a behaviour that the farmers took for granted. The rules were internalized, that is, they became internalized culture or, in the words of Bourdieu, predisposed dispositions in the form of a habitus. In this bottom-up process, the farmers financed their dairies themselves, making use of local, parish savings banks, just as they paid for all professional assistance required if they were unable to accomplish these various tasks themselves—just as was formerly the case with the wholesale companies (Bjørn, 1982: 100, See also Paldam and Svendsen, 2000).

The first outcome of the entrepreneurial activities and the accumulation of stocks of bridging social capital was a significant increase in economic growth in formerly poor rural areas. The second, as already indicated, was a general lubrication of mutual relations within the local communities, including cultural life. It is in this light that we shall investigate the formation of a multitude of cultural institutions during the second half of the nineteenth century, such as community folk high schools, village halls and military training halls—all of which enhanced the accumulation of various forms of capital in rural Denmark in addition to physical and economic capital such as education and human capital (Svendsen and Svendsen, 2004). This again strengthened the 'recruitment' of new generations of local entrepreneurs who provided collective goods, all the while continuing the process of amassing beneficial bridging social capital. This can be illustrated as shown in Figure 3.1.

Figure 3.1 shows that—in line with Ostrom's ideas—this development was set in motion by innovations in organizational structure (Rules of the Game), acting as a kick-starter for the formation of networks of associations and stocks of beneficial social capital, that is, bridging social capital that encouraged local entrepreneurs all over the country to provide collective non-excludable goods. Consequently, this development profited not only the individual local community, but the nation as a whole. As suggested in Figure 3.1, this again contributed to further accumulation of social capital and recruitment of new generations of entrepreneurs, and so on. Finally note that the historical sources indicate that three elements form the bedrock of this 'good circle of social capital-building': (1) Bottom-up voluntary self-organization; (2) A small group-size which facilitates regular face to face interaction; and (3) Physical meeting places securing social integration, here termed 'platforms' for bridging social capital. The case of the Danish Cooperative Movement suggests that this bedrock also is effected by innovations in organization, for example in the establishment of new meeting places and as a tool for self-organization.

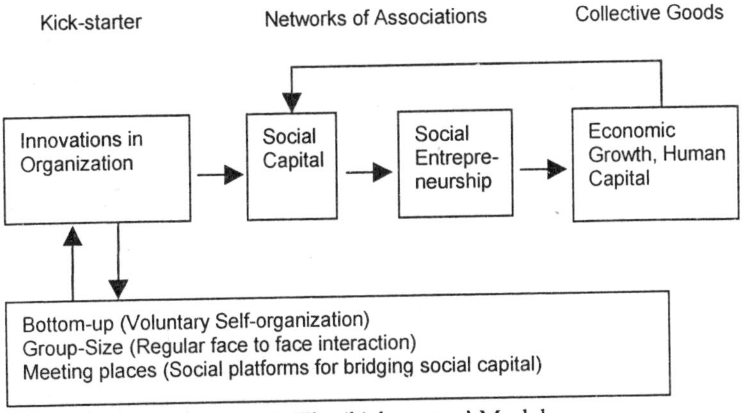

Fig. 3.1: The 'kick-starter' Model

Source: The Authors.

Overall, we see that strong common economic impulses mediating between political, religious and social differences, and regulated by 'rules of the game', are the primary core of this kind of co-operation. People in the countryside became richer and richer during this period despite the international economic crisis.

We have already shown that economic profit and democracy and trust appear to be crucial in starting the process of bridging social capital-building, which leads to the formation of social capital, to its 'cytogenesis', so to speak. This is in line with Sen's (1999) ideas of basic freedoms as the main factor for economic growth.

But bridging social-capital building involves another step: the spread of socio-economic networks or 'mytosis'. How was the idea and practice of co-operative dairies to be disseminated to the entire country? In order to understand this aspect we have to supplement the three core elements—profit, democracy and trust—with that of entrepreneurship. Most importantly, the entrepreneurs had to be reliable, best illustrated by the old Danish saying 'a word is a word' (*et ord er et ord*). The element of entrepreneurship is thus closely connected to the element of trust.

At the micro Level, the individual local entrepreneur had to have a reputation as a highly trustworthy person in every aspect if he was to succeed with his dairy project. The choice often would fall on the local school teacher, known by everybody, on a respected and well-to-do farmer, or on a dairy technical autodidact who had already proven his worth by contributing to the foundation of several dairies in other parts of the country. In short, the members wanted their leaders to be 'experienced men, inspiring confidence, whose participation was found to be valuable or even necessary for the foundation of the dairy' (Bjørn 1982: 104, *our translation*).

Local school teachers, who were especially active in the first year, rarely acted on the basis of pure philanthropic or socialist motives. They wanted to profit economically. Normally, the community gave the teacher a small piece of land, a so-called 'school-acre'. In order to supplement poor wages and thereby be able to provide for an often very large family, school teachers had to be very resourceful in cultivating this piece of land. Furthermore, this intensive form of agriculture involved raising domestic animals, including cows. Thus, the teacher himself became a milk supplier, thereby enlarging his source of income, not to speak of the fees paid in connection with the writing of association charters for the society, and contributing his technical know-how (*ibid*., 108).

The well-to-do farmer, who increasingly tended to take on the role as entrepreneur, had a special economic interest in the local dairy. First of all, he had many cows and was, therefore, able to increase his profit. But often he was simply 'head hunted' by smaller entrepreneurs with less social, political and economic prestige because he was seen as a man of honour, often with the power to gain access to the local savings bank and exercise major influence on the bank's board of directors.

Such head hunting was soon to become a common practice at the meso-level—that is, at a level where *groups* of entrepreneurs communicate and co-operate. So all these local consultants, experts and highly reputable men were invited to different corners of the country to talk about the revolutionary innovation, *andelsmejeriet*, the vast majority of them setting forth strictly economic arguments (*ibid*., 72). Moreover, after the talk, these men were often invited to participate in the foundation of a new dairy in the local area in question because of their history of successful enterprises. So, from functioning solely as individual local entrepreneurs, they joined entrepreneurial groups at the regional level, thus enlarging the common good of their activity to include other communities.

By first facilitating co-operation, trust and economic growth at a local micro-level and then on a regional, meso-level, the entrepreneurs were soon also to extend this particular stock of bridging social capital to the national, the *macro*-level.

Spreading to the national level, social capital first resulted in the promotion of the co-operative idea, and many dairies were built. Second, dairies across the country followed exactly the same pattern of development (*ibid*.). And third, but no less important: promotion and agitation metamorphosed into communication.

A common national interest was stimulated and a debate as well. Towards the end of the 1880s, newspapers and agricultural magazines that had formerly ignored the matter became interested, now criticizing, now defending the model. Educational institutions served as intermediaries of the co-operational idea—and in 1889 even the Government finally decided to recognize the movement by offering the co-operative dairies free technical support (*ibid*., 80).

By means of entrepreneurship the co-operative dairy movement thus went through the 'mytosis' process. A model of co-operation embedded in a specific local network was exported to other localities and even to other countries. (For example, the Danish co-operative movement strongly influenced the co-operative movements in Norway and Sweden.) Thus, the communication net was gradually spread out. Inter-regional relations based on mutual trust were created, uniting rural Denmark through strong socio-economic ties. Bridging social capital was accumulated, bringing benefits not only to the individual and the local community, but to the nation as a whole.

We have now seen that the process of social capital building in rural Denmark was set in motion by economic impulses in connection with two other elements, democracy and trust. This constitutes the initial part of the process, the cytogenesis of social capital. This is followed by the second part of the process, the spread of networks (or mytosis) through entrepreneurial agitation, promotion and export of a specific model of organization.

Such complexity is also noted by Putnam (1993b) who, in an article about democracy, notes in almost biblical fashion that 'those who have social capital tend to accumulate more'. 'Stocks of social capital', that is, the civic traditions of a society defined as its accumulated sum of trust, norms and networks, thus form the basis of further accumulation of social capital (*ibid.*).

In fact, in the Danish case it becomes evident that the *political system* (Capitalism) and the subsequent establishment of civic traditions gave impetus to the revolution and subsequent evolution. Thus, there is no doubt that the earlier land reforms that marked the final transition from feudalism to capitalism created the overall 'structural framework' for the development (Bjørn, 1988: 368). Also important for the movement were the Danish *folkehøjskoler*, folk high schools that since the 1840s had been important channels for disseminating knowledge to the rural population (See also Korsgaard 1997, for a more detailed analysis).

There is no doubt that once the organizational model had been established, it formed an almost physical, socio-economic structure that satisfied not only economic purposes, but also social and personal ones.

The Danish co-operative movement, *Andelsbevægelsen*, should be regarded as a socio-economic phenomenon whose social and economic factors are inextricably interwoven. Here we witness a specific co-operative 'spirit' or *Weltanschauung*, enhancing 'closure' and allowing neighbours tied together by strong socio-economic relations of trust to communicate, exchange visits and services and help one another—simply to participate in one another's lives.

IV

Conclusion

We focused on the role of entrepreneurship in the Danish Cooperative Movement and how it affected social capital in two parts, a theoretical and an empirical part. First, we argued theoretically how social capital as a positive externality is created and what the economic effects are. We then explained how social sanctioning could be imposed on uncooperative members in a group to help ensure trust between members and successful group action. Furthermore, the accumulation of social capital could be described as a positive externality resulting in an economic net gain for society. However, there is another side of the coin, namely bonding social capital, which is detrimental to economic growth. We, therefore, emphasized the crucial distinction between bridging and bonding social capital and the discussion of classical reciprocity theories.

We consider social capital a new production factor that should be added to the conventional concepts of human and physical capital. Social capital is productive because it increases the level of trust in a society and allows more transactions to take place without third-party enforcement. In fact, and as argued in the setting of new institutional economics, social capital compensates for the presence of asymmetrical information in real life. Theory, therefore, leads to the general recommendation that any loss in social capital must be deducted from the economic gain that accrues through market forces. For example, the voluntary organization of small-sized groups in the Danish co-operative dairy movement was eliminated by the economies of scale. It may be that an alternative means of production that took social capital into account could have increased economic growth even further.

The question why some countries are rich and others poor has been a core issue in research for centuries. We proposed that traditional production factors cannot fully explain the observed differences in the wealth of nations, and that the non-material and informal dimension of institutions had to be added. We also suggested how self-selection of local leaders can occur in a non-hierarchical setting such as self-selection among a number of potential entrepreneurs in, for example, the locally based voluntary co-operative movements. Such a self-selection process of entrepreneurs was arguably based on reputation.

Empirically, we analyzed why entrepreneurs emerge and organize larger groups in local areas, thereby contributing to voluntary collective good provision and the creation of bridging social capital beneficial to society. This question was important because voluntary collective good provision in a local area enhances economic growth and alleviates poverty. We argued that there is a gap in the economics literature. If an individual's economic gain from providing a collective good is negative, then it does not pay for that individual to act and organize. Nevertheless, larger groups actually *do* organize in local areas even though the individual net gain is clearly negative. This paradox cannot be explained in strict economic terms.

In an attempt to fill this gap in the literature, we offered another solution to this paradox, namely the presence of social incentives. Regular face-to-face interaction presumably encouraged co-operative relations among larger groups in local areas. Such relations, we argued, would be set in motion (kick-started) by innovations in organizational structure in the form of clear, written rules of the game. This formalization of co-operation included the imposition of sanctions, most prominently exclusion from the group, on members who violated the rules.

This theoretical proposal appeared to be confirmed by empirical evidence from rural Denmark since the late nineteenth century. We used the example of the rise of positive or beneficial social capital (bridging social capital) in the emergence of strongly inclusive farmers' networks organized in the co-operative movement during the second half of the nineteenth century. These networks were deeply rooted in the early economic associations formed by newly independent farmers in the first part of that century—that is, fully voluntary and self-enforced associations dating back to the initial emergence of a civic society in urban Denmark during the last decades of the eighteenth century.

How was bridging social capital generated during this period? First, we found that the initial establishment of networks—what we called the 'cytogenesis' of bridging social capital—is contingent upon the existence of the three key elements of democracy, trust and the equal opportunity to turn a profit. Here we observed that written rules in the form of the standardized founding charters of co-operative associations enhanced (kick-started) co-operation among farmers and thus gave rise to stocks of highly productive bridging social capital. As an outcome of this process, entrepreneurs provided collective goods, contributing to economic growth and education in formerly poor rural areas.

It was precisely these written rules of the game that facilitated self-organization in rural districts, a self-organization that brought with it a rapid accumulation of bridging social capital and, consequently, of other forms of capital, which ultimately achieved great socially beneficial significance. Moreover, the historical evidence suggested that a bedrock for such an organizational innovation was bottom-up voluntary self-organization, small group size and regular face-to-face interaction, and physical meeting places transcending group cleavages, termed 'platforms' for bridging social capital. Gradually, as farmers became accustomed to following the written rules of the game, the formalized framework for co-operation became 'naturalized', that is, adsorbed into informal exchange as well. In this way, co-operation according to the rules of the game, implying collective good provision secured by agreed-upon sanctions, became a natural way of behaving, that is, a behaviour the farmers no longer questioned.

The rules were internalized, turned into informal and unwritten rules, allowing the actors to engage in socio-economic strategies. In other words, they were turned into a specific 'habitus' that again further speeded up the accumulation of bridging social capital and promoted the recruitment of future generations of local entrepreneurs in a good circle, *cf.* our kick-starter model. In this way, bridging social capital-building was secured.

At a more general level, the combined theory and case study here demonstrated that because the only sanctioning mechanism in voluntary groups is a social sanctioning/reputation effect, then the setting for these effective social sanction mechanisms must be maintained. Three preconditions must be fulfilled: (1) voluntary groups should not be formally institutionalized, *i.e.* a bottom-up approach, (2) the size of such well-functioning voluntary groups should not be increased, and (3) physical meeting places ('social platforms') should be established. Otherwise the disciplining effect of repeated face-to-face interaction will be diminished. The presence of these three conditions should be considered in any organization, be it public and private, if it wants to enhance its stock of social capital.

NOTES

1. This article draws heavily on Svendsen and Svendsen 2004. We acknowledge financial support for our ongoing Social Capital Project (SoCap) from the Danish Social Science Research Foundation, the Rockwool Foundation and the World Bank. Thousand thanks to Else

Løvdal Nielsen for language revision and – as always – many constructive suggestions.

2. For a review of the bridging/bonding social capital literature, see Patulny and Svendsen, 2007.

REFERENCES

Balle-Petersen, M. (1976), 'Foreningstiden' [The era of associations], *Arv og Eje*, Year Book, 43-68. Copenhagen: Dansk Kulturhistorisk Museumsforening.

Bjørn, C. (1982), 'Dansk mejeribrug' [Danish dairywork], in C. Bjørn (ed.), *Dansk Mejeribrug 1882-2000* [Danish Dairywork 1882-2000], Odense, Denmark: De Danske Mejeriers Fællesorganisation, pp. 11-188.

Bjørn, C. (ed.) (1988), *Det Danske Landbrugs Historie* [History of the Danish Agriculture], vol. 3, Copenhagen: Det Danske Landboselskab.

Boix, C. and D.N. Posner (1998), 'Social capital: explaining its origins and effects on government performance', *British Journal of Political Science*, 28 (4), 686-93.

Bourdieu, P. (1977), *Outline of a Theory of Practice*, Cambridge: Cambridge University Press.

Bourdieu, P. (1986), 'The forms of capital', in J.G. Richardson (ed.) *Handbook of Theory and Research for the Sociology of Education*, New York, Westport, CT and London: Greenwood Press, pp. 241-58.

Bourdieu, P. (1989), *Distinction: A Social Critique of the Judgement of Taste*, London: Routledge.

Bourdieu, P. (1990), *The Logic of Practice*, Cambridge: Polity.

Coleman, J.S. (1988a), 'Social capital in the creation of human capital', *American Journal of Sociology*, 94, 95-121.

Coleman, J.S. (1988b), 'The creation and destruction of social capital: implications for the law', *Journal of Law, Ethics and Public Policy*, 3, 375-404.

Coleman, J.S. (1990), *Foundations of Social Theory*, Cambridge, MA: Harvard University Press.

Dollerup, P. (1966), *Brugsforeningerne 1866-1896. Sociale, Økonomiske og Politiske Undersøgelser i de Danske Brugsforeningers Historie fra 1866 til 1896* [The Co-operative Wholesale Societies 1866-1896. Social, Economic and Political Investigations in the History of the Danish Co-operative Wholesale Societies from 1866 to 1896], Albertslund, Denmark: Det Danske Forlag.

Feldbæk, O. (1988), 'Kongen bød—Enevælden og reformerne' [The king commanded—The absolute monarchy and the agricultural reforms], in C. Bjørn (ed.), *Landboreformerne—Forskning og Forløb* [The Agricultural Reforms—Research and Course], Odense, Denmark: Landbohistorisk Selskab, pp. 9-29.

Hansgaard, T. (1981), *Landboreformerne i Danmark i det 18. Århundrede. Problemer og Synspunkter* [The Agricultural Reforms in 18th Century Denmark. Problems and Opinions], Viborg, Denmark: Landbohistorisk Selskab.

Hume, D. [(1739) 1984], *A Treatise of Human Nature*, New York: Penguin Books.

Korsgaard, O. (1997), *Kampen om Lyset. Dansk Voksenoplysning gennem 500 År* [The Struggle for Light. Danish Adult Education through 500 Years], Copenhagen: Gyldendal.

Leisner, J. (1988), 'Den oplyste enevælde. Historien om en dansk succes' [The Enlightened Monarchy. The History of a Danish Success], in C. Bjørn (ed.), *Landboreformerne—forskning og forløb* [The Agricultural Reforms—Research and Course], Odense, Denmark: Landbohistorisk Selskab, pp. 30-43.

Manøe-Hansen (ed.) (1972), *Hjedding Andelsmejeri 1882-1905* [Hjedding Co-operative Dairy 1882-1905], Ansager, Denmark: Ølgod Museum.

Mingione, E. (1991), *Fragmented Societies: A Sociology of Economic Life Beyond the Market Paradigm*, Oxford: Basil Blackwell.

Nyhan, D. (2000), 'Book Review of *Bowling Alone*' in *Boston Globe*, www.BowlingAlone.com/reviews.php3, access date: September 20, 2000.

Ostrom, E. (1990), *Governing the Commons. The Evolution of Institutions for Collective Action*, Cambridge: Cambridge University Press.

Ostrom, E. (1992), *Crafting Institutions for Self-governing Irrigation Systems*, San Francisco, CA: Institute for Contemporary Studies Press.

Ostrom, E. (1994), 'Constituting social capital and collective action', *Journal of Theoretical Politics*, 6 (4), 527-62.

Ostrom, E., R. Gardner and J. Walker (1994), *Rules, Games, and Common-pool Resources*, Ann Arbor, MI: University of Michigan Press.

Paldam, M. and G.T. Svendsen (2002), 'Missing social capital and the transition in Eastern Europe', *Journal of Institutional Innovation, Development and Transition*, 5, 21-34.

Patulny, R. and G.L.H. Svendsen (2007) 'Exploring the social capital grid: Bonding, bridging, qualitative, quantitative', forthcoming in *International Journal of Sociology and Social Policy*, 2007, No. 2.

Portes, A. (1998), 'Social capital: origins and applications', *Annual Review of Sociology*, 24, 1-24.

Portes, A. (2000), 'The two meanings of social capital', *Sociological Forum*, 15, 1-12.

Portes, A. and P. Landolt (1996), 'The downside of social capital', *American Prospect*, 26, May–June, 18–21.

Portes, A. and J. Sensenbrenner (1993), 'Embeddedness and immigration: notes on the social determinants of economic action', *American Journal of Sociology*, 98 (6), 1320–50.

Putnam, R.D. (1993a), *Making Democracy Work. Civic Traditions in Modern Italy*, Princeton, NJ: Princeton University Press.

Putnam, R.D. (1993b), 'The prosperous community. Social capital and public life', *American Prospect*, 13, Spring, 35–42.

Putnam, R.D. (1995), 'Bowling alone: America's declining social capital', *Journal of Democracy*, 6 (1), 65-78.

Putnam, R.D. (1996), 'The strange disappearance of civic America', *American Prospect*, 24, Winter, 34–48.

Putnam, R.D. (2000), *Bowling Alone. The Collapse and Revival of American Community*, New York, London, Toronto, Singapore: Simon & Schuster.

Ravnholt, H. (1943), *Den danske Andelsbevægelse* [The Danish Co-operative Movement], Copenhagen: Det Danske Selskab.

Rørdam, T. (1983), *Fra Andelssamfundets Barndom.* [From the Childhood of the Co-operative Society], Jelling, Denmark: Dansk Friskoleforening.

Sen, A. (1999), *Development as Freedom.* Oxford, Oxford University Press.

Smith, A. [(1776) 1991], *The Wealth of Nations*, New York: Everyman's Library, A.A. Knopf.

Sobel, J. (2002), 'Can we trust social capital?', *Journal of Economic Literature*, 40, March, 139–54.

Sonne, H.C. (1867), *Om Arbejderforeninger. Til Oplysning og Veiledning* [About Workers' Associations. For Enlightenment and Instruction], Copenhagen: Louis Kleins Bogtrykkeri.

Svendsen, G.L.H. and G.T. Svendsen (2000), 'Measuring social capital: The Danish Co-operative Dairy Movement', *Sociologia Ruralis*, 40 (1), 72–86.

Svendsen, G.L.H. and G.T. Svendsen (2003), 'The wealth of nations: Bourdieuconomics and social capital', *Theory and Society*, 32 (5/6) (special double issue in memory of Pierre Bourdieu), 607-631.

Svendsen, G.L.H. and G.T. Svendsen (2004), *The Creation and Destruction of Social Capital: Entrepreneurship, Co-operative Movements and Institutions.* Edward Elgar, Cheltenham, UK, Northampton, USA.

Svendsen, G.L.H. (2006), 'Studying social capital *in situ.* An Anthropological Approach', *Theory and Society,* (1), 39-70.

Swedberg, R. (1994), 'Markets as social structures', in Neil Smelser and Richard Swedberg (eds.), *The Handbook of Economic Sociology*, Princeton, NJ: Princeton University Press, pp. 255–82.

Tietenberg, T.H. (2002), *Environmental and Natural Resource Economics*, 6th Edition, Reading, MA: Addison Wesley Longman Higher Education.

Williamson, O.E. (1975), *Markets and Hierarchies: Analysis and Antitrust Implications*, New York: Free Press.

Woolcock, M. (1998), 'Social capital and economic development: toward a theoretical synthesis and policy framework', *Theory and Society*, 27, 151-208.

4

Road Network Analysis of Atulia Union in Shyamnagar Thana of Satkhira District, Bangladesh

KHAN RUBAYET RAHAMAN, ABU SAYED and MD. ZAKIR HOSSAIN

Introduction

The integration of rural areas into the national economy can only be achieved through key urban-rural linkages. These are the connections which provide the network needed to facilitate important flows, such as the movement of agricultural products into agro-processing centres, the distribution of agricultural inputs or the spread of innovations and new ideas from centres to their hinterlands (ESCAP, 1979). Many poor villages in Bangladesh do not have all-weather road access and are often cut off for long periods during the wet season when access roads become impassable. The provision of basic, all-weather road access can thus serve as a valuable instrument for rural poverty alleviation. Road network has a part to play in the agricultural development of unpopulated but fertile areas. The best results are likely to be achieved if road network is planned in conjunction with other development inputs (Schelling and Liu, 2000). Rural roads are an important sector in rural development, which deals in all aspects of development including agriculture, health, education, forestry, fisheries, small-scale industries, trade, commerce etc. that depends on good communication. Rural transportation network will give shape to the living environment of villagers; rather roads of rural transportation are the connectivity elements in our society (Rao, 2003). Appropriate combination of various links both technically and economically can generate rural traffic infrastructure, which should be prepared for the measure of land development. Rural road connectivity is not only the key component of Rural Development; it is also recognized as an effective poverty reduction programme. An improved accessibility to all quarters of a village is an indispensable prerequisite for the provision of adequate living conditions in rural areas (Rao, 2003).

Good road network is one of the best key for development of any area. It helps by reducing our valuable time, expenses and distance. If we are not able to develop our road network, economy will not be strong as other developed countries. Flood is the common problem of our country. Every year millions of lives, livestock and corps are damaged by flood. To defense this situation good road networking is much effective. Most of the people in our country related with farming. They have to sale their goods in the market. Farmers need seed, fertilizer, plant, insecticide, animal aids for well production of agriculture. Eco-tourism is one of the best sources of earning foreign currency. If communication as well as road networking is developed for going to the remote area where natural sight or tourist spot is situated then tourists from other countries will be more interested to visit our natural sights. So, it is necessary to expand our plan for the road networking policy.

Shyamnagar, the largest thana of Satkhira district, in respect of area, was established in 1897. The thana occupies an area of 1968.24 sq. km. including 1534.88 sq. km. forest area. It is located between 21°36′ and 22°24′ north latitudes and between 89° 00′ and 89°19′ east longitudes. The thana is bounded by Kaliganj (Satkhira) and Assasuni upazilas on the north, Sunderbans and Bay of Bengal on the south, Koyra and Assasuni upazilas on the east, West Bengal of India on the west. The Atulia union is located at the north-eastern part of the Shyamanagar thana with the total area of 41.01 sq. km. The union is bounded on the north by Kashimarj union, on the east by Kholpetua river, on the south by Munshiganj and Buri Goalini union and on the west by Shyamnagar union. In Atulia union, shrimp farming is the principal occupation of the people irrespective of their income status. Agriculture is also a major source of income of the village. Since 1985, the agricultural farms are being converted to shrimp farms because of comparatively quick and higher rate of return from investment. This is the only reason behind the increasing involvement of the most inhabitants in shrimp cultivation. The interdependency in change of land use and transportation is not well appreciated in Atulia union and this keeps the economic system inactive in this area. The absence of good quality road network in Atulia union leads to stagnation of socio-economic conditions of the villagers.

The objectives of the study are identification and digital documentation of the existing road network, to analyze the problems related to existing road network and to recommend some guidelines to improve this road network, particularly through provision of basic, reliable all-weather road access to villages.

Methodology

At first a recognizance survey was conducted to get an overall idea about the study area. Primary data were collected by field survey and observation. While conducting the observation survey the researcher took some photographs to understand the existing situation. In field survey road condition, surface condition, transport mode related data were collected. Secondary data were collected from different transport related offices such as LGED office, Union Parisad, books and journals etc. Map of the study area has been collected from the Union Parisad. After data collection these data were processed manually. The processing of data was checking completed questionnaires for detecting and removing possible errors that might have crept in. For connectivity analysis, Atulia union was divided into seven zones. These zones were delineated on the basis of people's interest to go from the area to the nearest market or growth centre. Secondly, the accessibility of the important government and non-government social, economical and commercial infrastructures with the growth centres. The information from questionnaire survey, maps and secondary sources were interpreted and analyzed with the help of different statistical, mathematical and software tools. The findings were portrayed and arranged in various tables and figures.

Existing Road Network

Road Classification

According to the road classification of LGED, Feeder Road Type–B (FRB), Rural Road Class 1 (R1), Rural Road Class 2 (R2), Rural

Road Class 3 (R3) are included in rural road (World Bank, 1996). In the study area Rural Road Class 1 (R1), Rural Road Class 2 (R2) and Rural Road Class 3 (R3) are available.

Road Length according to Road Type

Table 4.1 shows that in the study area the total length of R3 is 80.16 kilometres which is 74.93 per cent of the total road length. On the other hand, R2 and R1 are 19.67 kilometres and 7.15 kilometres respectively. The percentage of the length of R2 is 18.39 and R1 is 6.68. Figure 4.1 shows the road network of Atulia union classified according to road types.

Table 4.1: Road Length according to Road Type

Types of Road	*Length (km)*	*Percentage*
Rural Road Class 1 (R1)	7.15	6.68
Rural Road Class 2 (R2)	19.67	18.39
Rural Road Class 3 (R3)	80.16	74.93
Total	**106.98**	**100.00**

Source: Field Survey, May 2005.

Road Width according to Road Type

Table 4.2 shows the standard road width defined by LGED. In the study area the crest width, pavement width and shoulder width of the rural road class 1 (R1) is as equal as the standard road width of the LGED. But the average crest width of the rural road class 2 (R2) is 2.90 meter which is less than the standard road width of the LGED. In case of rural road class 3 (R3), their average width (1.83 meter) is also less than the standard. Table 4.3 shows the existing road width of the study area according to road type.

Table 4.2: Road Width according to Road Type

Types of Road	*Crest Width (m)*	*Pavement Width (m)*	*Shoulder Width (m)*
Rural Road Class 1 (R1)	4.87	3.05	0.91
Rural Road Class 2 (R2)	3.72	–	–
Rural Road Class 3 (R3)	2.44	–	–

Source: LGED, 1993.

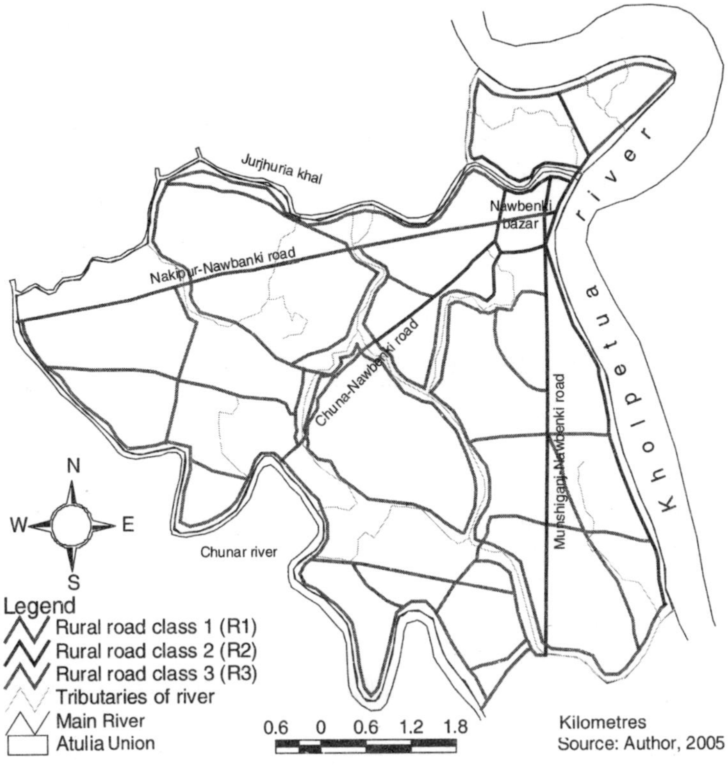

Fig. 4.1: Road Classification of Atulia Union

Table 4.3: Average Road Width of the Study area according to Road Type

Types of Road	*Crest Width (m)*	*Pavement Width (m)*	*Shoulder Width (m)*
Rural Road Class 1 (R1)	4.87	3.05	0.91
Rural Road Class 2 (R2)	2.90	0	0
Rural Road Class 3 (R3)	1.83	0	0

Source: Field Survey, November 2005.

Road Condition

Road Formation Condition

Condition of road is an important indicator of effective road network.

LGED defines three types of road condition. These are good, average and poor (World Bank, 1996). Here good refers to both formation and surface is in good condition, only routine maintenance needed, average refers to some periodical maintenance needed, but no major construction needed and poor refers to base and sub-base damaged, major maintenance needed in order to bring the road into a maintainable condition.

Table 4.4: Present Road Condition in the Study area according to Type and Length

Road Type / Condition	R1-type	R2-type	R3-type	Total (Km)	Percentage
	Length (km)	Length (km)	Length (km)		
Good	6.0	0.85	23.38	30.23	28.26
Average	0.0	6.63	11.41	18.04	16.86
Poor	1.15	12.19	45.37	58.71	54.88
Total	**7.15**	**19.67**	**80.16**	**106.98**	**100.00**

Source: Field Survey, May 2005.

Table 4.4 shows that 30.23 kilometres road is in good condition that is 28.26 per cent of the total in which R1-type is 6 kilometres, R2-type is 0.85 kilometres and R3-type is 23.38 kilometres which are 83.92 per cent, 4.32 per cent and 29.17 per cent of the respective roads. Again 18.04 kilometres road is in average condition that is 16.86 per cent of the total road in which R2-type is 6.63 kilometres and R3-type is 11.41 kilometres which are 33.71 per cent and 14.23 per cent of the respective roads. And 58.71 kilometres road is in poor condition that is 54.88 per cent of the total road in which R1-type is 1.15 kilometres, R2-type is 12.19 kilometres and R3-type is 45.37 kilometres which are 16.08 per cent, 61.97 per cent and 56.60 per cent of the respective roads. Figure 4.2 shows spatially the existing road condition of the Atulia union.

Road Surface Condition

Road surface is another indicator of effective rural road network. Easy, smooth and fast movement, types of mode, duration of travel time, transportation cost of people and goods, seasonal accessibility of roads etc. depend on the road surface. Paved roads fully engineered

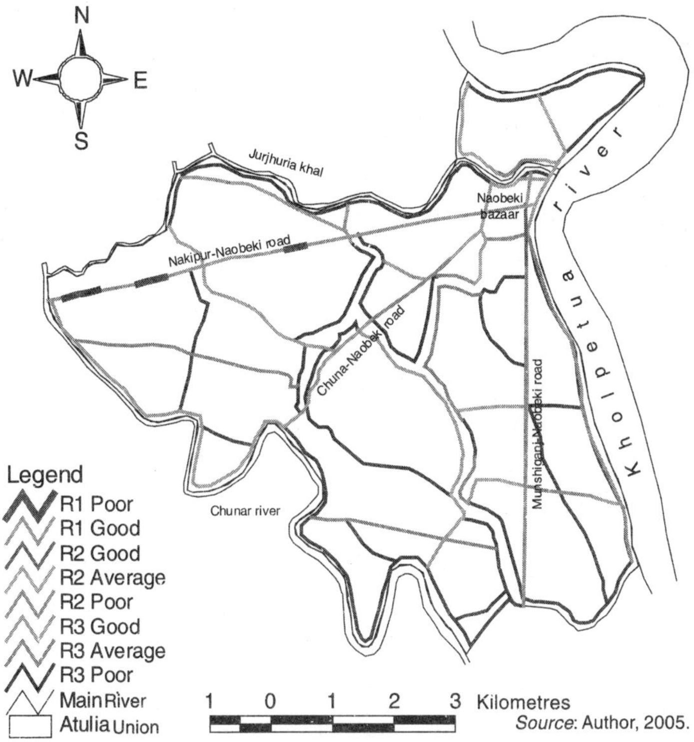

Fig. 4.2: Existing Road Condition of Atulia union

width adequate strength provided by a sub-base-wearing course construction on top of properly compacted and improved sub-grade. Herringbone bond roads are fully engineered width adequate strength provided by bricks on top of properly compacted and improved sub-grade. Brick soling roads also contain engineered width adequate strength provided by small pieces of bricks on top of properly compacted and improved sub-grade. Earthen roads, either predominantly clayey or sandy with the limited structural strength of the *in situ* material only (ESCAP, 1979). Paved surface is the indicator of good road condition. On the other hand earthen road is the symbol of worst condition of road. In the study area above four types of road are available. Figure 4.3 shows the existing surface condition of road of Atulia union.

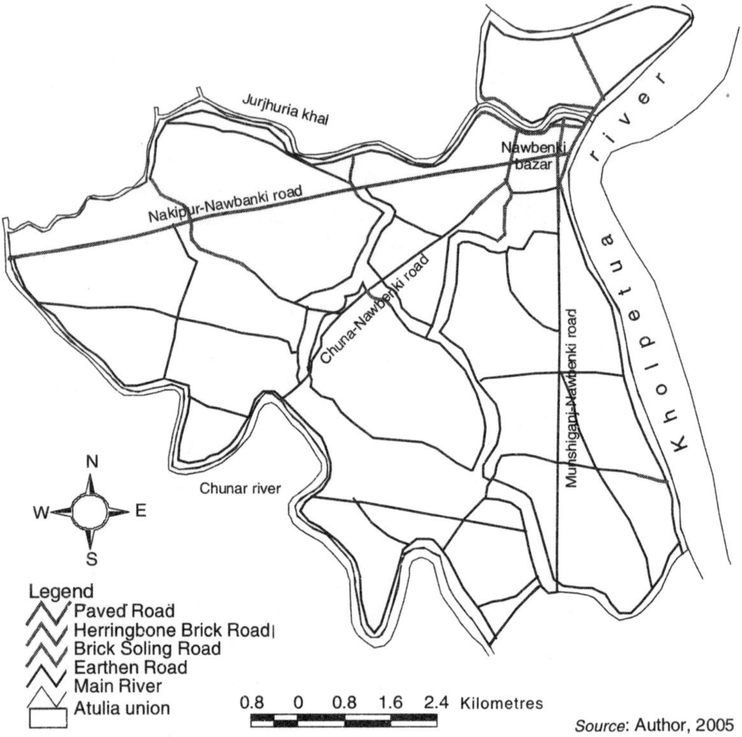

Fig. 4.3: Existing Road Surface Condition of Atulia union

Table 4.5: Existing Road Surface in the Study Area according to Type and Length

Road Type / *Surface*	*R1* *Length (km)*	*R2* *Length (km)*	*R3* *Length (km)*	*Total (Km)*	*Percentage*
Paved	7.15	0.85	0.0	8.0	7.48
Herringbone Brick	0.0	0.0	1.0	1.0	0.93
Brick Soling	0.0	6.63	2.87	9.5	8.88
Earthen	0.0	12.19	76.29	88.48	82.71
Total	**7.15**	**19.67**	**80.16**	**106.98**	**100.00**

Source: Field Survey, May, 2005.

Table 4.5 shows that in Atulia union has 8 kilometres paved road that is 7.48 per cent of the total in which rural road class 1

(R1) is 7.15 kilometres and rural road class 2 (R2) is 0.85 kilometre. Again 1 kilometre is herringbone bond road that is 0.93 per cent of the total in which rural road class 3 (R3) is 1 kilometre. Brick's soling road is 9.5 kilometres that is 8.88 per cent of the total in which rural road class 2 (R2) is 6.63 kilometres and rural road class 3 (R3) is 2.87 kilometres. And 88.48 kilometres is earthen road that is 82.71 per cent of the total in which rural road class 2 (R2) is 12.19 kilometres, rural road class 3 (R3) is 76.29 kilometres.

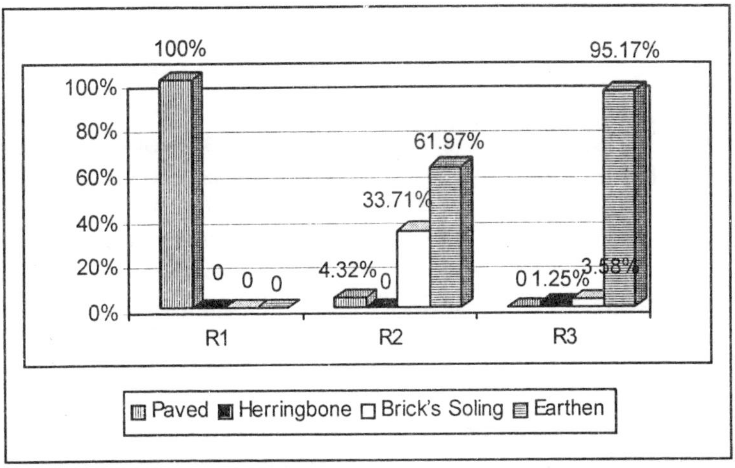

Source: Field Survey, May 2005.

Fig. 4.4: Percentage of Different Types of Road according to Surface Condition

Figure 4.4 shows that 100 per cent rural road class 1 (R1) is paved road. In rural road class 2 (R2) 4.32 per cent is paved, 33.71 per cent is brick soling and 61.97 per cent is earthen road. In rural road class 3 (R3) 1.25 per cent is herringbone brick, 3.58 per cent is brick soling and 95.17 per cent is earthen road. Figure 4.5 shows some photographs of existing road surface of the study area.

Culvert, Bridge and Sluice Gate

Culvert is an important element of road network. When the water

Fig. 4.5: Present Road Surface of Atulia union

line intersects the road, the point of that intersection of the road requires culvert, where the road is on very low land, there also requires culvert for frequent movement of water transport. Bridge links up the two sides of river or canals. Sluice gates are very much necessary for the irrigation purpose of agricultural production. In the study area there are 15 sluice gates and culverts. Among these 15 sluice gates and 3 culverts are on rural road class 1(R1), 7 are on rural road class 2 (R2) and rest 5 are on rural road class 3 (R3). Atulia union is situated on the bank of Kholpetua river. On the other side of this river Padma Pukur union is situated. From Padma Pukur union many people come to Atulia union and *vise versa* for business purpose. But there is no bridge between these two unions. If it can be established a bridge (*vide* figure 4.6 for proposed location) on the Kholpetua river then the road network of Atulia union will be more harmonized and the people will be benefited economically. Figure 4.6 shows the location of important establishments that are available in the Atulia Union.

Connectivity

Connectivity of establishments or infrastructures is one of the most important elements of road network. Figure 4.7 shows the zone-wise different establishment in Atulia union. Atulia union is divided into seven zones. These zones are delineated on the basis of accessibility of the important government and non-government social, economical and commercial infrastructures with the growth centres. These are zone1, zone 2, zone 3, zone 4, zone 5, zone 6 and zone 7. Table 4.6 shows the available infrastructure in every zone. Most of the infrastructures (31) are available in the zone 1 among these seven zones. This zone is well accessible from other regions. Every infrastructure is well connected by road network

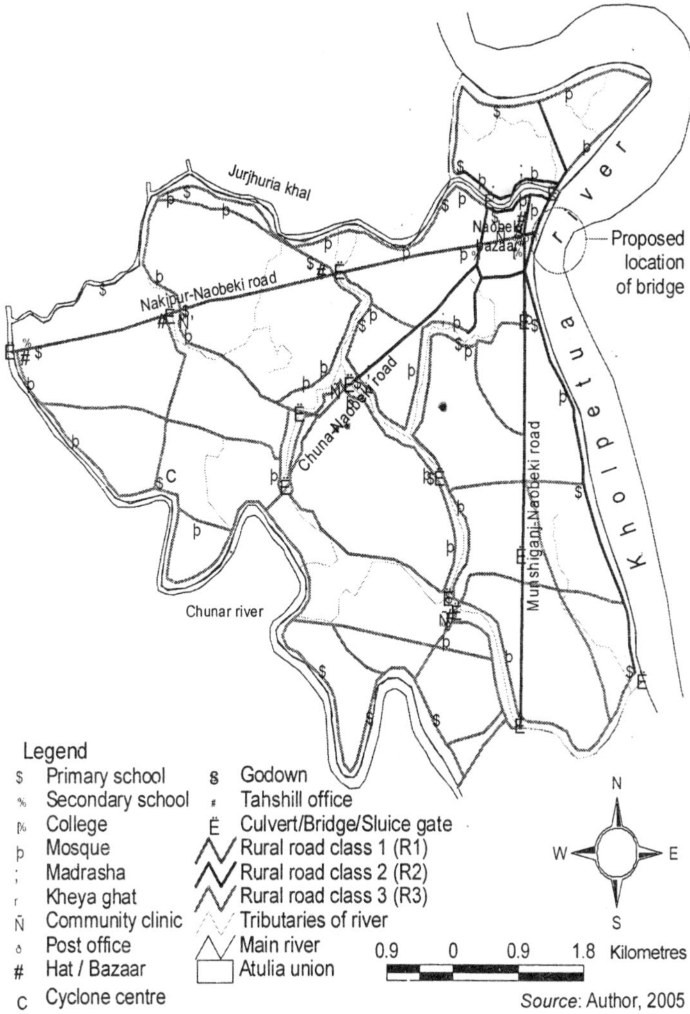

Fig. 4.6: Important Establishment of Atulia union

although there is still poor rural road class 3. Every settlement of this zone is also connected by road network. Fifteen infrastructures are available in the zone 2. Available infrastructure of this zone is well connected by road but 6 infrastructures are connected by the poor rural road class 3. One settlement in this zone is disconnected from the road (*vide* Figure 4.7). Fourteen infrastructures are available in the zone 3.

Table 4.6: Zone-wise Important Establishment in Atulia union

Establishment	*Zone 1*	*Zone 2*	*Zone 3*	*Zone 4*	*Zone 5*	*Zone 6*	*Zone 7*	*Total*
Kheya Ghat	1	0	0	0	0	0	0	1
Primary School	5	3	3	2	3	3	2	21
Secondary School	2	0	0	1	0	1	0	4
College	1	0	0	0	0	0	0	1
Mosque	11	7	4	3	4	3	0	32
Madrasha	3	1	1	0	0	0	0	5
Community Clinic	1	1	1	0	0	1	0	4
Post Office	1	0	1	0	0	1	0	3
Hat/Bazaar	1	1	1	1	0	1	0	5
Cyclone Centre	0	0	0	1	0	0	0	1
Godown	1	0	0	0	0	0	0	1
Tahshil Office	1	0	0	0	0	0	0	1
Culvert/Bridge/Sluice Gate	3	2	3	1	1	5	0	15
Total	**31**	**15**	**14**	**9**	**8**	**15**	**2**	**94**

Source: Field Survey, May 2005.

This zone is also well accessible from other region. Every infrastructure is well connected by road network but many people are not getting these service facilities as half of these service facilities (6) within this zone are located in the same place. Three settlements in this zone are not connected by road network (*vide* figure 4.7). Nine infrastructures are available in the zone 4. Only one cyclone shelter in the Atulia union is situated in this zone. Infrastructures of this zone are well connected by road network but the cyclone centre is connected by the poor rural road class 3 and only one settlement is disconnected from the road network (*vide* Figure 4.7). Eight infrastructures are available in the zone 5. This zone is nearer to the zone 1, zone 2 and zone 6. For this most of the infrastructures are not available in this zone. Every infrastructure and settlement in this is well connected by the rural road class 2 and rural road class 3. Fifteen infrastructures are available in the zone 6. This zone is well accessible from other region but this zone is far away from the union headquarters. Every infrastructure is well connected and only one settlement is not connected by road network (*vide* Figure 4.7). Among these seven zones, the lowest infrastructure is prevalent here. Only 2 infrastructures are available in the zone 7. This zone is not well connected from other regions of the Union and two settlements are disconnected from the road network (*vide* Figure 4.7).

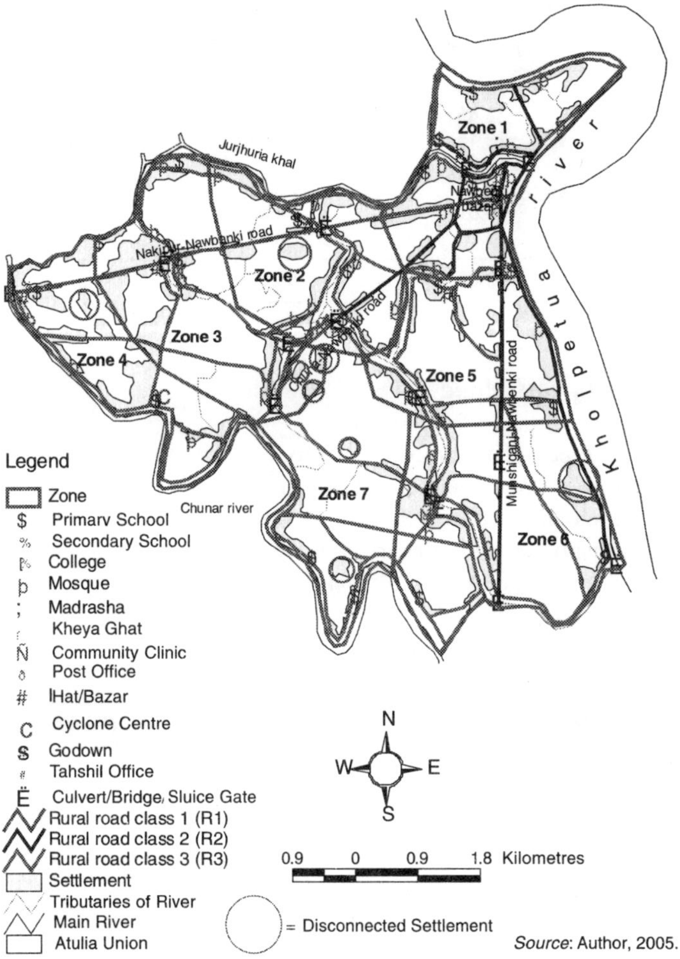

Fig. 4.7: Zone-wise Important Establishment of Atulia Union

Table 4.7 shows that 32.45 per cent R1-type roads are in zone 2. In the zone 5, 6 and 7, there is no R1-type roads. Most of the R2-type roads (56.95%) are in zone 1. The main growth centre (Naobeki Bazaar) is situated in this zone. There are no R2-type roads in the zone 3, 4 and zone 7. R3-type roads are available in every zone. In zone 6, there is 23.59 per cent of the total R3-type roads are available.

Table 4.7: Road Length according to Zone

Zone	R1-type (%)	R2-type (%)	R3 –type (%)
1	24.20	56.95	9.84
2	32.45	6.86	15.18
3	26.15	0.0	16.69
4	17.20	0.0	10.99
5	0.0	22.11	10.84
6	0.0	14.08	23.59
7	0.0	0.0	12.87
Total	**100.00**	**100.00**	**100.00**

Source: Field Survey, May 2005.

Transportation Mode

Different types of transportation mode are available in the Atulia union. Van, bicycle (helicopter), hackney motor cycle, and Engine Van are the main transportation modes that are available in this road. These transportation modes are mainly used for mobilization of rural resources such as fish, agricultural products. Every people of Atulia union are somehow depended with these transportation modes.

Table 4.8: Available Transportation Mode

Transport Mode	Number	Percentage
Van	213	48.74
Bicycle (Helicopter)	124	28.37
Hackney Motor Cycle	88	20.14
Engine Van	12	2.75
Total	**437**	**100.00**

Source: Field Survey, May 2005.

From Table 4.8, it is observed that van takes place first and bicycle (helicopter) takes place second as a mode of transport because the operator are poor, they can easily get van and helicopter than the other mode within their affordability. Other transportation modes are also available. These transportation modes are totally unfit to move on the rural road class 3 (R3) during the rainy reason. Because in Atulia Union, most of the rural road class 3 are made of earthen. Engine boat is the only transportation mode to move within the village during the rainy season.

Recommendations

The following are the recommendations of this study:

- Surface condition of the road R2 and R3 should be improved from earthen to herringbone brick or brick soling.
- Road should be improved from poor condition to good condition by maintaining regularly.
- As bridge is an important element of road network, therefore, it is important to establish a bridge at Naobeki Growth Centre which will connect this union with the Gar Padma Pukur union.
- Union Parisad may prepare a future road development plan considering the future development aspects of this region.

Conclusion

Rural roads are vital to the movement of agricultural production and fish from the production farm to the marketplace in context of the study area. In addition, these roads are used extensively in the secondary movement of grain from country elevators to terminal elevators or domestic processing plants. In Atulia Union there is sufficient road network to mobilize these resources. But the main problem is poor surface condition. 82.71 per cent of the total is earthen road deprived from all weather access. Another important problem of this road is that most of the road (about 54.88%) is in poor condition. That indicates base and sub-base damaged, major maintenance needed in order to bring the road into a maintainable condition. In the study area there are sufficient infrastructures which are closely related with the road network. Every infrastructure is well connected by road network but this road is not all-weather accessible. Due to the lack of technical guidance and weak funding mechanism for road maintenance, brick's soling and herringbone bond road is considered by local politicians and decision-makers as the only technical solution to ensure all-weather road accessibility. This analysis has confirmed the need for spatial development of road network configuration considering easy access of the users, which can achieve the desired results of economic, social interaction and overall development of the region.

REFERENCES

Atulia Union Parisad, 1979, *Map of Atulia Union.*

Author, (2005), *Author prepared the map for the present study, the base map collected from the Union Parishad, Atulia, Shyamnagar, Satkhira.*

Economic and Social Commission for Asia and the Pacific (ESCAP), (1979), *Guidelines for Rural Centre Planning,* New York, pp. 185-204.

Local Government Engineering Department (*LGED*), (1993), Second edition, June 1993.

Rao, L., (2003), *Rural Infrastructure Planning with emphasis on road network connectivity by Coplanar Concurrent Theory, Transportation, Map India 2003, URL: www.worldbank.org/transport/publicat, explored on September 9, 2005.*

Schelling, D., and Liu, Z., (2000), Designing a Rural Basic Access Road Project: The Case of Andhra Pradesh, India, *Journal of Infrastructure Notes, Transport No. RT-4,* January, 2000, pp. 1-4.

World Bank, (1996), Bangladesh Rural Infrastructure Strategy Study, *The University Press Limited,* Dhaka, Bangladesh, pp. 4-10.

5

Organizing Rural Elderly into Self-Help Groups: An Approach towards Sustainability

K. MANIKANDAN and S. SATHIYA BABU

Introduction

The elderly are marginalized both by family and communities in many parts of India. NGOs have been addressing to this issue through running homes for the aged, with or without collecting charges from the elderly (or from their families). The number of homes is increasing from time to time. However, these homes are not adequate to accommodate all the elderly who are neglected/ marginalized especially those elderly who are living in rural areas. This may be partly due to the fact that the rural elderly prefer to live in their own villages even being marginalized rather than offering themselves to be accommodated at these homes.

In rural areas one can find elderly those who do not have any source of income/livelihood opportunities depending fully on their offsprings and destitute elderly roaming about for mere subsistence. The condition of the elderly who live in the villages situated along the coastal area of south India particularly, Tamil Nadu and Kerala were further vandalized by the recent Tsunami. In this context, Helpage India's (HI) positive and ready response deserves mention. HI perceived that the impact of Tsunami was likely to be higher among elderly and make them more vulnerable. As such the areas of immediate concern of HI were the vulnerability of elderly in terms of losses of life, livelihood, possessions and emotional support, loss of coping mechanism and reduced access to relief assistance.

Keeping the above in view, HI embarked on a Tsunami Rehabilitation Project so as to address the specific needs of elderly in the Tsunami affected villages in Tamil Nadu and Kerala. The project was implemented in collaboration with Non Government Organizations called partner agencies in fifty five villages. In the process of implementation, HI followed a novel approach in the directions of sustainability of elderly care at the village level. The approach is, establishing and promoting Elders Self-Help Groups (ESHGs) and federating them at village and district level and thus ensuring the sustainability of elderly care. In this chapter, an attempt is made to highlight some of the issues related to the approach, to outline the challenges of the approach and to provide suggestions to overcome them.

Implications and Imperatives

HI started following this approach in the mid of 2005. The implications and imperatives of the approach are as follows:

- An approach to provide socio-economic and emotional care and support.
- Forming ESHG with a maximum of 20 members (men, women and mixed groups) above 55 years of age.
- Mobilizing savings from within and lending among members (as in women self-help groups).
- Savings operation is expected to build confidence among elderly in the terms of financial security to some extent.
- Loan operations are expected to help elderly to find suitable livelihood opportunities at the village level.
- Those who are destitute (elderly) and unable to offer themselves to be accommodated at homes are taken care of by the ESHGs at the village level to some extent.
- Elderly people are organized into groups. This gives a sense of moral strength and power and peer support among the elderly.
- When the ESHGs are federated at the village level as Village Level Federation, (VLF), their unity, strength and power are further enhanced. The representatives of each ESHG are

the members of VLF. It serves as a forum to take up issues of social protection with more vigour and strength and to create horizontal linkages for the betterment of elderly apart from financial aspects at the village level.

- Eventually at the district level, District Level Federations (DLFs) are formed to function as a strong organization to create networking and linkages in order to ensure sustainability of elderly care in terms of livelihood and social protection. DLF is a registered body with members drawn from each VLF to bring organic linkage. DLF, in the long run, would serve as an NGO which will be owned and managed by elderly.

Achievements

- The project staffs have established nearly 200 ESHGs in the project villages.
- Almost all the ESHGs have regular savings and also subscription.
- Major proportion of the loans is provided for productive purposes only. To quote a case, all the ESHGs in a village have so far lent 90 per cent of their funds for undertaking micro-enterprises such as, vegetable vending, fish vending, cattle rearing etc.
- The ESHG, have really made a great impact on the lives of elderly in the sense that they now earn a respect in the society. The very existence of ESHGs has brought positive changes in the mindset of family members towards elderly care too.
- At the village level, VLF discusses the ways and means to augment income to the groups and issues related to protect the interest of the elderly.
- The District level federations are established and in Cuddalore and Nagapattinam districts. In the DLF meetings, the members have full freedom to discuss whatever the issue they wish to. Thus it is a forum with real democracy of elderly people which is notable and could be seldom found elsewhere.
- In a few villages, even the women SHGs and youth group appreciated the manner of functioning of ESHGs.

Thus the approach has yielded good results in addressing the vulnerability of elderly in the project villages. However, while attempting to follow this approach one may encounter certain challenges/problems as discussed below:

Challenges/Problems

- Some of the elderly who are dependant on family members wholly, may not be able to join in the ESHGs.
- Frequent deaths of members of ESHGs and reduction in the numerical strength of the groups.
- Being dependent on outsiders for the maintenance of accounts and records in certain areas/groups.
- In some villages, there may not be healthy relationship among ESHGs particularly between women ESHGs and men ESHGs. Thus horizontal linkages could not be established.
- A few SHGs may deal with finance only and may not take upon other issues.

A Few Tips to Mitigate the above Challenges/Problems

- Understanding clearly the socio-economic and cultural conditions of all the elderly in the village.
- Flexibility in savings stipulated from group to group.
- Reorganization and strengthening of ESHGs in case of demise of the members.
- Involving community members, especially the youth to keep accounts and records on behalf of the elderly in case no member in the group can handle the task.
- Conducting sensitization sessions and generating awareness constantly among ESHG members and community members to establish horizontal as well as external linkages that could pave way for the betterment of elderly.

Conclusion

The approach of ESHGs to address to the problems of elderly has several merits including organizational strength and financial strength. It is a novel approach that could seldom be seen elsewhere than HI and has yielded positive results from the viewpoint of sustainability. Having highlighted this, this chapter has also outlined certain challenges/problems one may confront with while following this approach towards elderly care particularly in rural areas. The tips given above, if rightly followed, this approach would work well towards sustainability of livelihood and social protection of elderly.

REFERENCES

Dwaraki, B.R., (2006) Research and Documentation on the Traditional and Social Structures in the care of Elderly, Cuddalore: HI Tsunami Rehabilitation Project.

Help Age India (2005) Project Management Information Document, Cuddalore: HI Tsunami Rehabilitation Project.

Sathiya Babu, S., (2006) Community Based Elders Care System, project working document, Cuddalore: HI Tsunami Rehabilitation Project.

6

Application of Pragmatic Methodology for Generation of Rural Employment in India

M. SHIVAMURTHY

Introduction

Eminent Agricultural Scientist M.S. Swaminathan (1985), raised the issue of employment as follows: Developing countries with large rural population have already serious problems of unemployment and under-employment. This is reflected in the unplanned migration of rural poors to towns and cities seeking opportunities to earn their daily bread. Therefore, technologies which reduce labour use will have to be concurrently accompanied by the creation of alternative avenues of employment. Unless job destruction and job creation are concurrent events, considerable human hardship can be the outcome from the adoption of technologies which substitute capital and machines for human labour. In several countries of Asia, under nutrition or calorie inadequacy is the major problem. This in turn tends to be more related to inadequate purchasing power rather than to the lack of an adequate supply of food in the market. Hence, an employment revolution is important for families without assets in the form of land or livestock to derive economic and nutritional benefit from the green revolution. New technologies should hence be subjected to an employment impact analysis before they are recommended for large scale adoption.

There is also a growing skepticism regarding government policies of the present. To provide employment to rural poor through *ad hoc* programmes like "Jawahar Rojgar Yojana" which the Government has so much emphasized as a solution to the difficult task of providing rural employment. The question arises as to whether *ad hoc* supplementary schemes can solve the problems of employment and poverty. In fact the solutions of these problems of poverty and unemployment have to be found within the framework of the Development Plan itself (G.V.K. Rao, 1979).

The Government of India claims that more employment is created by its several measures undertaken through the planned programmes in IRDP. Its main argument is that the growth is taking place satisfactorily and this has resulted in more employment. The Union Finance Minister in his 1995 Budget speech stated: "Growth has created new jobs for our people. In 1991-92, total employment grew by about three million. The reason given for this optimistic view is that the guaranteed manpower employment programmes in rural areas have been strengthened which has ensured increased employment in rural areas. The above mentioned optimistic view is, however, not supported by statistics and empirical evidences. On the other hand, the evaluation reports of labour absorption in rural areas are not that encouraging.

According to Economic Advisory Council report, employment growth has not kept pace with growth in labour force in spite of G.D.P. growth exceeding 5 per cent. There has been a deceleration in rural employment growth, the annual growth declining steadily from 2.82 per cent during 1972-73 and 1977-78 to 2.22 per cent during 1977-78 and 1983, further to 1.55 per cent during 1983 and 1987-88 (Rural Development Report, NIRD, 1994). It is reported that the Planning Commission in its mid-term appraisal of the 8th plan is understood to have expressed concern over the adverse impact of the reforms started in 1991. The poverty level has increased, but needs and opportunities have shrunk from planned targets. Assessing the performance of the economy in the first three years of the Plan period, it is reported to have said that an employment generation during the period 1992-93 has fallen short of the targets envisaged in the Plan.

At present only a small beginning is made regarding this requirement in promoting dairy enterprise and oilseed cultivation and that too in limited areas. However, much more efforts are needed to remove this cause influencing poverty.

Causes for Unemployment in Rural Areas

1. *Poor Progress in establishing Small Scale Industries in Rural Areas*: Growth of small scale industries complements vigorous agricultural development policy by providing employment in rural areas. However, at present vigorous programmes for the development of small scale industries in rural areas are not being taken up.
2. *Low Wages of Agricultural Labourers*: Full employment will not be a complete solution to poverty unless it is accompanied by higher earnings. Real wage rates of agricultural commodities are generally lower than those of Minimum Wages Act. Unless, these real labour wages are brought to the level mentioned in the Minimum Wages Act, the problem of poverty cannot be alleviated. Government projects of providing rural employment do not provide adequate employment. The National Rural Employment Projects namely; Jawahar Rojgar Yojana has hardly provided adequate employment to the rural poor.
3. *Inability of Modern Agricultural Technology to provide More Employment:* In general the very technologies which are so essential to provide the food, to back wages goods payments provide only a small proportion of increased income directly to labour through increased employment. Mellor (1975) has quoted the results from his survey under 14 diverse situations in India wherein only 5 to 15 per cent of increased income came from new technologies represented by payment for increased labour.
4. *Absorption of Labour in Agriculture not Kept Pace with the Development:* The Government appointed High Powered Committee of 1990 observes that "there are also positive indications that absorption of human labour in agriculture has not kept pace with the increase in population. According to the Economic Advisory Council Report the employment growth had not kept pace with the growth in labour force in spite of GDP growth exceeding five per cent. This is so mainly because employment growth in agriculture has declined sharply from 2.32 per cent per annum during 1972-73 to 1977-78 to only 0.65 per cent during 1982-83 to 1987-88. The conclusion is reinforced by two other indications; (1) Intensity

of cultivation is almost stagnant in spite of expansion in irrigational facilities, (2) Secondly most of the gains in production can be attributed to a single factor, namely, application of larger doses of fertilizer for crop production.

5. *Employment in Cottage and Village Industries has declined:* Employment in the cottage and in the household industries has experienced a relative decline, due to shrinking markets on account of competition of modern products and often due to lack of technological upgradation to meet demands according to VIII Plan Document, 1992.
6. *Rural Employment is not Always Associated with High Income:* The VIII Plan document states that the incidence of poverty is much higher than that of unemployment. An overwhelming majority of the poors are thus those not apparently unemployed but are engaged for a major part of their time in some activity albeit at very low levels of productivity and earnings.
7. *So-called Small Industries Developed have not Provided More Employment for the Rural Unemployed:* "It has, however, been observed that the policy for the promotion of small-scale industry has not been very effective in serving the employment objective; the assumption that small capital necessarily implies high employment per unit of capital has not always been found valid.
8. *Small-Scale Industrial Policy has not Benefited Really Small Units:* Due to the cumbersome procedures and non-existence of the promotional and services network in small towns and villages the concessions and assistance have only reached not so small sectors.
9. *Government Support to Small-Scale Industries like Khadi and Village Industries has been found to be Inadequate:* The report of the working group of Khadi and Village Industries has pointed out that, "Although, there have been several policy announcements, according important place to KVI, in concrete terms, the policy support made available to KVI sector has been in the shape of concessional finance, small extent of subsidization and limited fiscal concessions. This policy support is quite inadequate, since the benefit conferred on the organized large and non-sector almost neutralize the benefits provided to KVI."

Implications about Performance of Employment Generation Programmes

The Integrated Rural Development Programme has been the principal plank of the poverty alleviation strategy since 1981. Evaluation of this programme has raised the question of whether asset distribution or direct employment generation was the more appropriate strategy for poverty alleviation. In this context, it was felt that both strategies should compliment each other. The mix of the two would also vary from area to area. Experience with implementation of rural works programme has highlighted some operational problems as well as some basic policy issues.

"Operationally, the programmes have faltered due to the cause of leakage, on account of corruption and administrative failure and inefficiency at local level. They have seldom succeeded in creating durable assets because of old material component in such projects and because of poor technical formulation. In spite of indirect indications of unutilized, underemployed labour, mobilization of labour for such employment has been quite inadequate. The programmes have, in general, operated as relief-cum-subsidy programmes rather than as programmes for increasing the productive potential of the community. Their implementation has clearly shown that the rural force is not a lump of mass of under-employed workers, who would come forward to work as soon as unskilled work opportunities are created for them. The basic issues in employment policy, therefore, relate to how best to incorporate the development of employment objectives in local level plans" (Kanta Ahuja, 1991).

In view of the above, it could be said that the problem of rural unemployment is still a gigantic one and needs very careful attention through well conceived plan programmes and their effective implementation.

Strategies for Generation of Employment in Rural Areas

Developing Rural Industries to provide Additional Employment

Among the objectives of developing the village and small industries have been the generation of employment opportunities on a decentralized and dispersed basis and the upgradation of the existing level of skills of artisans and quality of products (*Rural Development Report*—Rural Employment NIRD, 1994, p. 82).

The Government of India has stated in the VIII Plan Document that the employment policy through establishment of small industries in India has not succeeded so far. This report further states: "Promotion of small-scale industries has not been very effective in serving the employment objectives". It is not directly related to employment in so far as the eligibility for preferential treatment in terms of incentives and other assistance is related to fixed capital investment.

Employment in the cottage and household industries has experienced a relative decline due to shrinking markets on account of competition from modern projects and often due to lack of technological upgradation to meet the new demands.

There has been technological unemployment, caused in traditional industries by the growth of an intermediate sector between the traditional unorganized sector and the modern organized sector. An example of this is the power-loom sector which has caused technological unemployment in the traditional handloom sector. Efforts to strengthen the organizational base of the traditional industries by the formation of cooperative societies of artisans in order to provide economies of scale to small entrepreneurs and improve their bargaining power have also not succeeded. Most of the industrial and weavers cooperative societies are sick or dormant.

The non traditional industries coming up in rural areas are both agriculture related as well as those which have no connection with it. Examples are, agro-based and food processing industries, textile based industries and those producing construction materials like bricks, tiles etc. These are relatively better organized than the traditional household industries and the activities are generally pursued as main occupation. Although their locations may not be strictly rural, in the sense that they are tending to get located in smaller towns, they provide employment to rural workers.

To sum up it could be said that the objectives of increasing employment through small-scale and village industries have not been realized adequately.

Promoting Small Industries in the Rural Areas to generate Employment for the Rural Poors

(a) Modernizing Small Industries

Current Situation: In spite of promises to give priority to village industries, no concerted action has been taken in these areas to implement suitable measures to modernize them. There is a mistaken belief in the scientific sector that the village industries are only a passing phase in the process of economic development, till big national industries replace them. As a result machines used in village industries have still to be modernized. Even where some improvements have been made in selected village industries, new technology has not spread fast. For example, although the semi-automatic improved loom developed in 1972, even by 1990s 90 per cent of handloom weavers continued to use the old pit loom. No modernization is done in the case of spinning wheel for spinning low staple cotton. Even the improved model Amber *Charakha* is not suitable for small households which have little space to use for spinning. The KVIC experience has shown that the process of developing improved technology for village industries is very slow. There is also very little support from the National Government run and assisted industries to develop modern technology for village industries. For example, Hindustan Machine Tools (HMT) and National Small-Scale Industries Corporation (NSIC) have not been of much help to modernize tools for village industries. Even the Indian Institutes of Technology (IITs) have not made significant contribution to the development of new technologies for village industries. Unless the technologies of village industry are modernized to improve the production efficiency at little cost, these village industries will not be able to compete with large scale industries, manufacturing the same type of goods. Already many small-scale industries, like hand pounding of rice and thousands of handlooms, have been wiped out as a result of the competition.

Action Suggested: (a) IITs and CSIR institutions must take a lead in initiating research to modernize village industries. (b) Cottage and Village Industries Commission should allot more funds for undertaking research to modernize village industries. (c) There is a need to take up collaborative programmes with Japanese collaboration to develop research for modernizing village industries in India.

(b) Protection to Village Industries

Current Situation: Village industries in India cannot develop unless sufficient protection is given to them by the Government to avoid competition with big industries. What has however happened over the years is that the big industries have virtually steam rolled the small industries. The classic examples are the extinction of hand pounding rice industry, country *ghanis* in the villages and the handloom sector. As long as there is no restriction on the establishment of big industries, we cannot expect the small industries to develop. Years ago Gandhiji has suggested some kind of state intervention is required in promoting village industries, Sri Kamaraj Nadar requested the Government to give protection to small industries by preventing establishment of big industries and also suggested to prohibit the establishment of cotton mills in India and allow Khadi and Village Industries to manufacture cotton goods. However, this proposal was not accepted by the Government then. There are many industries like the paper manufacturing, soap manufacturing, spinning, weaving, rice milling, oil extraction industries which can be completely earmarked for the small industries sector. Thus there is supreme need to streamline Swadeshi movement in order to produce consumer goods by giving protection to small industries. However what has happened is that only big industries have been given protection by imposing import duty on manufactured goods from other developed countries. Big industries established in rural areas have been given special concessions by way of less taxation etc. This has resulted in the collapse of small industries.

Action Suggested: (a) The small industries protection committees set up by the Government of India from time to time should be asked to recommend more practical ways of protection to be given to small industries. (b) Steps should be taken by the Government of India to encourage small industries on the following programme, on the lines framed out in Japan, to promote small industries.

(i) Collective Projects: Raw materials needed for small industries,
(ii) Collective selling of products.

(c) *Promoting New Kinds of Organizations for Developing Village Industries as is done in Japan*

Current Situation: In small industries there is lack of innovativeness which is necessary to improve the working of small industries. Except providing subsidies to small industries to sell their products, no other action is taken to promote the small industries sector. No attempts have been made to study the experience of countries like Japan and Switzerland to promote small industries by developing a number of organizations.

Action Suggested: (a) In Japan small industries are promoted by providing new kinds of co-operative organisations namely; (i) The common facilities co-operatives, (ii) Credit co-operatives, (iii) Federation of co-operatives, (iv) Joint enterprise co-operatives, similar action is needed in India. (b) Japan has followed a new system of promoting production of few products in large quantities rather than spreading resources on a large variety of products in small quantities. This approach should be implemented in India. (c) The Japanese Government promoted a new policy of even merging a number of small industries into a larger one in order to have advantage of economy of scale Malgaonkar.

Undertaking Rural Works Programme

(*a*) *Promoting Public Works Programme to Improve Land Assets*

Current Situation: Presently public works programmes are primarily implemented to spend the budget allotted, without taking into consideration the real need for improving land assets in villages. Further no follow-up work is taken up to maintain this. The local Panchayats and village people are not consulted in developing these programmes. Most of the money was spent on road work, that too on *kutcha* roads, which were again washed off during the rains following the undertaking of rural work. Hence assets created were mostly not durable. Although the implementation of the schemes required preparation of shelf of projects, this has been rarely implemented.

Action Suggested: (a) No public works programme should be implemented without discussing this with the local Panchayats and Gram, Sabhas, (b) Assets created must have clear plans of maintenance, otherwise assets cannot become durable, (c) Assets must be developed in the lands of poor people on priority basis, (d) No land development scheme or bunding should be taken up without complete plan of levelling the land and maintaining the bund after construction, (e) Watersheds should be selected for development of land in stages. (f) Desiltation of existing tanks should be taken up in the programme as priority item, and (g) Without active participation of the land owning families, no developmental works should be taken up.

(b) Implementing Pragmatic Labour Policies in Rural Areas

Current Situation: The Government itself has enacted the Minimum Labour Wages Act, but is not implementing it faithfully in rural areas. Many labour engaging projects in rural areas are given exemptions from implementing the Minimum Wages Act. Wage revision does not take place in consideration of the rise in Wholesale Price Index (WPI) from time to time. As a result of these shortcomings, even if the rural poors are given full labour employment in rural areas, they will not be able to come above the poverty line due to inadequate labour wages earned by them. Labour absorption in agriculture has not satisfactorily increased in India with the introduction of new agricultural practices, as is the case in Japan and some other South Asian Countries (SAC). Priority is not given to development of non-foodgrain agriculture, where agriculture had already developed.

Action Suggested: (a) Minimum Wages Act should be enforced in all rural areas without exception, (b) The minimum wages fixed should be revised, (c) New kind of research to improve the labour absorption in agriculture should be explored on a priority basis, (d) Employment audit should be introduced in research systems so as to avoid recommending new practices which displace labour, and (e) New schemes for processing agricultural products in rural areas should be taken up to increase the labour requirement in rural areas.

REFERENCES

Ahuja, Kanta (1991), "Agricultural Labour and Rural Employment" in Dantwala (Editor), *Indian Agricultural Development since Independence, op. cit.*, pp. 367-398.

FAO (1994), *Agriculture Production Year Book.*

Government of India, 1985, *Report of the Committee to review the existing administrative arrangements of Rural Development and Poverty Alleviation Programmes* (Chairman G.V.K. Rao), Ministry of Agriculture, Department of Rural Development, New Delhi.

Government of India, Planning Commission: VIII *Plan Document*, 1992.

Government of India, Planning Commission, New Delhi (1983), *Draft Report of the Working Group on KVI.*

Malgavkar, P.D., 1970, How small industries in Japan meet the challenges, paper presented in the souvenir brought out on the occasion of Inauguration of Technocrates Industrial Estate, Balanagar, Hyderabad, First Week Aug. 1970, pp. 49-53.

M.K. Gandhi, *Village Industries*, Compiled by R.K. Prabhu, Navjeevan Publishing House, 1966.

Padmanabhan, M. and Swaminathan, M.S., 1994, Rural Development Report: *Rural Employment*, NIRD, Hyderabad.

Rao, G.V.K., 1979, "Employment expansion among agricultural labour and small farm households—An Indian experience", paper presented at the ILO Seminar organised at the University of Agricultural Sciences, Bangalore on Agricultural Labour Employment.

Swaminathan, M.S., 1985, Achieving rural-urban harmony in agricultural development, Guest Lecture Series, No. 3, Institute of Rural Management, Anand, Gujarat, pp. 5-8.

7

Trends in Extent, Depth and Severity of Poverty: An Analysis of Economic Inequalities in India

NIRANKAR SRIVASTAV and AMARESH DUBEY

Introduction

The Approach Paper to the Eleventh Five Year Plan (2007-2012) prepared by the Planning Commission (2006) propose to dedicate towards faster and more inclusive growth. It envisages doubling the real income of average Indian in ten years with sustained economic growth by 8 to 9 per cent per year during Plan period. While mentioning major strengths, it also highlighted the crucial challenges are being faced by the economy. Foremost challenge is the economic inequality between rich and poor. Though it admits that poverty is declining but pace of poverty reduction is to be accelerated. From this point of view it is imperative to have an in-depth analysis of the trends in extent, depth and severity of poverty to highlight the inter- and intra-State disparities within the country.

The objective of this paper is to investigate the inter-state and inter-regional disparities in poverty incidence and levels of living in the rural and urban sectors of India. It is established in the literature that the economic development process follows an inverted U-shape curve (Williamson, 1969). This implies that in the initial stages of economic development, inter-regional disparities tend to increase before declining again. Besides, Williamson (1969) there are several researchers, *e.g.* Barro and Sala-i-Martin (1992), Sala-i-Martin (1996), who had tried to study regional disparities and its changes over time in the theoretical framework of "convergence". But the empirical evidence on regional convergence is mixed at best.

In India too there had been several attempt to study the changes in regional disparities (Mathur, 1983; Marjit and Mitra, 1996; Dasgupta *et al.*, 1997; Ghosh *et al.*, 1998). A common feature of these studies is that they use normalized state income as summary indicator of regional (State level) development. Most of these researchers do not find any evidence of regional convergence while some report an evidence of divergence.

Their results could be due to methodological problems that are inherent in the data that these researchers have used. First, the data used by these researchers is Per-Capita State Domestic Product (PCSDP). The PCSDP is a summary indicator that does not take into account the distribution profile of the income over population. Secondly, the PCSDP data is not comparable over time in scope and coverage. Moreover, most of the studies are restricted to so-called major states in the Indian Union, thereby leaving out a large number of States and Union Territories from their calculations. Thirdly, some of the researchers, *e.g.* Ghosh *et. al.* (1998), have used CPIAL as the deflator to derive real SDP series. As it is, CPIAL is not a representative deflator even for the rural sector (Suryanarayana, 1996). Its appropriateness for the entire population is clearly questionable.[1]

In this chapter, we propose to analyse regional disparities using a more disaggregated data. It is known that there are significant variations in the agro-climatic conditions within the States. Therefore, a more disaggregated analysis of NSS region-wise indicators would be worth trying. In this chapter we investigate whether regional disparities are also present in the incidence of poverty and, in consumption levels of the population. In this chapter we look at the disparities across States and also in the rural and urban sectors of States. Next, we consider the regions within a State, and also the rural and urban sectors within each NSS region. Specifically, we concentrate on two sets of variables; average per capita consumption of the households and the poverty measures of the population in the geographical unit of interest.

Rest of the chapter is organised as follows. In section 2, we discuss the data and methodological issues. Section 3 deals with the regional disparities at State/region level. This is followed by the analysis of disparities among the regions divided into rural and urban regions in section 4. Conclusions and policy implications of the chapter are given in section 5.

Data and Methodological Issues

Data

In this chapter we use data from the socio-economic survey conducted by the National Sample Survey Organization (NSSO) for two quinquennial rounds. The reference years are 1987-88 and 1993-94. During these two rounds of survey, the NSSO collected data on household level consumption expenditure for the agriculture year *i.e.,* from July to June. In order to cover entire territory in the Indian Union, the country is divided into 78 NSS regions in rural and urban sectors separately. The details on number of regions formed in different States, abbreviations and State and region codes are given in Appendix Table 7.1.

The socio-economic survey data of NSS has its reputation for reliability and suitability for the type of study at hand. This data set has two major advantages; firstly, this is in the form of unit record or household level. Secondly, this is the only detailed data that covers almost entire territory of India.[2] All the States and Union Territories are being referred to as States for the sake of convenience, which are 32 in numbers.

Methodology

The official poverty incidence in India is reported at the State level, divided into rural and urban sectors in a number of studies, *e.g.* GOI (1993, 1997 and 2001). But, in the situation where there exists substantial inter- and intra-State differences in the level of development and incidence of poverty, the State level analysis do not provide enough insight into the process leading to change in poverty incidence. As pointed above, we wanted to carry out the analysis at a more disaggregated level. Therefore, we use sub-State (NSS Region) level poverty incidence in the rural and urban sector. It is worth-mentioning that many bigger States in India are divided into more than one NSS Regions, for example, the Madhya Pradesh is divided into seven number of regions, whereas, Maharashtra in six and Uttar Pradesh and Gujarat are divided into five regions each (See Appendix 7.1 for details). This enables us to do the regional disparity analysis at fairly disaggregated level.

Level of Living and Poverty Line

For measuring welfare of the population, traditionally per person income or expenditure has been used. The consumption expenditure is preferred indicator of standard of living and in turn indicates the welfare at the household level. To capture this the Average Per Capita Consumption Expenditure (APCTE) is estimated for entire population disaggregated by States and NSS Regions for rural and urban sectors separately. For details, See section 2.2.3 below.

The poverty norm, z, which we use in this chapter, is the Official Poverty Line (OPL) based on the official norm that was derived by the Task Force in 1979 (GOI, 1979). The all-India Poverty Norm for rural and urban sector was derived using food energy intake method. The task force estimated that on an average a representative Indian needs 2435 K. calories in the rural sector and 2095 K. calories in the urban sector per day. The cost of these many calories worked out to be Rs. 49.07 and Rs. 56.64 per person at 1973-74 prices for the rural and urban sector, respectively, assuming that education and healthcare will be provided by the State.[3] The Expert Group (GOI, 1993) recommended that the all-India poverty norm is to be deflated using State-wise price indices keeping the average calorie requirement fixed.[4] We use the State-wise poverty line that were derived by the Expert Group (1993) and reported in GOI (1997).

It is to be noted that the GOI (1997) recommended that for smaller States and Union Territories, the poverty ratios of neighbouring larger states be adopted, as the price data for these States and UTs are not available. For example, the poverty ratios of Assam have been assigned to remaining six north-eastern States and Sikkim. The modification that we introduced in this chapter is that we used the poverty line of the neighbouring larger States [in place of poverty ratios as suggested in GOI (1997)] and expenditure distribution of the concerned States to calculate the poverty incidence.

Poverty Measures

The simplest index of poverty is Head Count Ratio (HCR), which is defined as:

$$HCR = \frac{q}{n} \times 100 \qquad \text{... (1)}$$

where the population consists of *n* individuals with Per Capita Total Expenditure (PCTE), y_i, ranked in ascending order. *q* is the number of persons who are below the poverty line '*z*'. HCR gives the proportion of the population that has PCTE below the poverty line.

One of the main shortcomings of HCR is that it is insensitive to the depth of poverty of the poor person, thus violating what Sen (1976), defined as the monotonicity axiom. This axiom ensures that any poverty index should increase if there is a drop in the income of any poor individually, *cteris paribus*.

The weighted Poverty Gap Index (PGI) satisfies the above axiom, which is defined as:

$$PGI = \frac{1}{q.z}\sum_{i=1}^{q}(z - y_i) \qquad \text{... (2)}$$

where *n*, *q*, y_i and *z* are as defined above. But this measure is insensitive to income transfer against the poor, thus violating Sen's Weak Transfer Axiom—the requirement that any transfer of income from a poor person to any one richer should increase poverty, so long as no one crosses the poverty line as a result. There are several such measures described in the literature, which satisfy the transfer axioms. Foster, Greer and Thorbecke (1984) index (henceforth, FGT) has almost become standard in the literature for its simplicity and useful properties.[5] FGT (α), a generalized index, is a normalized weighted sum of the poverty gaps of the poor, with weights given by those poverty gaps themselves raised to an appropriate power. The FGT index is defined as:

$$FGT(\alpha) = \frac{1}{n.z^{\alpha}}\sum_{i=1}^{q}(z - y_i)^{\alpha},\ \alpha \geq 0 \qquad \text{... (3)}$$

where *n*, *q*, y_i and *z* are same as defined above. For α=0, the FGT (α) equals HCR, for α=1, the index equals PGI. For greater values of α, it satisfies the criteria of diminishing transfer sensitivity. In case of α=2, FGT index is defined as:

$$\text{FGT}(z) = \frac{1}{n.z^2}\sum_{i=1}^{q}(z - y_i)^2 \qquad \text{... (4)}$$

The advantage of using weights independent of position in the distribution ensures decomposability of the index across different household types.

In this chapter we have estimated all the three poverty indices, namely, HCR, PGI and FGT using FGT generalised index. Recall that for α =0, from equation 3 we get HCR; for α =1 it yields PGI and for α =2 it is FGT as shown in equation 4.

Recall that we have access to unit record data on all the households surveyed by the NSS in the two rounds, 43rd and 50th. Consequently, the per capita consumption expenditure of every surveyed household is available and has been used to calculate all three poverty measures described above.

Average Per-Capita Monthly Total Expenditure

Average expenditure is considered to be a good summary indicator of the standard of living of population. In this chapter we report the average expenditure calculated for three groups, entire population (APCTE), only the poor (APCTEP) and non-poor (APCTENP) separately at various level of disaggregation. The disaggregation is for all the States and all the NSS regions. Also, each State/NSS Region is further considered in two sectors namely, rural and urban.

The NSSO collects the expenditure data at market prices. For comparing the change in average expenditure of 1993-94 over 1987-88, we deflated 1993-94 expenditure distribution at 1987-88 prices. The deflator that we have used in this chapter is implicit price deflator derived from the official State-wise poverty line reported in GOI (1997).

Disparity Measures

The measure of disparity that is used in this chapter is coefficient of variation or CoV. This is defined as:

$$CoV = \frac{1}{\mu}\sqrt{\sum_{j=1}^{m}\frac{n_j}{n}(y_j - \mu)^2} \qquad \text{... (5)}$$

where μ is the mean (expenditure or poverty measure as the case may be), n is total number of people equal to sum of n_j and y is once again welfare indicator, which is taken as APCTE for the population, APCTEP for the poor persons and APCTENP for the non-poor in our calculations. The coefficient of variation measures the degree of dispersion and variability of mean between two different groups/ time points of the data set.

Regional Disparities

Table 7.1 reports the State–wise poverty incidence (HCR) for the years 1987-88 and 1993-94. The all-India HCR has declined from 39.31 to 35.95, which is about 8.5 per cent during the above mentioned period. During the same period the depth (PGI) and severity (FGT) declined at a significantly faster rate, 13.5 per cent and 17.5 per cent, respectively. Smaller States like Mizoram, Chandigarh, Manipur and Himachal Pradesh and medium size States like Punjab and Haryana were showing low level of poverty incidence in 1987-88. Whereas Bihar, Orissa, Pondicherry and Madhya Pradesh were having higher level of poverty.

In year 1993-94 poverty level has reduced in most of the States in India but there are some States that do not follow the trend. For example, Arunachal Pradesh, Assam, Bihar, Haryana, Himachal Pradesh, Manipur, Mizoram and Punjab are the States where incidence of poverty has in fact increased instead of declining. But increase in some of the States is only marginal. It is important to note that most of the States belong to north-eastern part of India where substantial poverty increase is observed. Ironically, Assam and Arunachal Pradesh[6] have joined the list of four most poor States in the year 1993-94, where the remaining two States are Bihar and Orissa.

Table 7.1 also reports the poverty incidence for the rural and urban sectors of the States. Rural poverty was concentrated in the States like Bihar, Orissa, West Bengal and Pondicherry in the year 1987-88. We see a general trend in reduction of poverty in the rural sector in most of the States in India in the year 1993-94. The poverty incidence in the urban sectors was lowest among the smaller States like Mizoram, Meghalaya, Himachal Pradesh and Pondicherry in 1987-88. The poverty incidence has, in general, declined in the urban sector of almost all the States of India too except in the case of

Table 7.1: State-wise Incidence of Poverty (HCR) (1987-88 and1993-94)

(In Percentage)

States	1987-88			1993-94		
	Rural	Urban	Total	Rural	Urban	Total
APR	21.07	41.19	25.47	15.93	38.80	21.91
ARP	26.43	16.22	26.04	41.29	6.05	37.10
ASS	39.75	11.45	37.45	45.26	7.93	41.45
BIH	53.81	51.89	53.57	57.88	34.88	55.09
GOA	15.53	36.08	22.54	5.00	28.26	14.85
GUJ	28.48	38.52	31.24	22.23	28.28	24.20
HAR	13.15	18.57	14.29	27.99	16.47	25.02
HPR	10.98	7.20	10.73	30.37	9.26	28.59
J&K	25.85	14.98	23.91	18.24	5.13	13.34
KAR	34.77	49.19	38.95	30.08	39.73	32.84
KER	31.64	38.69	32.81	25.39	24.31	25.12
MPR	42.01	47.25	43.02	40.72	48.01	42.44
MAH	40.91	40.52	40.78	38.11	34.97	36.94
MAN	15.81	6.52	13.11	18.94	6.89	15.65
MEG	36.18	2.04	31.39	24.35	1.81	21.26
MIZ	3.93	0.62	2.81	6.22	0.00	4.26
NAG	NA	0.00	0.00	2.30	0.00	1.69
ORI	58.62	42.58	56.75	49.78	40.64	48.61
PUN	8.94	13.71	10.24	11.49	10.89	11.31
RAJ	33.30	37.89	34.25	26.36	31.05	27.44
SIK	41.00	7.72	34.94	31.70	0.96	29.25
TND	46.38	40.27	44.21	32.98	39.95	35.43
TRI	23.73	11.22	22.31	23.64	6.04	21.29
UPR	42.65	45.04	43.08	42.32	34.83	40.85
WEB	48.80	33.74	45.14	41.18	22.95	36.94
ANI	5.20	6.86	5.65	1.06	5.22	2.24
CHA	18.65	5.36	6.49	11.79	2.08	3.34
DNH	69.40	NA	69.40	51.67	38.83	50.74
DAD	NA	NA	NA	4.71	21.66	11.42
DEL	9.11	16.74	15.85	2.00	16.11	14.58
LAD	26.94	38.31	31.69	0.00	15.93	8.06
PON	44.07	56.06	50.78	19.99	36.47	30.26
All-India	**39.36**	**39.16**	**39.31**	**37.28**	**31.70**	**35.95**

Source: Special tabulation by the authors using household level consumer expenditure data of 43rd round and 50th round collected by the NSSO.

Manipur where poverty level has actually increased marginally from 6.52 per cent to 6.89 per cent during the reference period. The state-wise PGI and FGT are reported in Tables 7.2 and 7.3 respectively. These measures more or less follow the trend that we observed in the case of HCR.

Table 7.2: State-wise Poverty Index (PGI) (1987-88 and 1993-94)

	1987-88			*1993-94*		
States	*Rural*	*Urban*	*Total*	*Rural*	*Urban*	*Total*
APR	0.0438	0.1067	0.0576	0.0291	0.0926	0.0457
ARP	0.0539	0.0275	0.0529	0.0907	0.0136	0.0816
ASS	0.0750	0.0163	0.0703	0.0830	0.0092	0.0755
BIH	0.1293	0.1300	0.1294	0.1462	0.0789	0.1381
GOA	0.0248	0.0764	0.0424	0.0094	0.0492	0.0262
GUJ	0.0558	0.0823	0.0631	0.0415	0.0622	0.0482
HAR	0.0266	0.0367	0.0287	0.0557	0.0305	0.0492
HPR	0.0168	0.0073	0.0162	0.0557	0.0125	0.0520
J&K	0.0450	0.0243	0.0413	0.0322	0.0101	0.0239
KAR	0.0839	0.1409	0.1004	0.0627	0.1128	0.0770
KER	0.0683	0.0999	0.0736	0.0562	0.0553	0.0560
MPR	0.1058	0.1354	0.1115	0.0950	0.1339	0.1041
MAH	0.0956	0.1237	0.1049	0.0934	0.1015	0.0964
MAN	0.0200	0.0057	0.0158	0.0231	0.0059	0.0184
MEG	0.0924	0.0021	0.0797	0.0334	0.0019	0.0291
MIZ	0.0061	0.0033	0.0052	0.0086	0.0000	0.0059
NAG	NA	0.0000	0.0000	0.0021	0.0000	0.0015
ORI	0.1632	0.1112	0.1572	0.1195	0.1141	0.1189
PUN	0.0134	0.0229	0.0160	0.0188	0.0168	0.0183
RAJ	0.0864	0.0964	0.0885	0.0519	0.0701	0.0560
SIK	0.0722	0.0106	0.0609	0.0547	0.0004	0.0503
TND	0.1266	0.1155	0.1227	0.0731	0.1027	0.0835
TRI	0.0506	0.0248	0.0477	0.0532	0.0117	0.0476
UPR	0.1015	0.1227	0.1054	0.1037	0.0858	0.1002
WEB	0.1161	0.0744	0.1060	0.0829	0.0455	0.0742
ANI	0.0035	0.0083	0.0048	0.0007	0.0086	0.0030
CHA	0.0131	0.0085	0.0089	0.0130	0.0045	0.0056
DNH	0.1645	NA	0.1645	0.1074	0.1404	0.1098
DAD	NA	NA	NA	0.0089	0.0335	0.0187
DEL	0.0560	0.0302	0.0333	0.0016	0.0392	0.0351
LAD	0.0539	0.0529	0.0535	0.0000	0.0311	0.0157
PON	0.1210	0.1618	0.1439	0.0320	0.0904	0.0684
All-India	**0.0943**	**0.1040**	**0.0964**	**0.0845**	**0.0798**	**0.0834**

Source: As in Table 7.1.

Note: The Figures are Ratios.

Table 7.3: State-wise Poverty Index (FGT) (1987-88 and 1993-94)

	1987-88			*1993-94*		
States	*Rural*	*Urban*	*Total*	*Rural*	*Urban*	*Total*
APR	0.0144	0.0396	0.0199	0.0090	0.0320	0.0151
ARP	0.0195	0.0053	0.0189	0.0302	0.0046	0.0272
ASS	0.0207	0.0043	0.0193	0.0222	0.0023	0.0202
BIH	0.0450	0.0456	0.0451	0.0505	0.0266	0.0476
GOA	0.0054	0.0241	0.0118	0.0025	0.0143	0.0075
GUJ	0.0172	0.0257	0.0195	0.0124	0.0197	0.0148
HAR	0.0095	0.0119	0.0100	0.0174	0.0085	0.0151
HPR	0.0045	0.0012	0.0043	0.0162	0.0026	0.0151
J&K	0.0120	0.0063	0.0110	0.0088	0.0027	0.0065
KAR	0.0297	0.0565	0.0375	0.0203	0.0433	0.0268
KER	0.0223	0.0386	0.0250	0.0185	0.0189	0.0186
MPR	0.0380	0.0520	0.0407	0.0328	0.0503	0.0369
MAH	0.0321	0.0519	0.0386	0.0337	0.0416	0.0367
MAN	0.0041	0.0007	0.0031	0.0047	0.0013	0.0038
MEG	0.0335	0.0004	0.0289	0.0073	0.0003	0.0064
MIZ	0.0016	0.0030	0.0021	0.0018	0.0000	0.0013
NAG	NA	0.0000	0.0000	0.0002	0.0000	0.0002
ORI	0.0627	0.0416	0.0602	0.0407	0.0429	0.0410
PUN	0.0044	0.0062	0.0049	0.0049	0.0041	0.0047
RAJ	0.0340	0.0344	0.0341	0.0155	0.0226	0.0171
SIK	0.0193	0.0031	0.0164	0.0138	0.0000	0.0127
TND	0.0480	0.0466	0.0475	0.0250	0.0397	0.0302
TRI	0.0165	0.0073	0.0155	0.0171	0.0035	0.0153
UPR	0.0341	0.0452	0.0361	0.0353	0.0300	0.0343
WEB	0.0402	0.0239	0.0362	0.0245	0.0141	0.0221
ANI	0.0004	0.0018	0.0008	0.0001	0.0024	0.0007
CHA	0.0014	0.0029	0.0027	0.0020	0.0014	0.0015
DNH	0.0509	NA	0.0509	0.0305	0.0603	0.0327
DAD	NA	NA	NA	0.0023	0.0065	0.0039
DEL	0.0349	0.0087	0.0118	0.0001	0.0143	0.0127
LAD	0.0130	0.0117	0.0124	0.0000	0.0084	0.0043
PON	0.0456	0.0627	0.0552	0.0106	0.0326	0.0243
All-India	**0.0329**	**0.0391**	**0.0343**	**0.0281**	**0.0291**	**0.0283**

Source: As in Table 7.1.
Note: The Figures are Ratios.

Tables 7.4, 7.5 and 7.6 report the region-wise poverty measures for 1987-88 and 1993-94 for rural and urban sectors for 77 NSS regions.[7] At all-India level 31 regions out of 74 comparable regions had poverty incidence above the national average in 1987-88. This

Table 7.4: Region-wise Incidence of Poverty (HCR) (1987-88 and 1993-94)

(In Percentage)

State/Regions	*1987-88*			*1993-94*		
	Rural	*Urban*	*Total*	*Rural*	*Urban*	*Total*
21	17.24	38.50	21.78	17.13	43.46	24.10
22	21.53	37.73	25.10	14.00	30.59	18.28
23	19.04	52.92	27.55	20.72	42.95	26.81
24	40.81	56.54	43.91	12.97	44.62	20.75
31	26.43	16.22	26.04	41.29	6.05	37.10
41	35.25	6.42	32.93	37.06	3.50	33.49
42	43.28	14.47	40.86	50.53	11.05	46.55
43	26.68	9.49	25.88	41.43	3.54	38.30
51	52.70	34.65	49.00	62.25	26.53	55.34
52	54.74	64.98	55.30	58.46	49.35	57.87
53	53.08	63.24	54.82	53.62	35.43	51.07
61	15.53	36.08	22.54	5.00	28.26	14.85
71	34.20	39.16	34.48	26.02	33.91	26.75
72	25.87	33.06	28.59	23.49	29.17	25.91
73	22.85	30.12	25.56	26.20	20.16	23.76
74	46.95	51.97	47.85	26.19	25.28	26.03
75	18.95	51.17	27.49	11.99	32.60	19.52
81	17.52	19.69	18.10	31.91	17.43	27.65
82	7.96	15.16	8.87	22.25	14.09	20.64
91	10.98	7.20	10.73	30.37	9.26	28.59
101	23.28	16.64	21.71	9.87	4.69	7.80
102	35.45	17.56	34.51	43.90	7.39	33.62
103	20.70	13.78	19.18	NA	NA	NA
111	13.43	55.64	25.68	9.30	15.52	10.74
112	24.53	40.70	27.65	14.53	37.14	19.54
113	37.38	39.94	38.30	29.27	28.81	29.09
114	40.39	59.56	45.37	37.96	57.23	42.58
121	39.58	48.82	40.82	27.81	28.44	27.96
122	26.27	34.07	27.73	23.77	21.91	23.30
131	46.72	35.99	45.27	44.36	44.25	44.34
132	36.42	64.56	39.74	36.53	50.85	38.54
133	44.46	59.39	48.32	49.40	52.05	50.23
134	37.36	45.57	39.40	27.32	45.59	33.40
135	51.34	38.76	48.25	46.38	50.71	47.62
136	50.93	67.60	54.08	67.83	56.76	65.84
137	22.95	41.49	27.22	16.57	44.15	23.50
141	29.75	18.96	22.89	15.24	12.45	13.31
142	31.47	44.07	34.73	25.13	40.20	29.46

(Contd.)

Table 7.4:—*Contd.*

State/Regions	1987-88			1993-94		
	Rural	Urban	Total	Rural	Urban	Total
143	45.48	55.20	47.68	47.90	58.34	50.69
144	48.34	67.28	52.17	50.03	61.54	52.62
145	49.50	59.98	52.99	49.18	59.18	52.71
146	45.57	60.78	47.56	49.53	52.73	50.00
151	9.39	5.82	8.08	13.69	6.19	11.09
152	25.19	10.16	23.07	27.28	11.53	25.49
161	36.18	2.04	31.39	24.35	1.81	21.26
171	3.93	0.62	2.81	6.22	0.00	4.26
181	NA	0.00	0.00	2.30	0.00	1.69
191	48.37	42.11	47.67	45.31	47.23	45.55
192	82.98	52.93	80.29	68.84	41.94	66.07
193	61.01	39.90	58.16	45.79	32.45	43.88
201	7.72	12.46	9.07	7.03	8.29	7.43
202	10.73	15.88	12.03	17.31	15.60	16.88
211	27.95	37.98	29.98	25.51	23.38	25.02
212	28.81	41.40	31.89	17.99	33.57	22.10
213	61.10	33.41	58.95	46.30	26.59	44.11
214	31.32	25.05	30.05	33.03	42.75	35.17
221	41.00	7.72	34.94	31.70	0.96	29.25
231	60.73	39.78	51.16	44.23	38.57	41.87
232	39.50	38.53	39.28	20.81	43.00	26.05
233	51.44	52.07	51.65	37.16	48.38	40.95
234	30.39	29.55	30.11	22.35	32.10	25.71
241	23.73	11.22	22.31	23.64	6.04	21.29
251	13.38	20.36	14.98	24.83	17.85	23.40
252	32.60	46.60	36.02	29.29	32.41	30.10
253	44.48	43.16	44.21	50.19	29.31	45.75
254	50.79	45.22	50.24	48.79	40.21	47.79
255	65.02	64.22	64.88	67.36	66.79	67.23
261	33.88	18.37	31.83	58.42	32.63	55.51
262	60.45	47.22	59.24	47.49	35.14	45.96
263	43.75	32.21	39.02	31.41	18.24	26.29
264	47.59	42.08	47.09	40.73	41.78	40.82
271	5.20	6.86	5.65	1.06	5.22	2.24
281	18.65	5.36	6.49	11.79	2.08	3.34
291	69.40	NA	69.40	51.67	38.83	50.74
301	NA	NA	NA	4.71	21.66	11.42
311	9.11	16.74	15.85	2.00	16.11	14.58
321	26.94	38.31	31.69	0.00	15.93	8.06
331	44.07	56.06	50.78	19.99	36.47	30.26
All-India	**39.36**	**39.16**	**39.31**	**37.28**	**31.70**	**35.95**

Source: As in Table 7.1.

Table 7.5: Region-wise Poverty Index (PGI) (1987-88 and 1993-94)

State/Regions	*1987-88*			*1993-94*		
	Rural	*Urban*	*Total*	*Rural*	*Urban*	*Total*
21	0.0372	0.0959	0.0497	0.0324	0.1046	0.0515
22	0.0391	0.0965	0.0518	0.0233	0.0669	0.0345
23	0.0339	0.1416	0.0609	0.0432	0.1114	0.0618
24	0.1086	0.1676	0.1203	0.0217	0.1183	0.0454
31	0.0539	0.0275	0.0529	0.0907	0.0136	0.0816
41	0.0573	0.0091	0.0535	0.0686	0.0024	0.0616
42	0.0868	0.0206	0.0812	0.0937	0.0136	0.0856
43	0.0620	0.0130	0.0597	0.0564	0.0077	0.0524
51	0.1359	0.0783	0.1241	0.1614	0.0524	0.1403
52	0.1261	0.1975	0.1299	0.1477	0.1204	0.1459
53	0.1296	0.1500	0.1331	0.1322	0.0834	0.1254
61	0.0248	0.0764	0.0424	0.0094	0.0492	0.0262
71	0.0743	0.0893	0.0751	0.0588	0.0652	0.0594
72	0.0443	0.0629	0.0513	0.0387	0.0641	0.0495
73	0.0544	0.0535	0.0540	0.0514	0.0509	0.0512
74	0.0966	0.1227	0.1013	0.0448	0.0635	0.0480
75	0.0304	0.1284	0.0564	0.0202	0.0664	0.0371
81	0.0408	0.0378	0.0400	0.0627	0.0314	0.0535
82	0.0097	0.0335	0.0127	0.0454	0.0280	0.0420
91	0.0168	0.0073	0.0162	0.0557	0.0125	0.0520
101	0.0436	0.0297	0.0403	0.0129	0.0102	0.0118
102	0.0700	0.0315	0.0680	0.0914	0.0096	0.0684
103	0.0291	0.0206	0.0272	NA	NA	NA
111	0.0152	0.1484	0.0539	0.0142	0.0299	0.0178
112	0.0439	0.0677	0.0485	0.0267	0.0931	0.0414
113	0.0850	0.0985	0.0898	0.0575	0.0664	0.0609
114	0.1091	0.2005	0.1328	0.0830	0.1855	0.1075
121	0.0882	0.1435	0.0956	0.0683	0.0609	0.0666
122	0.0549	0.0800	0.0596	0.0481	0.0520	0.0491
131	0.1041	0.0977	0.1033	0.0857	0.1153	0.0909
132	0.0821	0.2082	0.0970	0.0770	0.1225	0.0834
133	0.1038	0.1760	0.1225	0.1191	0.1683	0.1345
134	0.1054	0.1244	0.1101	0.0533	0.1141	0.0735
135	0.1497	0.1179	0.1419	0.1187	0.1469	0.1268
136	0.1506	0.1999	0.1599	0.2263	0.1975	0.2211
137	0.0533	0.1028	0.0647	0.0355	0.1201	0.0567
141	0.0659	0.0392	0.0489	0.0255	0.0237	0.0242
142	0.0609	0.1210	0.0764	0.0502	0.0991	0.0642
143	0.1112	0.1980	0.1308	0.1105	0.1687	0.1261
144	0.1299	0.2432	0.1527	0.1603	0.2304	0.1761
145	0.1202	0.2034	0.1480	0.1153	0.2007	0.1454

(Contd.)

Table 7.5—*Contd.*

State/Regions	*1987-88*			*1993-94*		
	Rural	*Urban*	*Total*	*Rural*	*Urban*	*Total*
146	0.0973	0.2012	0.1109	0.1072	0.1238	0.1096
151	0.0107	0.0046	0.0084	0.0162	0.0059	0.0126
152	0.0337	0.0115	0.0305	0.0340	0.0057	0.0308
161	0.0924	0.0021	0.0797	0.0334	0.0019	0.0291
171	0.0061	0.0033	0.0052	0.0086	0.0000	0.0059
181	NA	0.0000	0.0000	0.0021	0.0000	0.0015
191	0.1151	0.1017	0.1136	0.1032	0.1307	0.1066
192	0.2918	0.1458	0.2787	0.1886	0.1506	0.1847
193	0.1675	0.1112	0.1599	0.1053	0.0815	0.1019
201	0.0106	0.0224	0.0140	0.0104	0.0115	0.0108
202	0.0176	0.0238	0.0192	0.0298	0.0265	0.0290
211	0.0592	0.0993	0.0673	0.0430	0.0427	0.0430
212	0.0622	0.1046	0.0726	0.0347	0.0800	0.0467
213	0.2452	0.0881	0.2330	0.0977	0.0589	0.0934
214	0.0619	0.0589	0.0613	0.0770	0.1071	0.0836
221	0.0722	0.0106	0.0609	0.0547	0.0004	0.0503
231	0.1756	0.1147	0.1478	0.1049	0.1055	0.1051
232	0.0922	0.0982	0.0935	0.0402	0.1069	0.0559
233	0.1541	0.1619	0.1567	0.0871	0.1321	0.1023
234	0.0704	0.0762	0.0723	0.0398	0.0641	0.0482
241	0.0506	0.0248	0.0477	0.0532	0.0117	0.0476
251	0.0202	0.0422	0.0253	0.0436	0.0397	0.0428
252	0.0738	0.1279	0.0870	0.0608	0.0753	0.0646
253	0.1037	0.1137	0.1057	0.1379	0.0785	0.1252
254	0.1231	0.1175	0.1226	0.1198	0.0956	0.1170
255	0.1809	0.2211	0.1879	0.2017	0.1992	0.2011
261	0.0442	0.0268	0.0419	0.1156	0.0747	0.1110
262	0.1573	0.1305	0.1548	0.1015	0.0712	0.0977
263	0.1094	0.0688	0.0928	0.0674	0.0343	0.0545
264	0.1023	0.0911	0.1013	0.0693	0.0932	0.0713
271	0.0035	0.0083	0.0048	0.0007	0.0086	0.0030
281	0.0131	0.0085	0.0089	0.0130	0.0045	0.0056
291	0.1645	NA	0.1645	0.1074	0.1404	0.1098
301	NA	NA	NA	0.0089	0.0335	0.0187
311	0.0560	0.0302	0.0333	0.0016	0.0392	0.0351
321	0.0539	0.0529	0.0535	0.0000	0.0311	0.0157
331	0.1210	0.1618	0.1439	0.0320	0.0904	0.0684
All-India	**0.0943**	**0.1040**	**0.0964**	**0.0845**	**0.0798**	**0.0834**

Source: As in Table 7.1.

Note: The Figures are Ratios.

Table 7.6: Region-wise, State-wise Poverty Index (FGT) (1987-88 and 1993-94)

State/Regions	*1987-88*			*1993-94*		
	Rural	*Urban*	*Total*	*Rural*	*Urban*	*Total*
21	0.0132	0.0347	0.0177	0.0103	0.0366	0.0172
22	0.0109	0.0353	0.0163	0.0070	0.0211	0.0107
23	0.0111	0.0541	0.0219	0.0147	0.0435	0.0226
24	0.0387	0.0678	0.0444	0.0053	0.0421	0.0144
31	0.0195	0.0053	0.0189	0.0302	0.0046	0.0272
41	0.0143	0.0022	0.0133	0.0187	0.0003	0.0167
42	0.0248	0.0056	0.0232	0.0251	0.0036	0.0230
43	0.0167	0.0029	0.0161	0.0106	0.0020	0.0099
51	0.0507	0.0261	0.0456	0.0559	0.0156	0.0481
52	0.0422	0.0782	0.0442	0.0514	0.0438	0.0510
53	0.0453	0.0496	0.0461	0.0450	0.0285	0.0427
61	0.0054	0.0241	0.0118	0.0025	0.0143	0.0075
71	0.0250	0.0299	0.0253	0.0199	0.0180	0.0197
72	0.0114	0.0180	0.0139	0.0100	0.0203	0.0144
73	0.0181	0.0135	0.0164	0.0151	0.0182	0.0163
74	0.0276	0.0396	0.0297	0.0121	0.0203	0.0135
75	0.0108	0.0455	0.0200	0.0069	0.0199	0.0117
81	0.0155	0.0125	0.0147	0.0201	0.0091	0.0169
82	0.0024	0.0101	0.0034	0.0134	0.0071	0.0121
91	0.0045	0.0012	0.0043	0.0162	0.0026	0.0151
101	0.0125	0.0088	0.0116	0.0027	0.0028	0.0027
102	0.0203	0.0074	0.0196	0.0276	0.0023	0.0205
103	0.0063	0.0048	0.0060	NA	NA	NA
111	0.0031	0.0479	0.0161	0.0038	0.0094	0.0051
112	0.0113	0.0190	0.0128	0.0094	0.0316	0.0143
113	0.0290	0.0351	0.0312	0.0180	0.0210	0.0192
114	0.0410	0.0898	0.0537	0.0271	0.0776	0.0392
121	0.0285	0.0588	0.0325	0.0241	0.0199	0.0231
122	0.0181	0.0294	0.0202	0.0148	0.0183	0.0157
131	0.0338	0.0363	0.0342	0.0247	0.0409	0.0276
132	0.0275	0.0846	0.0342	0.0235	0.0395	0.0258
133	0.0339	0.0680	0.0427	0.0398	0.0705	0.0494
134	0.0413	0.0461	0.0425	0.0161	0.0388	0.0237
135	0.0599	0.0485	0.0571	0.0425	0.0560	0.0464
136	0.0588	0.0763	0.0621	0.1010	0.0894	0.0990
137	0.0177	0.0367	0.0221	0.0114	0.0436	0.0195
141	0.0215	0.0117	0.0153	0.0066	0.0068	0.0068
142	0.0174	0.0456	0.0247	0.0162	0.0363	0.0220
143	0.0385	0.0873	0.0495	0.0366	0.0675	0.0449
144	0.0475	0.1138	0.0609	0.0696	0.1114	0.0790

(Contd.)

Table 7.6—*Contd.*

State Regions	*1987-88*			*1993-94*		
	Rural	*Urban*	*Total*	*Rural*	*Urban*	*Total*
145	0.0408	0.0927	0.0581	0.0371	0.0873	0.0548
146	0.0313	0.0866	0.0385	0.0342	0.0433	0.0355
151	0.0021	0.0005	0.0015	0.0032	0.0015	0.0026
152	0.0070	0.0016	0.0063	0.0071	0.0004	0.0064
161	0.0335	0.0004	0.0289	0.0073	0.0003	0.0064
171	0.0016	0.0030	0.0021	0.0018	0.0000	0.0013
181	NA	0.0000	0.0000	0.0002	0.0000	0.0002
191	0.0394	0.0354	0.0390	0.0330	0.0460	0.0346
192	0.1285	0.0597	0.1224	0.0706	0.0634	0.0699
193	0.0629	0.0429	0.0602	0.0354	0.0319	0.0349
201	0.0033	0.0065	0.0042	0.0026	0.0029	0.0026
202	0.0060	0.0056	0.0059	0.0079	0.0063	0.0075
211	0.0182	0.0363	0.0219	0.0120	0.0116	0.0120
212	0.0198	0.0371	0.0241	0.0105	0.0263	0.0146
213	0.1278	0.0297	0.1202	0.0289	0.0197	0.0279
214	0.0185	0.0208	0.0190	0.0249	0.0376	0.0277
221	0.0193	0.0031	0.0164	0.0138	0.0000	0.0127
231	0.0691	0.0456	0.0584	0.0372	0.0449	0.0404
232	0.0313	0.0372	0.0326	0.0133	0.0375	0.0190
233	0.0622	0.0697	0.0647	0.0304	0.0504	0.0372
234	0.0228	0.0286	0.0248	0.0114	0.0195	0.0142
241	0.0165	0.0073	0.0155	0.0171	0.0035	0.0153
251	0.0047	0.0119	0.0064	0.0108	0.0115	0.0110
252	0.0243	0.0465	0.0297	0.0185	0.0256	0.0203
253	0.0340	0.0411	0.0354	0.0501	0.0290	0.0456
254	0.0412	0.0418	0.0412	0.0403	0.0315	0.0393
255	0.0698	0.1020	0.0754	0.0809	0.0801	0.0807
261	0.0096	0.0062	0.0092	0.0319	0.0246	0.0310
262	0.0566	0.0480	0.0558	0.0314	0.0224	0.0303
263	0.0389	0.0213	0.0317	0.0210	0.0107	0.0170
264	0.0333	0.0313	0.0331	0.0181	0.0276	0.0189
271	0.0004	0.0018	0.0008	0.0001	0.0024	0.0007
281	0.0014	0.0029	0.0027	0.0020	0.0014	0.0015
291	0.0509	NA	0.0509	0.0305	0.0603	0.0327
301	NA	NA	NA	0.0023	0.0065	0.0039
311	0.0349	0.0087	0.0118	0.0001	0.0143	0.0127
321	0.0130	0.0117	0.0124	0.0000	0.0084	0.0043
331	0.0456	0.0627	0.0552	0.0106	0.0326	0.0243
All India	**0.0329**	**0.0391**	**0.0343**	**0.0281**	**0.0291**	**0.0283**

Source: As in Table 7.1.

Note: The Figures are Ratios.

declined to 26 in 1993-94. Similarly, in the rural sector number of regions reporting poverty incidence above the national average was 32 in 1987-88 that reduced to 26 in 1993-94. In the urban sector the number of regions reporting higher poverty levels than the national average were 36 and 35 in 1987-88 and 1993-94 respectively.

The above observations imply that there is overall reduction in the incidence of poverty at every level. It also implies that there could have been reduction in inter-regional disparities also. The reduction in inter-regional disparities appears to be favouring rural than urban sector (This issue is investigated in detail below).

Besides the poverty measures, we are also interested in analyzing the changes in the welfare levels of the households at State and regional levels compared to at all-India level. These calculations were done at the State level, rural and urban sectors of each State, NSS region level and for rural and urban sectors of each region for the reference years. These are reported in Tables 7.7 and 7.8 for States and Tables 7.9 and 7.10 for the regions.

APCTE was highest among the States Like Delhi, Chandigarh, Nagaland, Mizoram and Punjab and lowest among the Orissa, Bihar, Madhya Pradesh, Uttar Pradesh, Karnataka and Assam in that order in 1987-88. It is to be noted that APCTE was found lower in those Sates which are bigger in size with higher population. At all-India level APCTE has grown from Rs. 176.75 in 1987-88 to Rs. 184.15 in 1993-94 at constant (1987-88) prices. This shows a significant rise in the average real consumption expenditure at national level.

If we arrange the States in descending order of APCTE (real) in 1993-94 and compare their relative positions in 1987-88, we find that Pondicherry has improved its rank from 19th to 13th, Karnataka from 28th to 22nd, Madhya Pradesh from 30th to 25th and West Bengal from 25th to 21st. These are the States, which also show relatively better performance in improving the average standard of living. On the other hand there are some States, which have depicted the relative poor performance on this account. Though in absolute sense their APCTE has gone up but there relative rank has gone down significantly. For example, Arunachal Pradesh that was having tenth highest APCTE at national level in 1987-88 has slipped down to 26th position in 1993-94. Similarly, Manipur has slipped from 17th to 27th, Mizoram from 5th to 11th, Nagaland from 3rd to 9th and Tripura from 15th to 19th. Incidentally, all these States belong

Table 7.7: State-wise Average Per Capita Monthly Total Expenditure (1987-88)

States	*APCTEP*			*APCTENP*			*APCTE*		
	Rural	*Urban*	*Total*	*Rural*	*Urban*	*Total*	*Rural*	*Urban*	*Total*
APR	72.82	112.54	86.85	181.84	308.72	203.72	158.87	227.92	173.9
ARP	101.47	105.16	101.55	261.78	295.14	263.23	219.41	264.34	221.1
ASS	103.38	108.59	103.51	194.65	274.52	203.87	158.37	255.52	166.2
BIH	91.44	112.61	94.03	185.98	267.66	196.67	135.10	187.21	141.6
GOA	97.14	149.12	125.51	203.06	386.01	254.53	186.61	300.53	225.4
GUJ	92.46	136.18	107.28	194.17	295.80	219.15	165.20	234.32	184.2
HAR	90.08	114.89	96.87	241.33	306.81	254.42	221.44	271.17	231.9
HPR	95.63	129.47	97.15	222.76	342.30	231.10	208.80	326.98	216.7
J&K	102.67	124.31	105.09	228.58	290.08	240.86	196.03	265.25	208.4
KAR	79.26	122.16	94.95	175.63	321.61	210.80	142.12	223.50	165.6
KER	102.40	121.13	106.07	241.88	350.38	258.35	197.75	261.69	208.3
MPR	80.05	127.24	90.05	180.71	328.80	207.17	138.42	233.56	156.7
MAH	88.59	131.42	102.62	205.99	369.66	260.22	157.96	273.13	195.9
MAN	111.31	115.57	111.93	197.56	208.53	201.00	183.92	202.47	189.3
MEG	94.91	113.35	95.08	211.79	341.95	237.90	169.50	337.28	193.0
MIZ	107.58	60.42	104.06	247.08	349.01	282.29	241.59	347.22	277.2
NAG	NA	NA	NA	NA	390.93	390.93	NA	390.93	390.9
ORI	87.61	122.21	90.63	188.34	296.00	204.96	129.30	222.01	140.0
PUN	95.93	120.78	105.00	253.30	300.25	265.60	239.23	275.64	249.1
RAJ	87.02	123.30	95.28	217.92	319.41	237.65	174.33	245.11	188.8
SIK	105.01	109.25	105.18	194.43	295.61	220.58	157.76	281.22	180.2
TND	85.95	118.28	96.42	217.25	330.36	260.31	156.36	244.95	187.8
TRI	100.25	98.58	100.16	213.31	280.03	221.96	186.49	259.67	194.7
UPR	87.30	112.15	92.00	194.74	297.34	212.67	148.91	213.94	160.6
WEB	98.47	116.87	101.81	201.02	314.73	234.39	150.98	247.97	174.5
ANI	110.28	145.75	121.79	273.22	430.06	314.55	264.74	410.55	303.6
CHA	134.83	122.03	125.16	310.76	439.01	429.52	277.95	422.02	409.7
DNH	88.21	NA	88.21	215.23		215.23	127.07	NA	127.0
DAD	NA	NA	NA	NA	NA	NA	NA	NA	NA
DEL	43.48	144.95	138.12	337.74	485.95	467.21	310.94	428.86	415.0
LAD	104.46	140.76	122.78	264.49	276.85	269.15	221.38	224.72	222.7
PON	85.75	117.95	105.65	250.24	298.22	274.21	177.75	197.15	188.6
All-India	**88.70**	**121.00**	**95.94**	**200.74**	**326.53**	**229.10**	**156.64**	**246.04**	**176.7**

Source: As in Table 7.1.

Note: The figures are at current prices.

Table 7.8: State-wise Average Per Capita Monthly Total Expenditure (1993-94)

States	APCTEP			APCTENP			APCTE		
	Rural	*Urban*	*Total*	*Rural*	*Urban*	*Total*	*Rural*	*Urban*	*Total*
APR	75.16	115.63	93.89	179.22	291.60	202.23	162.64	223.31	178.50
ARP	99.44	98.11	99.41	226.27	306.59	240.51	173.90	293.99	188.16
ASS	104.06	111.98	104.21	172.90	287.19	191.23	141.74	273.30	155.16
BIH	89.95	116.26	91.98	170.75	279.13	189.82	123.98	222.33	135.92
GOA	93.93	156.23	144.14	298.85	355.24	318.97	288.60	299.00	293.01
GUJ	93.55	135.11	109.34	194.59	315.71	231.85	172.13	264.64	202.21
HAR	90.45	116.74	94.91	222.03	291.66	242.03	185.20	262.85	205.22
HPR	92.20	124.72	93.09	203.12	454.96	230.14	169.43	424.38	190.96
J&K	102.39	119.17	104.80	213.52	326.77	259.88	193.25	316.12	239.19
KAR	82.68	122.58	96.47	179.78	316.75	214.90	150.57	239.61	176.01
KER	101.72	126.14	107.50	245.66	339.25	268.80	209.12	287.44	228.27
MPR	82.05	128.62	94.47	179.31	323.20	209.95	139.70	229.77	160.94
MAH	87.27	134.28	103.84	207.06	396.79	279.92	161.41	304.99	214.88
MAN	111.89	115.83	112.37	177.14	196.05	182.84	164.78	190.52	171.81
MEG	109.96	113.58	110.00	223.65	319.64	240.10	195.97	315.91	212.45
MIZ	109.90	NA	109.90	220.82	327.57	256.05	213.92	327.57	249.84
NAG	115.77	NA	115.77	243.85	303.13	259.94	240.90	303.13	257.51
ORI	92.26	118.94	95.10	182.46	294.69	198.99	137.56	223.27	148.49
PUN	94.38	122.60	102.23	224.66	312.95	250.32	209.70	292.23	233.56
RAJ	94.41	128.02	103.13	204.62	304.97	226.50	175.57	250.03	192.65
SIK	105.46	120.62	105.50	190.60	310.87	204.03	163.61	309.04	175.21
TND	92.01	123.19	104.39	217.82	325.87	253.21	176.33	244.90	200.48
TRI	98.78	102.00	98.90	215.99	304.17	230.01	188.29	291.96	202.09
UPR	86.49	116.16	91.45	191.88	296.91	214.58	147.28	233.95	164.29
WEB	103.19	120.26	105.65	205.19	337.02	242.64	163.18	287.27	192.03
ANI	110.23	138.38	128.79	300.30	527.22	362.45	298.28	506.91	357.22
CHA	128.95	113.72	120.71	282.86	597.71	560.29	264.71	587.64	545.58
DNH	91.59	120.81	93.22	189.65	340.73	203.35	138.98	255.33	147.48
DAD	93.75	159.85	143.38	277.58	305.02	287.19	268.92	273.58	270.77
DEL	104.02	133.86	133.42	296.10	515.86	488.50	292.26	454.31	436.73
LAD	NA	131.41	131.41	282.89	326.92	303.25	282.89	295.77	289.40
PON	99.33	124.70	118.37	242.52	297.87	273.91	213.89	234.71	226.85
All-India	**91.18**	**123.92**	**98.05**	**198.68**	**331.68**	**232.48**	**158.60**	**265.83**	**184.15**

Source: As in Table 7.1.

Note: The figures are at constant (1987-88) prices

Table 7.9: Region-wise Average Per Capita Monthly Total Expenditure (1987-88)

States/ Regions	*APCTEP*			*APCTENP*			*APCTE*		
	Rural	*Urban*	*Total*	*Rural*	*Urban*	*Total*	*Rural*	*Urban*	*Total*
21	72.11	114.05	87.95	182.10	303.49	202.51	163.14	230.56	177.55
22	75.24	113.02	87.76	182.07	332.31	209.60	159.07	249.57	179.02
23	75.58	111.26	92.79	185.67	253.84	196.80	164.72	178.38	168.15
24	67.47	106.85	77.46	173.12	268.84	187.73	130.01	177.25	139.31
31	101.47	105.16	101.55	261.78	295.14	263.23	219.41	264.34	221.14
41	106.71	108.66	106.74	200.84	300.55	212.00	167.66	288.23	177.34
42	101.90	108.55	102.10	189.86	256.36	197.96	151.79	234.97	158.79
43	97.83	109.22	98.02	200.35	319.50	207.11	172.99	299.55	178.88
51	89.31	116.30	93.22	188.93	290.41	215.55	136.43	230.09	155.60
52	92.65	104.58	93.41	189.14	234.67	191.08	136.32	150.14	137.07
53	90.96	114.61	95.64	178.06	241.44	186.90	131.83	161.24	136.87
61	97.14	149.12	125.51	203.06	386.01	254.53	186.61	300.53	225.45
71	90.02	133.69	92.87	211.11	257.99	213.61	169.70	209.32	171.98
72	95.32	140.25	114.95	192.44	299.62	230.39	167.31	246.93	197.39
73	87.63	142.43	111.75	201.61	329.91	246.60	175.57	273.45	212.13
74	91.33	132.31	99.36	184.64	243.76	194.47	140.83	185.83	148.96
75	96.53	129.71	112.90	184.71	267.23	199.44	168.00	196.86	175.65
81	86.60	115.71	95.15	237.90	315.78	258.52	211.40	276.38	228.94
82	99.19	111.61	101.87	244.97	280.91	249.19	233.37	255.25	236.13
91	95.63	129.47	97.15	222.76	342.30	231.10	208.80	326.98	216.73
101	101.04	121.92	104.82	247.23	306.50	262.14	213.19	275.78	227.99
102	99.77	121.78	100.36	221.60	311.92	227.62	178.41	278.53	183.71
103	106.84	126.24	109.90	223.82	279.09	236.77	199.61	258.03	212.43
111	92.61	125.51	113.30	181.62	294.66	201.21	169.67	200.55	178.63
112	85.78	142.72	101.96	174.50	284.25	191.88	152.74	226.65	167.01
113	80.72	128.96	98.76	177.29	346.48	236.33	141.19	259.59	183.64
114	76.24	113.56	88.96	173.01	298.69	197.16	133.93	188.42	148.07
121	101.50	115.28	103.70	219.22	309.93	229.73	172.62	214.91	178.29
122	103.32	124.96	108.29	254.45	364.70	273.24	214.75	283.02	227.51
131	83.15	129.94	88.18	163.16	337.34	190.71	125.78	262.70	144.30
132	82.87	120.85	90.16	183.44	302.49	191.71	146.81	185.22	151.35
133	82.01	125.50	95.82	160.61	318.54	192.66	125.67	203.90	145.87
134	76.81	129.65	92.01	201.60	325.65	229.32	154.99	236.33	175.22
135	75.80	124.08	85.34	178.42	348.59	227.94	125.73	261.57	159.14
136	75.35	125.61	87.21	180.16	289.30	194.70	126.78	178.65	136.57
137	82.14	134.18	100.41	197.64	324.35	221.10	171.14	245.45	188.25
141	90.02	150.07	121.64	194.18	394.49	328.02	163.19	348.14	280.77
142	93.25	137.23	107.67	226.17	355.96	254.91	184.34	259.57	203.78
143	87.36	121.32	96.23	199.19	313.46	221.27	148.32	207.39	161.65

(Contd.)

Table 7.9—*Contd.*

States/ Regions	APCTEP			APCTENP			APCTE		
	Rural	Urban	Total	Rural	Urban	Total	Rural	Urban	Total
144	84.56	120.79	94.00	211.29	323.98	226.87	150.03	187.28	157.55
145	87.53	125.01	101.68	183.38	338.41	227.41	135.94	210.42	160.78
146	90.92	126.55	96.88	181.06	296.74	192.37	139.98	193.30	146.96
151	112.99	116.68	113.96	203.84	206.53	204.85	195.31	201.31	197.51
152	110.40	112.30	110.52	186.45	219.33	191.87	167.30	208.46	173.10
161	94.91	113.35	95.08	211.79	341.95	237.90	169.50	337.28	193.08
171	107.58	60.42	104.06	247.08	349.01	282.29	241.59	347.22	277.27
181	NA	NA	NA	NA	390.93	390.93	NA	390.93	390.93
191	92.54	125.45	95.79	182.64	288.54	195.74	139.06	219.87	148.10
192	78.73	119.84	81.15	182.68	274.34	202.24	96.42	192.57	105.01
193	88.08	119.31	90.98	200.20	309.44	221.38	131.79	233.58	145.53
201	97.40	118.95	105.86	257.44	300.39	269.25	245.09	277.77	254.43
202	94.38	123.26	104.00	247.04	299.99	259.81	230.66	271.93	241.06
211	92.61	122.15	100.19	219.16	309.41	235.34	183.79	238.28	194.82
212	92.15	123.60	102.15	223.78	330.37	246.25	185.86	244.76	200.29
213	70.37	121.75	72.62	182.70	329.46	201.15	114.07	260.07	125.38
214	94.28	126.48	99.72	216.82	302.80	235.49	178.44	258.64	194.69
221	105.01	109.25	105.18	194.43	295.61	220.58	157.76	281.22	180.26
231	84.05	118.01	96.12	191.60	339.44	274.90	126.29	251.35	183.44
232	90.64	123.57	98.04	200.69	302.09	224.20	157.23	233.30	174.65
233	82.82	114.26	93.25	201.81	308.85	236.73	140.60	207.52	162.62
234	90.85	123.05	101.49	257.77	343.56	286.87	207.05	278.40	231.05
241	100.25	98.58	100.16	213.31	280.03	221.96	186.49	259.67	194.79
251	97.24	122.19	104.98	223.64	354.79	251.68	206.73	307.42	229.71
252	88.62	111.83	95.95	207.27	287.22	223.55	168.59	205.49	177.60
253	87.86	113.55	93.00	183.62	313.47	210.72	141.02	227.18	158.67
254	86.79	114.09	89.22	181.70	280.97	192.49	133.50	205.51	140.61
255	82.70	101.08	85.89	178.83	303.38	201.10	116.33	173.45	126.36
261	112.37	128.06	113.56	176.34	268.56	190.91	154.66	242.75	166.29
262	95.59	108.52	96.53	192.61	237.30	197.92	133.96	176.49	137.86
263	96.89	117.92	104.00	216.33	331.15	268.64	164.07	262.48	204.40
264	101.43	117.50	102.72	196.51	240.26	200.81	151.27	188.60	154.62
271	110.28	145.75	121.79	273.22	430.06	314.55	264.74	410.55	303.67
281	134.83	122.03	125.16	310.76	439.01	429.52	277.95	422.02	409.77
291	88.21	NA	88.21	215.23	NA	215.23	127.07	NA	127.07
301	NA	NA	NA	NA	NA	NA	NA	NA	NA
311	43.48	144.95	138.12	337.74	485.95	467.21	310.94	428.86	415.06
321	104.46	140.76	122.78	264.49	276.85	269.15	221.38	224.72	222.77
331	85.75	117.95	105.65	250.24	298.22	274.21	177.75	197.15	188.61
All-India	**88.70**	**121.00**	**95.94**	**200.74**	**326.53**	**229.10**	**156.64**	**246.04**	**176.75**

Source: As in Table 7.1.
Note: The Figures are at Current Prices.

Table 7.10: Region-wise Average Per Monthly Total Expenditure (1993-94)

States/ Regions	APCTEP			APCTENP			APCTE		
	Rural	Urban	Total	Rural	Urban	Total	Rural	Urban	Total
21	74.54	115.31	93.99	173.36	279.96	194.36	156.42	208.41	170.18
22	76.64	118.68	94.79	181.65	309.96	209.76	166.95	251.45	188.75
23	72.79	112.48	90.19	189.89	283.52	209.86	165.63	210.06	177.79
24	76.56	111.63	95.09	187.16	264.75	200.48	172.81	196.42	178.61
31	99.44	98.11	99.41	226.27	306.59	240.51	173.90	293.99	188.16
41	103.84	117.86	103.99	174.71	306.20	195.03	148.44	299.61	164.54
42	103.80	111.01	103.98	171.76	274.99	189.05	137.42	256.86	149.44
43	110.09	99.17	110.01	169.72	268.03	182.44	145.02	262.05	154.70
51	89.15	120.59	92.06	175.73	308.18	217.84	121.83	258.42	148.23
52	89.95	113.59	91.24	167.99	246.24	174.00	122.37	180.77	126.11
53	90.68	114.86	93.03	171.26	257.31	187.17	128.05	206.84	139.09
61	93.93	156.23	144.14	298.85	355.24	318.97	288.60	299.00	293.01
71	89.03	139.65	94.95	185.05	287.26	193.57	160.07	237.21	167.18
72	96.04	135.13	114.79	198.10	325.75	250.10	174.13	270.15	215.04
73	92.44	129.43	105.16	198.45	340.71	258.76	170.68	298.11	222.27
74	95.33	129.66	101.12	192.50	395.42	228.11	167.05	328.25	195.05
75	95.65	137.91	121.44	197.51	260.36	216.74	185.30	220.44	198.14
81	90.72	117.39	95.66	206.20	284.47	232.46	169.35	255.35	194.64
82	89.87	114.76	93.23	242.32	308.73	256.53	208.40	281.39	222.83
91	92.20	124.72	93.09	203.12	454.96	230.14	169.43	424.38	190.96
101	108.14	116.13	110.06	218.13	334.27	266.04	207.28	324.04	253.87
102	98.44	129.15	100.34	190.84	286.73	228.53	150.28	275.08	185.44
103	NA	NA	NA	NA	NA	NA	NA	NA	NA
111	88.53	138.15	105.16	216.97	357.20	247.77	205.03	323.21	232.45
112	85.26	128.26	103.35	180.93	300.36	201.57	167.03	236.43	182.38
113	83.93	131.73	102.06	174.88	325.21	232.68	148.26	269.47	194.68
114	81.62	115.71	92.59	172.70	291.25	193.84	138.13	190.79	150.73
121	98.55	128.30	105.50	228.10	323.81	249.94	192.07	268.21	209.56
122	104.18	124.51	109.04	256.72	347.49	280.22	220.46	298.63	240.33
131	86.34	131.90	94.36	157.31	309.01	184.12	125.83	230.63	144.32
132	84.45	135.38	93.86	171.50	332.91	189.58	139.70	232.47	152.69
133	81.21	120.69	94.04	155.66	343.69	212.49	118.88	227.62	152.99
134	86.13	133.73	107.76	186.00	332.58	225.87	158.71	241.92	186.42
135	79.62	126.70	93.96	212.52	311.95	239.28	150.88	218.00	170.08
136	71.30	116.29	78.25	168.91	318.09	202.76	102.70	203.56	120.78
137	84.08	129.84	105.67	206.34	322.33	227.60	186.07	237.35	198.95
141	96.26	153.17	133.12	235.39	422.67	366.35	214.19	389.12	335.32
142	92.51	142.54	112.12	204.83	373.75	245.94	176.61	280.80	206.52
143	88.93	134.47	102.95	182.19	314.62	212.12	137.52	209.51	156.78
144	78.57	118.34	89.05	231.93	388.42	260.55	155.21	222.20	170.30
145	88.52	125.02	102.96	183.46	349.07	233.84	136.76	216.47	164.86
146	90.58	144.77	98.86	180.76	312.22	198.77	136.09	223.92	148.82
151	112.33	114.57	112.76	174.32	196.21	182.34	165.83	191.16	174.63

(Contd.)

Table 7.10—*Contd.*

States/ Regions	*APCTEP*			*APCTENP*			*APCTE*		
	Rural	*Urban*	*Total*	*Rural*	*Urban*	*Total*	*Rural*	*Urban*	*Total*
152	111.55	120.30	112.00	182.44	194.91	184.13	163.10	186.31	165.74
161	109.96	113.58	110.00	223.65	319.64	240.10	195.97	315.91	212.45
171	109.90	NA	109.90	220.82	327.57	256.05	213.92	327.57	249.84
181	115.77	NA	115.77	243.85	303.13	259.94	240.90	303.13	257.51
191	93.76	119.63	97.11	181.61	290.03	194.72	141.81	209.54	150.26
193	93.49	123.86	96.72	188.92	291.82	206.69	145.22	237.31	158.43
201	96.14	124.86	106.30	226.63	321.01	256.25	217.45	304.74	245.10
202	93.44	120.40	99.66	221.78	297.02	240.85	199.57	269.46	217.01
211	97.70	135.16	105.81	190.99	292.92	215.12	167.19	256.03	187.77
212	94.84	125.96	107.31	206.55	313.03	230.50	186.46	250.24	203.28
213	92.73	128.74	95.14	217.11	325.13	232.87	159.52	272.91	172.12
214	90.12	123.95	99.17	223.53	300.90	238.56	179.46	225.26	189.54
221	105.46	120.62	105.50	190.60	310.87	204.03	163.61	309.04	175.21
231	90.20	120.47	101.84	237.35	332.62	279.37	172.26	250.79	205.03
232	95.41	124.60	106.78	223.86	336.75	244.39	197.13	245.52	208.55
233	90.52	120.56	102.50	192.98	294.12	222.84	154.91	210.15	173.57
234	97.18	132.68	112.46	216.21	336.30	254.04	189.60	270.95	217.64
241	98.78	102.00	98.90	215.99	304.17	230.01	188.29	291.96	202.09
251	94.43	119.87	98.42	187.95	305.15	213.80	164.73	272.08	186.81
252	90.78	118.33	98.51	203.67	307.21	229.76	170.60	245.99	190.25
253	83.09	112.89	87.16	187.83	291.61	216.60	135.27	239.23	157.38
254	86.44	117.50	89.52	179.95	275.75	192.85	134.32	212.11	143.47
255	80.27	108.18	86.44	197.04	283.66	216.60	118.38	166.46	129.09
261	103.65	115.61	104.44	160.01	245.62	174.63	127.08	203.20	135.67
262	101.60	119.57	103.30	211.80	297.51	224.53	159.47	234.98	168.81
263	101.48	121.80	106.95	209.88	351.77	271.02	175.83	309.83	227.89
264	107.21	116.50	108.00	202.17	269.72	207.69	163.49	205.70	167.00
271	110.23	138.38	128.79	300.30	527.22	362.45	298.28	506.91	357.22
281	128.95	113.72	120.71	282.86	597.71	560.29	264.71	587.64	545.58
291	91.59	120.81	93.22	189.65	340.73	203.35	138.98	255.33	147.48
301	93.75	159.85	143.38	277.58	305.02	287.19	268.92	273.58	270.77
311	104.02	133.86	133.42	296.10	515.86	488.50	292.26	454.31	436.73
321	NA	131.41	131.41	282.89	326.92	303.25	282.89	295.77	289.40
331	99.33	124.70	118.37	242.52	297.87	273.91	213.89	234.71	226.85
All-India	**91.18**	**123.92**	**98.05**	**198.68**	**331.68**	**232.48**	**158.60**	**265.83**	**184.15**

Source: As in Table 7.1.
Note: The Figures are at constant (1987-88) prices.

to NER of India. This reflects slow growth of APCTE among north-eastern States in comparison to some other States of the rest of India. One possible explanation could be that these States have very poor industrial base. As a result these States have not benefited from the opening up of the economy.

Increase in APCTE does not always reveals the improvement of standard of living for all the households belonging to different expenditure classes, as it is insensitive to changes in the distribution of expenditure. In other words, we cannot say with certainty that by improving APCTE (as we noted earlier) would benefit poor and non-poor households equally. In order to capture this, in Tables 7.7 and 7.8 we have reported the APCTE for poor and non-poor separately for the years 1987-88 and 1993-94.

There are about nine States, which show lower APCTE for poor than national average Rs. 95.94 in 1987-88 (Table 7.7). Out of these Andhra Pradesh, Orissa, Madhya Pradesh and Uttar Pradesh are the prominent States belong to this category. But, the APCTE for poors (Rural) at all-India level has increased by about 3 per cent, from Rs. 88.70 in 1987-88 to Rs. 91.18 in 1993-94. This clearly shows some improvement in the consumption expenditure level of poors in the rural sector of most of the States. Similar trends are also observed for the urban sector where APCTEP increased by about 2.4 per cent. During the same period the APCTE for non-poors has increased from Rs. 229.10 to 232.48 (1.5 per cent) at all-India level (Tables 7.7 and 7.8). In urban sector, the increase was just about the same, less than 1.6 per cent). The implication of these observations on regional inequality could be that for poors, there might be narrowing down of regional disparities. This might have some rural bias compared to urban areas.

These observations are further strengthened when we look at the shift in the distribution of population along the expenditure scale shown in Figures 7.1 and 7.2. The figures clearly indicate the overall increase in the real consumption expenditures at per capita household level for almost all segments of the population during 1987-88 to 1993-94 for both the rural and urban sectors. But this increase is more uniform and steady in the case of rural population than urban population. These trends were also followed while analyzing the data at sub-State level reported in Tables 7.9 and 7.10.[8]

Relative Performance over Time

In this section we carry out two types of analysis in order to capture the extent of change in regional disparities among the States/regions over two time points, 1987-88 and 1993-94. First, we look at the regional disparities by calculating rank correlations and the Coefficients of Variation (CV) of all the three poverty measures, the HCR, PGI and FGT and the APCTE, APCTEP and APCTENP. Secondly, a differential band analysis introduced to highlight the

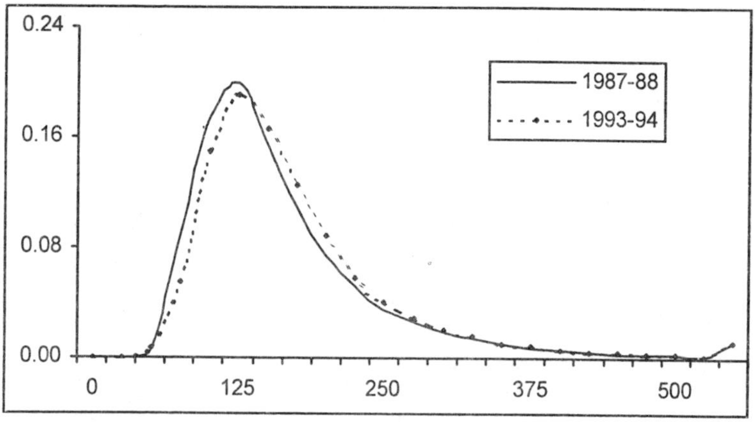

Fig. 7.1: Distribution of Population at Different Expenditure Levels (Rural)

Note: The 1993-94 PCTE is in constant (1987-88) prices. *See* section 2 for details.

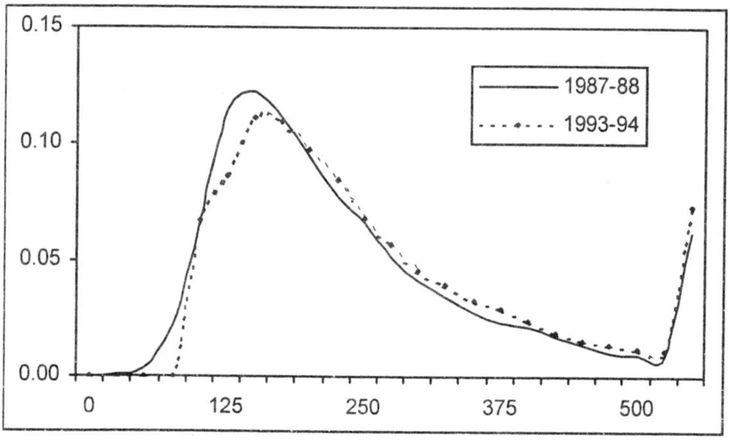

Fig. 7.2: Distribution of Population at Different Expenditure Levels (Urban)

Note: As in Figure 7.10

degree of poverty reduction within the regions during this period. This analysis provides us a disaggregated view of regional disparities. In this way, actually, we are intending to investigate within States and the regional disparity can be viewed with respect to other regions in the country, as well.

Regional Disparities: Rank Correlation and Coefficient of Variation Analysis

Tables 7.11 and 7.12 report the rank correlation across the States/regions for poverty measures and for various consumption expenditure levels for two years. The strong positive rank correlation coefficient (0.84), when States/regions are arranged according to their respective HCR reveals that during this period there are no major changes in the relative position of the States/regions. But the value of this coefficient is relatively lower for rural sector (0.76) compared to urban sector (0.92). This suggests that rural sector of some of the States improved their relative position on account of HCR.

Table 7.11: Rank Correlation of Poverty Measures (1987-88 and 1993-94)

	State			*State/Region*		
Sector	*HCR*	*PGI*	*FGT*	*HCR*	*PGI*	*FGT*
Rural	0.76	0.71	0.64	0.80	0.75	0.72
Urban	0.92	0.93	0.95	0.85	0.86	0.88
Total	**0.84**	**0.85**	**0.84**	**0.84**	**0.82**	**0.83**

Source: As in Table 7.1.

Table 7.12: Rank Correlation of Average PCTEs (1987-88 and 1993-94)

	State			*State/Region*		
Sector	*APCTEP*	*APCTENP*	*APCTE*	*APCTEP*	*APCTENP*	*APCTE*
Rural	0.73	0.83	0.84	0.80	0.69	0.77
Urban	0.87	0.82	0.93	0.77	0.66	1.00
Total	**0.84**	**0.93**	**0.85**	**0.80**	**0.84**	**1.00**

Source: As in table 7.1.

Table 7.12 has the rank correlations of States/regions of APCTEs. The rank correlation of APCTEP supports the observation regarding improvement in the ranking of the States. The rank correlation of the regions, however, shows relative stability. In other words, the rank correlation of HCR and APCTEP in case of regions is same in the rural sector. In the urban sector, the ranking of States as well as regions is relatively stable when we consider the correlation in case of HCR. The stability of ranks among the States is maintained when we look at the rank of PCTEP. There is a lot of happening, though, among the ranking of the regions where the coefficient has declined from 0.85 to 0.77. This implies that in some regions level of living of poor has improved.

Table 7.11 also reports the rank correlation of other two poverty measures, PGI and FGT, among the States as well as the regions. It is interesting to note that in the rural sector the correlation is highest for HCR (0.76) and lowest for FGT (0.64). It implies that there are several States, which have been able to raise the condition of the poorest households faster than others. The similar rank correlation is observed in case of regions also but the gap in the correlation between HCR and FGT is relatively lower. The rank correlation of level of living of entire population (APCTE) and of non-poor (APCTENP) does not show much variability between States and regions. These observations need to be examined in greater detail.

This analysis is indicative of increasing regional disparities at State/region level. We have investigated this issue further by calculating the Coefficient of Variation (CoV). The CoV quantifies the degree of dispersion and variability of mean between two groups of data set. Table 7.13 reports the CoV of the poverty measures for the States. The CoV for urban is higher than rural sector, which shows the higher disparity on account of poverty measures in urban than rural sector among the States in 1987-88. We find the same trend in 1993-94. Comparing the result we notice that CoV has remained constant over two periods for the States as a whole. However, it has increased from 43.70 to 46.62 for rural sector and from 52.89 to 56.85 for urban sector for HCR among the States. This indicates that there is some evidence of increase in regional disparities in both the rural and urban sectors of the States during this period.

Table 7.14 reports the CoV of the poverty measures for comparable regions for the two years. We find a similar change in the CoV in case of regions also. It could be seen that the difference in CoV is more in case of regions (Table 7.14) than for the States (Table 7.13), for both the rural and urban sectors. This implies that the regional disparities have increased sharply among the regions than the States. Other interesting observation is that in the rural sector the CoV of FGT has declined across the regions in 1993-94 compared

Table 7.13: Coefficient of Variation across States

Sector	*1987-88*			*1993-94*		
	HCR	*PGI*	*FGT*	*HCR*	*PGI*	*FGT*
Rural	43.70	51.98	56.25	46.62	54.57	59.05
Urban	52.89	60.83	65.27	56.85	63.64	67.38
Total	**43.39**	**52.01**	**56.57**	**43.08**	**50.19**	**54.62**

Source: As in Table 7.1.
Note: The figures are in per cent.

Table 7.14: Coefficient of Variation across NSS Regions

Sector	*1987-88*			*1993-94*		
	HCR	*PGI*	*FGT*	*HCR*	*PGI*	*FGT*
Rural	42.45	58.61	74.12	46.29	59.50	71.22
Urban	47.60	61.49	72.12	54.63	70.25	83.37
Total	**44.01**	**61.46**	**75.75**	**49.54**	**63.06**	**75.56**

Source: As in Table 7.1.
Note: The figures are in per cent.

to 1987-88. Exactly opposite is the case in case of urban regions. This could mean that in rural sector, the severity of poverty has declined whereas it has increased in the case of urban poors.

In Table 7.15, we have reported the CoV of APCTEs of the States for two years. The CoV of APCTE was 41.96 in 1987-88 that increased to 52.72 in 1993-94 indicating a sharp increase in inter-State disparities. During the same period, there is only marginal increase in the rural sector but it is in the urban sector that recorded significant increase in the disparities. When we look at the APCTEP, we find that CoV has declined marginally in rural sector whereas it has remained unchanged in urban sector. In other words, the inter-State disparity among the poors does not show any deterioration during this period. Among the non-poors, CoV remained almost same in rural sector. But in the urban sector, the CoV of APCTENP recorded significant increase from 17.28 to 25.73.

Table 7.16 reports the CoV of APCTEs at the region level. The calculated CoV for all the three groups, APCTE, APCTENP and APCTEP for entire population and in the two sectors is similar to the observations recorded above in the case of States.

Table 7.15: Coefficient of Variation across States

Sector	*1987-88*			*1993-94*		
	APCTEP	*APCTENP*	*APCTE*	*APCTEP*	*APCTENP*	*APCTE*
Rural	18.25	21.96	33.99	13.63	21.25	34.68
Urban	9.90	17.28	27.60	9.20	25.73	36.26
Total	**14.69**	**28.87**	**41.96**	**15.56**	**38.34**	**52.72**

Source: As in Table 7.1.
Note: The figures are in per cent.

Table 7.16: Coefficient of Variation across NSS Regions

Sector	*1987-88*			*1993-94*		
	APCTEP	*APCTENP*	*APCTE*	*APCTEP*	*APCTENP*	*APCTE*
Rural	14.28	16.32	25.90	11.63	16.07	25.49
Urban	12.37	15.36	22.82	8.94	19.32	26.64
Total	**9.11**	**20.93**	**30.31**	**12.63**	**26.40**	**36.38**

Source: As in Table 7.1.
Note: The Figures are in per cent

In sum, if we divide the households into the poor and non-poor sections, we find that the increased disparity is among the non-poor persons only. But in the case of both the urban and rural poors the disparity on the basis of APCTEP, has gone down as CoV has in fact decreased. And this reduction, in inter-State disparities is more in the case of urban than rural poors. This implies that increase in regional disparities is mainly due to increase in the disparity of APCTE for non-poors, whereas disparities on the basis of APCTE have actually declined in the case of poors. As a matter of fact the Dubey and Gangopadhyay (1998) have reported that the average per capita consumption of the poors had actually increased significantly in 1993-94 over that of 1987-88. Thus, as far as the poors are concerned, their per capita consumption expenditure has become more homogeneous across regions and, the level is higher. This is a significant point. Some people maintain that in the nineties, the poors have become worse off, and the rich better off. The consumption expenditure data for 1993-94, compared to that of 1987-88, suggest otherwise.

Regional Disparities: Differential Band Analysis

The foregoing analysis of inter-regional disparities is based on variation in the rank correlation and coefficient of variation. The major limitation of this approach is that this gives the aggregate view of regional disparity. If we intend to find out the inter-regional (intra-State) disparity, then this approach is not of much help. In this section we introduce an approach where extent of regional disparity is categorized in differential bands for an in-depth analysis.

Recall that the all-India HCR in the rural sector as measured by the OPL and given in Table 7.1, declined by 2.08 percentage points (*i.e.,* 39.36 to 37.28). We now check the performance of each region against this national average. We define six bands, three below, and three above, the national average. If the (national) average reduction in poverty is denoted x, then keeping in mind that x is negative, define one band as the interval $(x + 0.5x, x)$, and a corresponding one as $(x, x - 0.5x)$. Similarly, define two other intervals as $(2x, x + 0.5x)$ and $(x - 0.5x, 0)$. The other two intervals are $(-\infty, 2x)$ and $(0, \infty)$. Similarly, we have defined six bands for the urban regions also. The all-India urban HCR, as given in Table 7.1, declined by 3.36 percentage points (*i.e.,* 39.31 – 35.95) during the period. The corresponding six bands were defined and used for further analysis.

These six bands help us in understanding the extent and degree of increase or decrease of poverty incidence among the 74 NSS regions during the period 1987-88 to 1993-94. First band shows the regions where reduction in poverty incidence is more than two times of national average. Second band shows the regions where reduction in poverty is more than 1.5 times and less than double. Third band shows the reduction in poverty more than national average but less than 1.5 times of national average. Similarly, fourth band shows reduction in poverty less than national average but above than 0.5 times of national average and fifth band shows reduction in poverty but less than 0.5 times of national average. Finally, sixth band shows those regions in which the poverty incidence has actually increased.

Table 7.17 reports the band-wise distribution of regions for rural and urban sectors. In the rural sector, in 52 out of 74 comparable regions (above 70 %) the incidence of poverty has declined. But 22 regions belonging to sixth band the incidence of poverty has increased. So, in fact 42 out of the 74 comparable regions are in the two extreme bands.[9] There are 20 regions where poverty level has reduced more than two times of national average, belonging to the first band.

Table 7.17: Distribution of Regions from Average (All-India) HCR

	Bands					
	1	*2*	*3*	*4*	*5*	*6*
Rural Regions	20	11	9	6	6	22
Urban Regions	14	10	8	13	12	17

Note: *See* section 3.1 for the definition of the bands.

Similarly, in the urban sector, the record of reduction of poverty is slightly better in a sense that in 57 out of 74 comparable regions (above 77 %) the incidence of poverty has declined. There are 17 regions belonging to the category of sixth band, where HCR has actually increased during this period. In the rural sector, we observe more regional heterogeneity than in urban sector. These results are also plotted in a bar diagram in Figure 7.3.

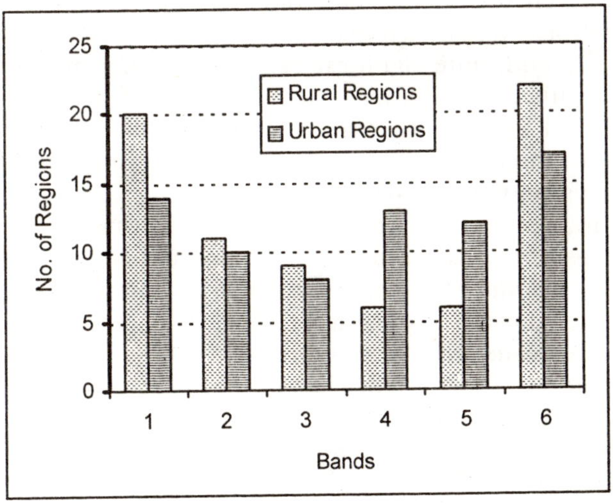

Fig. 7.3: Distribution of Regions

Note: We have considered comparable regions only. *See* section 3.1 for details. *See* note in Table 7.17 for definition of bands.

What is the regional disparity within a State? We look at a simple measure. We check whether or not, there is any State, which has regions that have performed the best and the worst over time. Only MPR and APR satisfy this criterion. Three (131, 132 and 134)[10] out of seven regions in MPR have the best relative performance over all regions in the country.[11] It also has one region (136), where the HCR has gone up. APR has one (024) in the top group, and one, (021), where the poverty has actually increased.

Conclusion

In this chapter, we have studied the regional disparities in poverty incidence and other poverty indices and in the levels of living, captured by average per capita consumption expenditure of households divided into three groups. One of our major findings is that poverty, as measured by the three indices in this chapter, has declined for the entire country. This is true for both the rural and urban sectors of the country.

If we divide the country into the administrative boundaries of the States and the Union Territories, then the changes in the poverty levels turn out to be more revealing and meaningful. The inter-State disparity, measured using Coefficient of Variation (CoV) is found quite significant and it is further magnified if we look within the States, *i.e.,* across the NSS regions. Indeed, we did find States with regions at the extreme ends of the spectrum—those with the best and worst performing among all regions within the country.

We also looked at the disparities in the level of living by comparing the average per capita consumption expenditures across States and regions. Using the coefficient of variation as a measure, we show that regional disparities in the standards of living of the poors have come down, while urban disparities are lower than rural disparities. At the State level, however, in 1987-88, urban disparities among the urban poors were higher; in 1993-94, they were lower. For the non-poors, disparities fell over time, but the urban disparities were consistently higher than in the rural sector.

Our findings have important implications in identifying the poor regions within the State and call for the appropriate role of the State administrations to play in reducing the disparities across regions within the States.

NOTES

1. Suryanarayana (1996) has argued that the CPIAL is based on a weighting diagramme of 1956-57 consumption pattern. Since the consumption patterns have changed for all population groups over the last four decades, CPIAL might not be a representative index even for agricultural labour.
2. It is to be noted that the PCSDP data is available for only about 25 States and Union Territories out of a total of 32. However, the NSS data is collected from almost entire territory in the Indian Union. For details on the geographical areas not covered in the survey, See Dubey and Gangopadhyay (1998).
3. For further details, please refer to GOI (1979) or Dubey and Gangopadhyay (1998).
4. The methodology recommended by the Expert Group (GOI, 1993) is based on Minhas *et al.* (1988).
5. Besides satisfying various poverty axioms, this measure is population sub-group consistent. Recall that we are computing aggregate poverty measures as weighted sum of population sub-groups, State and NSS region.
6. Observe that these States had poverty incidence lower than the all-India average.
7. In 1987-88, the NSSO had divided the entire country into 77 agro-climatic regions. In 1993-94, there were 78 such regions. However, in 1993-94 one NSS region in Jammu and Kashmir could not be surveyed. Consequently, there were 77 NSS regions surveyed in both the rounds.
8. Dubey and Gangopadhyay (2002) have shown that there is first order stochastic dominance in the expenditure distribution in both rural and urban sectors.
9. For the description and identification of regions, See Dubey and Gangopadhyay (1998).
10. See the Appendix for the region and State codes.
11. Dubey and Gangopadhyay (1998).

REFERENCES

Barro, R.J. and X. Sala-i-Mratin (1992), Convergence, *Journal of Political Economy*, Vol. 100 (3).

Dasgupta, D.; P. Maiti; R. Mukherjee and S. Sarkar (1997), *Inter-regional Disparities and Growth in India*, Public Policy Research Unit (PPRU), Indian Statistical Institute, New Delhi, December.

Dubey, A. and S. Gangopadhyay (1998), Counting the Poor: Where are the Poor in India?, *Sarvekshana*: Analytical Report, No. 1, February.

Ghosh, B.; S. Marjit and C. Neogi (1998), Economic Growth and Regional Divergence in India, 1960 to 1995, *Economic and Political Weekly*, Vol. 33 (26), pp. 1623-30.

Government of India (1979), Report of the Task Force on Projections of Minimum Needs and Effective Consumption Demand, Planning Commission, Perspective Planning Division, January.

Government of India (1993), Report of the Expert Group on Estimation of Proportion and Number of Poor, Planning Commission, Perspective Planning Division, July.

Government of India (1997), *Estimates of Poverty*, Press Information Bureau, March 11.

Marjit, S. and S. Mitra (1996), Convergence in Regional Growth Rates, *Economic and Political Weekly*, Vol. 31 (33), pp. 1723-30.

Mathur, A. (1983): *Regional Development and Income Disparities in India: A Sectoral Analysis, Economic Development and Cultural Change*, Vol. 31 (2), April, 475-505.

Mazumdar, D. and H.H. Son (2001), *Vulnerable Groups and Labour Markets in Thailand*, University of Toronto, October (mimeo.).

Suryanarayana, M.H. (1996), Economic Reforms, Nature and Poverty, *Economic and Political Weekly*, Vol. 31 (11), pp. 617-24.

UNDP (1999): *Diversity and Disparities in Human Development: Key Challenges for India*, UNDP, New Delhi, January.

APPENDIX TABLE 7.1

ABBREVIATIONS AND STATE AND REGION CODES

Code and Acronym	*Name of the State and UTs*	*Regions within a State (Codes)*
02 APR	Andhra Pradesh	021, 022, 023, 024
03 ARP	Arunachal Pradesh	031
04 ASS	Assam	041, 042, 043
05 BIH	Bihar	051, 052, 053
06 GOA	Goa	061
07 GUJ	Gujarat	071, 072, 073, 074, 075
08 HAR	Haryana	081, 082
09 HPR	Himachal Pradesh	091
10 J&K	Jammu and Kashmir	101, 102, 103
11 KAR	Karnataka	111, 112, 113, 114
12 KER	Kerala	121, 122
13 MPR	Madhya Pradesh	131, 132, 133, 134, 135, 136, 137
14 MAH	Maharashtra	141, 142, 143, 144, 145, 146
15 MAN	Manipur	151, 152
16 MEG	Meghalaya	161
17 MIZ	Mizoram	171
18 NAG	Nagaland	181
19 ORI	Orissa	191, 192, 193
20 PUN	Punjab	201, 202
21 RAJ	Rajasthan	211, 212, 213, 214
22 SIK	Sikkim	221
23 TND	Tamil Nadu	231, 231, 233, 234
24 TRI	Tripura	241
25 UPR	Uttar Pradesh	251, 252, 253, 254, 255
26 WEB	West Bengal	261, 262, 263, 264
27 ANI	Andaman and Nicobar Islands	271
28 CHA	Chandigarh	281
29 DNH	Dadra and Nagar Haveli	291
30 DAD	Daman and Diu	301
31 DEL	Delhi	311
32 LAD	Lakshadweep	321
33 PON	Pondicherry	331

Note: The State and Regions Codes reported above are based on the 1993-94 consumption expenditure survey. For matching of State and Region Codes in 1987-88 and 1993-94, See Dubey and Gangopadhyay (1998).

8

Poverty Determinants in the Rainfed Traditional Farms in Western Sudan: Rural Kordofan State

RAGA M. ELZAKI, SHAMS ELDEIN H. AHMED,
ALI M. EISSA and ALI A.A. SALIH

Introduction

African people have continued to suffer from hunger, malnutrition, starvation, diseases and preventable death (Sullivan, 2006 and Benson, 2004). Lofgren and Richards (2003) reported that in Middle East and North Africa (MENA) as well as elsewhere in the developing world poverty is disproportionately a rural phenomenon. Dar *et al.* (2003) confirmed that around 70 per cent of the poors and food-insecure people reside in rural areas. Many researchers argued that rural poverty lines were set slightly higher than urban poverty lines (Datt and Jolliffe, 1999 and Grootaert, 1996). Satterthwaite (2005) suggested that because they were based on food expenditure, with an assumption that activity levels were higher in rural areas, so rural populations needed more calories per person.

Poverty in Sudan is widespread and pervasive, particularly in rural areas owing to the relatively low incomes, inequality in income distribution and in face of continuous rise in the prices of goods and services. According to the United Nations Human Development index, Sudan ranked as the 144th out of 174 poor countries in the world (IFAD, 2004). Poverty in the Sudan is deeply ingrained and is largely rural. In 2002 about 20 million people were living below the poverty line of less than US$ 1 a day (IFAD, 2007). The same source indicated that poverty in Sudan has clear sub-national trends. There are strong regional disparities, where States of Kordofan, Darfur, Blue Nile, and the Red Sea are the poorest. Furthermore, the south as whole is worse than the north in poverty census. The decade of the 1980s signified a period of disappointing macro-economic performance and the decade of the 1990s witnessed increasing numbers of poors among the rural people in Sudan, the largest and the richest, in natural resources, among the sub-Saharan countries. The Sudanese economy has had suffered secular regress during the 1980s when judged by all macro-economic indicators. A steady declining of income and consumption per capita, persistence deficit in the balance of payment and huge external debt have also characterized the 1980's and most of 1990's. The poor economic performance during the last two decades had been triggered mainly by the spreading long civil war, an ethnic conflict and recurrent famine. Famines were often initiated by the frequent drought episodes that struck Sudan and complicated by poor policies. Poverty in Sudan is a multi-dimensional problem involving economic, political, social as well as ecological factor (Fergany, 1997 and Deng, 2004).

The estimation of the national poverty trend in Sudan by Ali (1994) over the period (1968-1992) was demonstrated in Table 8.1. The Table 8.1 depicts the rural poverty was highly significant than the urban poverty. The rate of growth of poverty incidence in the rural Sudan is piercingly increased during the period (1968-1992); it ranged from 0.23 per cent during (1968-1978) to 0.21 per cent during (1986-1992). Even though, the rate of growth of poverty gap in rural areas had increased from 0.84 per cent during (1968-1978) to 6.79 per cent in period (1978-1986) and then decreased to 3.2 per cent in period (1986-1992).

The urban poverty incidences were greater than those of the rural poverty by 2.35 per cent during (1968-1978), by 9.27 per cent during (1978-1986). It then increased by 7.81 per cent than that of the rural poverty during (1986-1992). The indication of a high urban poverty incidence during the period (1978-1986) may be attributed to the introduction of the Structural Adjustment Programmes in 1978.

Table 8.1: Rural, Urban and National Poverty Trends in Sudan (1968-1992)

Poverty Indicator	*Poverty Trends (1968-1978)*			*Poverty Trends (1978-1986)*			*Poverty Trends (1986-1992)*		
	1968	*1978*	*α_1(%)*	*1978*	*1986*	*α_2 (%)*	*1986*	*1992*	*α_3(%)*
1. P_o(%)									
Rural	62.68	64.17	0.23	64.17	83.12	3.29	83.12	93.16	0.21
Urban	15.90	20.51	2.58	20.51	52.86	12.56	52.86	84.43	7.81
Sudan	51.59	54.26	0.50	54.26	77.8	4.61	77.8	91.41	2.69
2. P_1(%)									
Rural	28.11	30.56	0.84	30.56	51.67	6.79	51.67	62.61	3.20
Urban	4.56	8.58	6.53	8.58	24.38	13.94	24.38	47.78	11.21
Sudan	24.66	23.12	–0.64	23.12	45.43	8.81	45.43	59.35	4.45
3. H (000)									
Rural	1181.0	1575.0	2.92	1575.0	2309	4.9	2309	2725	2.76
Urban	51.7	127.4	9.44	127.4	370	14.3	370	705	10.74
Sudan	1305.8	1669.0	2.48	1669.0	2706	6.23	2706	3430	3.95
4. µ (ls)									
Rural	75	407	18.43	407	2415	24.93	2415	85450	59.44
Urban	97	452	16.63	452	3440	28.88	3440	117200	58.81
Sudan	71	446	20.17	446	2656	24.99	2656	90200	58.75
5. Z (ls)	136	777	19.04	777	6384	30.12	6384	270000	62.41

Source: Ali (1994). ***H:*** the number of poor households. ***P^o:*** the head count index ***$P^o = H/n$.µ:*** the mean income of the poor families. ***Z:*** the poverty line per household per year. **P^1**: the poverty gap ratio. ***$P^1 = P^o (1 - \mu/z)$.αj:*** annual growth rate of poverty over period *j*.

Study Motivations and Objectives

Sudan economy like other African economies depends mainly on traditional rainfed agriculture, which is characterized by high risk and uncertainty and continued fluctuation in the agricultural output. Thus food insecurity becomes a prominent feature in the traditional rainfed of rural Sudan. Before two decades productivity or yield was high and rural household used to cover all grain and cereal needs from farm production through direct or physical access. Over the years crop production has fluctuated due to many factors such as low/erratic rainfall, pest infestation and low soil fertility, as well as ill perceived macro-policies. As a result rural Sudan has continuously been facing food deficits in many of its regions. In spite, of the existence of livestock ownership by some families, the indirect food access through exchange is low, due to limited ownership of small ruminants by many rural families. On the other hand, during the recent past a number of key changes have occurred that combined to profoundly affect the lives of over 20 million poor inhabitants' rural areas of Sudan. In broad terms these changes can be grouped into two categories:

(a) The high environmental degradations, which result in low production of food crops and depletion of large livestock herds.
(b) The formulation of pricing policy in direction disfavouring the main food and export producers such as monopolizing of gum Arabic, oilseeds and livestock marketing and trade.

In addition to that, rural Sudan continuously has food gaps and is receiving food aids. Therefore, studying poverty in traditional farms in rural Sudan will be valuable to policy-makers and to donors of development projects. In addition to Sudan suffers from quality due to the civil war of 1983 to present (Ali, 2002).

The objectives set of the study are twofolds:

1. To establish poverty lines, indicators and profiles in the rural household focusing on the traditional farms.
2. To identify the poverty causes of the poor rural tenants in traditional farms.

Methodology and Techniques

The data used in this study are based on household cross-section survey conducted in the traditional rainfed farms named rural Kordofan State in western Sudan for the agricultural season 2005-06. Households' locations within specific geographic areas constituted two provinces named Sheickan and Bara to represent the Kordofan State. The sample selection was based on stratified random sampling with multi-stage selection. The key information of the rural poverty had been collected included: Socio-economic factors of the household-headed, assets owned by the rural household, housing, land use and ownership patterns, food issues, economic activities, drinking water and health information.

Poverty Line Approaches

Two approaches are applied to establish the poverty line in the rural areas, these are Food Energy Intakes (FEI) approach and Costs of Basic Needs (CBN) approach. The basic needs approach concentrates on the degree of fulfilment of basic human needs in terms of health, food, education, water, shelter and transport (Streeten *et al.,* 1981). In this study the food poverty line is calculated from the main common food basket used in rural areas of Kordofan State and the daily consumption is calculated based on adult equivalent (Table 8.2). The prices of such common food basket were obtained from survey. Based on the WHO caloric values, the number of calories for each kilogram of food basket is determined. Then, the total calories consumed per adult are calculated, then required calories per adult per day and the amount of Kg required is calculated based on daily minimum caloric requirement of 2300 kilo calories per person per day as determined by the WHO to establish food poverty line.

Table 8.2: Actual Consumed and Required Calories in the Traditional Farms (Rural Kordofan State)

Main Diet	*Per Day Actual Consumed Calories**	*Per Day Required Calories*	*No. of Calories Per Kg of Diet*	*Per Required Kg*	*Price Per Kg of Diet*
Sorghum	597.8	664.7	3350	0.2	106
Wheat	309.5	344.2	3350	0.1	121
Millet	522.9	581.5	3630	0.2	133
Meat	40.8	45.4	2020	0.02	854
Milk	48.7	54.2	640	0.08	197
Sugar	206.3	229.4	4000	0.06	301
Tea	4.9	5.5	1070	0.005	782
Okra	31.1	34.6	220	0.2	755
Onion	59.4	66.1	220	0.3	559
Tomatoes	17.5	19.5	220	0.08	73
Salt	11.2	12.5	710	0.02	88
Oil	163.3	181.6	9000	0.02	448
Chicken	45.0	50.04	1500	0.03	350
Egg	1.3	1.5	1200	0.001	448
Vegetables	8.7	9.7	220	0.04	217
Total	**2068.4**	**2300**	**31350**	**1.356**	**SD 5432**

Source: Field Survey, 2005-2006 and * WHO (2003).
Note: Price in SD. SD 1= US$ 200.230 at time of the survey.

According to the cost of basic need that takes into consideration (both food and non-food items) is used to establish the extreme poverty line by adding up the cost of non-food items (education, health, water etc.) to food poverty line.

FGT Measures

Maxwell (1999) indicated that there are various ways in which poverty can be assessed, each with their own merits. The standard of US$ 1 a day has become a powerful tool to draw attention to global poverty. It is increasingly being used to highlight where most poverty is concentrated. There are advantages to the universality of this measure. Lipton and Litchfield (2001) argued that such as standard is both widely available and enables international comparison.

Given the intra-group income distributions a number of poverty indices may be computable (Ravallion, 1994). The most widely used class of poverty indices in the literature is the FGT, following Foster, Greer and Thorbecke (1984). The FGT indicators, denominated by *p*, belong to a class of additively decomposable poverty measures. These indicators allow the measurement of the headcount ratio as well as the gap ratio and the severity of poverty at both the group and the national levels. The study used FGT measures to estimate the poverty measures. The FGT poverty measure is defined as in the following equation[1]:

$$p^{\alpha} = \frac{1}{n}\sum_{1}^{q}\left[\frac{z-y}{z}\right]^{\alpha} \qquad \ldots (1)$$

where n is the total number of individuals under consideration, q is the total number of poors, y is the income of the ith poor individual, z is the poverty line, and α is a parameter characterizing the degree of poverty aversion *i.e.* the parameter α determines the precise measure of poverty to be used.

Researchers are concerned with the absolute poverty line concept, *i.e.* the bundle of basic consumer goods required, in addition to other expenditure on health, education, housing etc. (Ibrahim, 2003). Absolute poverty is perceived as subsistence below the minimum requirements for physical well-being, generally based on a quantitative proxy indicator such as income or calories, but sometimes taking into account a broader package of goods and services (Hulme *et al.*, 2001).

For z, most of the literature uses the national absolute poverty line. The absolute poverty line can either be assumed as exogenous in the analysis, *e.g.*, using the one or two dollars World Bank estimates adjusted or unadjusted for purchasing power, or generated endogenously using the national basket of basic needs and the commodity prices.

When the parameter α is equal to zero the headcount ratio (H) is generated, which gives the proportion of the population for which consumption or income y is less than the poverty line z.

$$H = \frac{q}{n} \qquad \text{... (2)}$$

When parameter α equals one, the poverty gap ratio (PG) is generated, which is often considered as representing the depth of poverty. It is meant the distance separating the population from the poverty line as follows:

$$PG = \frac{1}{n}\sum_{i=1}^{q}\left[\frac{z-y_i}{z}\right] \qquad \text{... (3)}$$

Where: y_i is the income of individual (i), often work with household rather than individuals, but the individual still be considered as being equal.

The poverty severity (PS) takes the square of the distance and it reflects the inequality among the poors. It obtained when the parameter α is equal to as follows:

$$PS = \frac{1}{n}\sum_{i=1}^{q}\left[\frac{z-y_i}{z}\right]^2 \qquad \text{... (4)}$$

Binary Logistic Regression Technique

In past decays many researchers estimated the causes of poverty using different regressions models (Kyereme and Thorbecke, 1991; Rodriguez and Smith, 1994; Coulombe and McKay, 1996; Dudek, 2006; Krishna *et al.*, 2006 and Francis, 2006).

A Binary Logistic Regression (BLR) analysis was undertaken to determine which factors were significantly associated with poverty movements (Kristjanson *et al.*, 2006). The BLR used to build a model to directly estimated the probability of an occurring event. The dependent variable (the status of the household livelihood) is dichotomous (1 for extremely poor and 0 for non-poor). The model used to derive estimates of the odd ratios for each factor contributing to the poverty incidence. The independent variables considered in the analysis were: age, occupation, households' size, education level of the household head, disease affected the households' members, water sources, gender, etc.

The binary logistic regression is specified as:

$$Z_i = \breve{a}_j + \beta_i W_{hij} + \varepsilon_{hi} \qquad \ldots (5)$$

Where:

z_i is the value of the unobserved explanatory variable for the ith case, it is a binary variable indicating whether a household is below the extreme poverty line or not (1 if extremely poor, zero if not). W_{hi} is the ith predictor for the hth and it is a vector of the rural household's characteristics.

β_i is the ith coefficient of W_{hi}, $\breve{a}$ = a cluster fixed or random effect (constant), ε_{hi} = is a random error term assumed uncorrelated with the regressors. The probability of being extremely poor depends on a set of variables W so that:

$$\text{Prob } (z_i\ 1)\ F\ (\beta_i W_{hi}) \qquad \ldots (6)$$

$$\text{Prob } (z_i\ 0)\ 1 - F\ (\beta_i W_{hi}) \qquad \ldots (7)$$

Where:

Z_i is the household total expenditure. So the probability of a household should be:

$$\text{Prob } (z_i = 1) = p\ (z_i > 0) = f\ (\tilde{a}_j + \beta_i W_{hij}) \qquad \ldots (8)$$

Result and Discussions

Poverty Line, Indicators and Profile

Our estimated food poverty line in traditional farms is equal \$ 0.34 for person per day. Similarly the extreme poverty line of the traditional farms is \$ 0.41 for per person per day. IFAD (2004) reported that in

Sudan the small-scale farmers and herders in the traditional rainfed farms and livestock sectors are more prone to poverty than those in irrigated areas.

Highest number of the rural poors is found in the traditional farms (rural Kordofan) which amounted to 91 per cent (Table 8.3) mainly attributable to recurrent droughts in such areas and to recent civil war in the southern and western parts of the Kordofan region.

Table 8.3: Proportions of the Rural Non-Poor and Poor Households in the Traditional Farms in Sudan

Poverty Status	*No. of Households*	*Percentage*
Non-poor	19	8
Poor	218	91
Total	**237**	**100.0**

Source: Field Survey, 2005-2006.

Many observers have noted that poverty and violence go hand in hand (Miguel, 2003). Furthermore, the very famous recent civil war in Darfur enforced the rural people to migrate from their residence to neighbouring State (Rural Kordofan State) which consequently increased the numbers of the rural poors in the State.

From Table 8.4, it is obvious that the *H*, *PG* and *PS* in the traditional farms (Rural Kordofan State) are high. The poverty incidence, depth and severity in the Sheickan province from rural Kordofan (traditional farms households), which is located in the northern part of the State had a low percentage than Bara province which is located in the southern part of Kordofan State (Table 8.4).

Table 8.4: Poverty Indicators in Traditional Farm (%)

Province	*Poverty Index (H)*	*Poverty Depth (PG)*	*Poverty Severity (PS)*
Sheickan	85	81	72
Bara	90	83	81
Overall	97.8	93.7	89.7

Source: Field Survey, 2005-2006.

These results imply that poverty in rural Sudan over the agricultural year 2005-06 had been more widely spread and deep in traditional farms. The variations in the standard of living and the incidence of poverty are related to the differences in the agro-climatic/geographical conditions (Gunasena, 2003).

The socio-economic characteristics of the rural poor households are expected to have great effects on the poverty incidences in the study areas. The educational attainment of the head of the household is found to be among the important factors that are associated with poverty (Elsheikh and Siwar, 2004; Chadha, 2002 and Dasgupta, 1989). The results indicate that more of the poor rural households-headed are illiterate. Consequently, the opportunities for continuing education beyond the primary level are limited, as many rural poors cannot attend secondary schooling. Travelling for long distances for school and lack of financial resources to pay fees or purchase uniforms and notebooks are the main reasons faced by the rural poors for sending their children to schools. More than half of the poor children are enrolled in schools and unable to resume their education for tuition fees.

Roushdy (2004) argued that in Egypt about 11 per cent of children above the age of 6 have never attended school. Furthermore the parents with education positively and significantly affect children's schooling attainment in comparison to parents with no education.

The poorest people in most countries spend most of their money on food, in some places as much as three-quarters (Deaton, 2004). Poor people in India spend 60-80 per cent of their incremental income on food (Brown, 1979). Our results reveal that the rural households in the study areas spend about 85 per cent of their income on food, as they obtain not-enough money to satisfy their basic needs. Yet, even the poorest buy things other than food, such as, clothing and housing, as well as an increasing number of goods that are not usually classified as necessities.

Most rural villagers have a low and sporadic income (Howells *et al.*, 2002 and Williams, 1994). Besides the income growth in rural areas is extremely unpredictable and is likely to depend on agricultural growth (Nyoro, 2002).

Agriculture remains as the main source of livelihood of the rural people in the surveyed farms the rural population derive their livelihoods from land. Majority of the poor rural households in the farm were fully occupied with their tenancies (had no off-farm occupation). Occupational categories are abject poverty (Dreze *et al.*, 1992 and Angelsen and Kaimowitz, 1999). Generally, having a job offers protection against poverty, but having only one off-farm income earner in the family unit is often not enough.

In rural economies a stock of household wealth typically consists of agricultural land, human capital and labour endowment (Fuwa, 2006). In the MENA regions, as well as in developing world, the poor lack of education and control little or no land and capital. Predominantly, they live in rural areas (Lofgren and Richards, 2003). Rural people in extreme poverty are largely landless (Mellor, 1985). A small percentage of the rural poor tenants in traditional farms are landless. Nevertheless, owning land under control of the governmental authorities. These results indicate that the poor households owned agricultural land but lack of appropriate technology and removal of subsidies from the production inputs (*e.g.* from fertilizers) which make them as the main factors for being poor in these farms. Most of land is not occupied efficiently to satisfy the rural household's needs.

The traditional farms are greatly depending on the family labour for most of their agricultural practices, and this normally associated to the big size of the households' members in this farm, the phenomena of the numerous wives are common in this region of Sudan.

Thornton *et al.* (2002) and Peden *et al.* (2005) reported that livestock are one of the major assets that households accumulate as a result of their efforts to climb out poverty. The study result indicates that high incidence of poverty links with poor households who do not own livestock. Furthermore, the survey results found that about 90 per cent of the poor household suffered from water borne diseases specially malaria.

Water resource scarcity is a major constraint in the traditional rainfed farms. As well a small percentage of the rural poors rely on piped water indoors (public taps), for their water supply.

Hafeer is the main source of water in the western Sudan filled from rainfall water. The Hafeer storage water is more prominently found in the traditional farms. Besides the impurity of its water (because it is reserved for long time and use in the dry seasons) it almost suffers from water loss due to evaporation during stormy summers. This finding indicates the importance of accessing water inside the household. In addition, from the survey it is noted that there is significant correlation between water sources and the incidence of diseases especially the water borne diseases.

The water within the Hafeer is often used to supply water to the whole community, for agriculture, livestock to domestic washing and drinking. Contamination is, therefore, a major consideration. Poor sanitation and the lack of access to clean water explain in large part why diarrhoea related diseases are major sources of illness in the surveyed farms.

For the last three decades, many women's advocates have been arguing that women are poorer than men (Cagatay, 1998; Székely, 1998; Beneria and Bisnath, 1996; Chant, 2003 and Regehr 2006). The results show that female-headed households are poorer than male-headed households. The familiar type of a house of the poor in traditional farms is constructed from collected wild dry straw (shrub and scrub) and residues of crop product or mud.

Causes of Poverty in Rural Sudan

World Bank (1991) and Lanjouw and Ravallion (1994) argued that the large households tend to be associated with poverty. In the traditional farms it denotes that the positive estimate of parameters (β) occurs at variables of marital status, family size, numbers of males and females children in the households and diseases effected the households members

Table 8.5 shows the risk of poverty was on average higher in households with a large number of individuals and of being households suffering from the ill health increase the likelihood of being in a higher poverty status category. While the negative estimate of parameters (β) occurs at the variables: gender, age, education level, secondary occupation and sharing of the households' members in the agricultural activities. Poverty is reducing by the age of the household-headed, *i.e.* the risk of poverty was on average lower in households with male-head and young of the households-head. As well the risk of poverty was on average lower in households with head with at least vocational education comparing with households where head had only informal or primary education. Also in the traditional farms the household of being with extra occupation and of being more working family members in the farms reduces the likelihood of being in a higher poverty.

Table 8.5: Poverty Causes in the Traditional Farms (Rural Kordofan State)

Variable	*Estimated Coefficient (β)a*	*Standard Error*	*Wad*	*Odds Ratio Exp (β)*	*95% of C.I. for Odds Ratio*	
					Lower	*Upper*
GENDER	–1.046	1.371	0.582	0.351	0.024	5.158
AGE	–0.005	0.039	0.015	0.995	0.922	1.074
EDUCALEVEL	–0.246	0.426	0.332	0.782	0.339	1.803
MERITALS	1.478	1.004	2.167	4.384	0.613	31.372
SECDOCCU	– 1.660	1.049	2.502	5.258	0.672	41.120
FAMSIZE	1.897	1.405	1.822	1.150	0.010	2.356
NOMALE	2.081	1.445	2.074	8.016	0.472	136.180
NOFEMAL	1.789	1.402	1.629	5.983	0.384	93.331
DIDYOUW	–0.584	0.999	0.342	0.558	0.079	3.950
HAVDISEA	0.79	1.290	0.004	1.924	0.074	11.574
CONSTANT	1.276	4.396	0.084	3.581		

Regression Statistics:

Number of observation = 240
Likelihood ratio test: $X^2_{0.05}(10) = 11.407$
Adjusted R-squared: 0.270
2-Log likelihood = 39.465

Source: Survey findings and Authors' calculations. a ★ indicates statistical significance at the level α =0.05.

The variables list in Table 8.5 is defined as follows:

A. Dependant Variable:

A binary variable indicates whether a household is below the extreme poverty line or not (1 if extremely poor, zero if not). Poverty is estimated based on consumption per adult equivalent.

B. Explanatory Variables:

GENDER: Binary variable indicating whether the household-head is female or male (1 if female, zero if male).

AGE: Age of the household-head.

EDUCALEVEL: Binary variable indicating whether the household-head received education (primary, secondary, higher or professional education) or not (1 if educated, zero otherwise).

MERITALS: Binary variable indicating whether the household head is married or not (1 if married, zero otherwise).

SECDOCCU: Binary variable indicating whether the household-head works in a secondary occupation or not (1 have secondary occupation, zero otherwise).

FAMSIZE: Size of the household.

NOMALE: Number of males children in the household.

NOFEMAL: Number of females children in the households.

DIDYOUW: Performance of the agricultural activities by the households members (1 work in the field by themselves, zero otherwise).

HAVDISEA: Suffering from the diseases last year (1 suffering from the diseases, zero otherwise).

Conclusions and Policy Implications

- Highly significant proportion of the rural population in the traditional farms are living or lived below the poverty line, without access to sufficient food or income to maintain a healthy and productive life.
- The incidence of poverty varies considerably according to region. The southern regions of the farms are poorest than the northern regions of the farms. The diverse of poverty incidences is mainly due to uneven distribution of economic growth and severe inequalities in terms of access to education, clean water, natural resources, public services, justices and political protection in the regions.
- Majority of the children of the poor households enrolled in the school and were unable to resume their education for many reasons; chief of which is the high tuition fees paid for school and resettlement due to civil war.
- The chances of a household being poor were related to size and demographic structure. Households with large number of female or male children were more likely to be poor than those with less number of female or male children.

Generally the study concluded that the poverty existing in the traditional farms were due to (i) unavailable other off-farm opportunities, (ii) female-headed households, (iii) poor housing condition, (iv) deficits in health care, (v) lack of own livestock, (vi) civil war and environmental instability, (vii) low yielding farm practices and shortage in modern agricultural inputs and information. All these factors impede access to use new technology in agriculture to produce sufficient food for self-sufficiency and increase income.

The results of this study have important policy implications for future priorities in poverty reduction as the results of the outcome of the research findings:

- Rural education should be afforded the highest priority, *i.e.* the Government should gear up its attention to rural education. The education programmes should be improved in the rural areas, because it is the main factor affecting the poverty incidence in such areas. Improved education helps farmers gain access to and use new technology generated by the research system, thereby promoting agricultural growth. But more importantly, education helps farmers to gain and improve their skills for non-farm employment and reduce rural poverty and regional inequality.

- There is an urgent need to reduce the incidence of diseases and mortality by establishing and/or increasing supply of health services centres in rural areas, especially to enhance the programmes of eliminating and fighting diseases. Combating major diseases of the rural areas such as Malaria should acquire a high priority.
- The drinking water sources should be safe with adequate sanitation.
- The Government should continue efforts to increase its over all development in rural areas.

NOTE

1. Equation (1) is referred to as the Foster-Greer-Thorbecke (FGT) equation. It defines a family of measures of absolute poverty in any one welfare dimension, which vary according to the choice of poverty line and the choice of the parameter α.

REFERENCES

Ali, A.G.A. (1994). *Structural Adjustment Programmes and Poverty in the Sudan*. Arab Research Centre, Cairo (in Arabic).

Ali, A.G.A. (2002). *Poverty in the Arab Region: A Selective Review Background,* paper prepared for the IFPRI/API Collaborative Research Project on: "Public Policy and Poverty Reduction in the Arab Region."

Angelsen, A. and Kaimowitz, D. (1999). Rethinking the Causes of Deforestation: Lessons from Economic Models. The International Bank for Reconstruction and Development World Bank. *The World Bank Research Observer*, vol. 14, no. 1.

Beneria, L.; Bisnath, S. (1996). *Gender and Poverty: An Analysis for Action*. UNDP Gender in Development Monograph Series, No. 2.

Benson, T. (2004). *Assessing African's Food and Nutrition Security Situation.* International Food Policy Research Institute (IFPRI). 2020 Africa Conference Brief 1. Washington, U.S.A. *www.ifpri.org.*

Brown, G. (1979). Agricultural Pricing Policies in Developing Countries. In *Distortions of Agricultural Incentives.* Bloomington: Indiana Univ. Press.

Cagatay, N. (1998). *Gender and Poverty.* Social Development and Poverty Elimination Division, United Nations Development Programme (UNDP), Rome.

Chadha, G.K. (2002). *Indian Agriculture in the New Millennium.* Human Response to Technology Challenge. Presidential Address, 62nd Annual Conference of the Indian Society of Agricultural Economics. New Delhi, India.

Chant, S. (2003). *Female Household Headship and the Feminization of Poverty*: Facts, Fictions and Forward Strategies. Gender Institute. London.

Coulombe, H. and McKay, A. (1996). *Modelling Determinants of Poverty in Mauritania.* World Development; 24(6).

Dar, W.D.; Gowda, C.L.L.; and Sharma H.C. (2003). Role of Modern Science and Technologies in *Agriculture for Poverty Alleviation in South Asia.* International Crops Research Institute for the Semi-Arid Tropics Andhra Pradesh, India.

Dasgupta, B. (1989). *Diffusion of Agricultural Innovations in Village India.* New Delhi, Wiley Eastern.

Datt, G. and Jolliffe, D. (1999), *Determinants of Poverty in Egypt: 1997*, FCND Discussion Paper No 75, IFPRI, Washington, U.S.A.

Deaton, S. (2004). Measuring Poverty. Research Programme in Development Studies. Princeton University.

Deng, L.A. (2004). The Challenges of Post-conflict Economic Recovery and Reconstruction in the Sudan Institute of Development, *Environment and Agricultural Studies* (IDEAS). Washington, U.S.A.

Dreze, J.; Lanjouw, P. and Stern, N. (1992). Economic Mobility and Agricultural Labour in Rural India: a case study, *Indian Economic Review*, India.

Dudek, H. (2006). *Determinants of Poverty in Polish Farmers' Households—Binary Choice Models Approach.* Electronic Journal of Polish Agricultural Universities. Economics, volume 9, issue 1. Poland. http://www.ejpau.media.pl/volume9/issue1/art-08.html

Elsheikh, S. and Siwar, C. (2004): *Tenant Households and Poverty in the Gezira Irrigated Area*, Sudan: Analysis and Implications. Faculty of Economics, University Kebangsaan, Selangor, Malaysia.

Fergany, N. (1997). *Towards Poverty Eradication in the Sudan: An Analysis of Human Capability Failure*, Draft Report. Khartoum. Sudan.

Foster, J.; Greer, J. and E. Thorbecke, (1984). A New Class of Decomposable Poverty Measures. *Econometrical*, vol. 51, no. 1.

Francis, E. (2006). *Poverty: Causes, Responses and Consequences in Rural South Africa.* Development Studies Institute. London School of Economics. CPRC Working Paper No. 60. Chronic Poverty Research Centre, London.

Fuwa, N. N. (2006). Pathways out of Rural Poverty: A case study in Socio-Economic Mobility in the Rural Philippines. *Cambridge Journal of Economics Advance Access*, Oxford University, UK.

Grootaert, C. (1996). *Analyzing Poverty and Policy Reform: The Experience of Côte d'Ivoire*, Avebury, Aldershot, Hants, England; Brookfield, Vt. USA.

Gunasena, H.P.M. (2003). *Food and Poverty: Technologies for Poverty Alleviation*. Council for Agriculture Research and Policy (CARP). Sri Lanka.

Howells M.; Alfstad, T.; Cross N.; Jeftha L. and Gary Goldstein (2002). *Rural Energy Modelling*. Environmental Science and Policy Encina Hall East, University Stanford, CA 94305-6055. http://www.pesd.stanford.edu/

Hulme, D. Moore K. and Shepherd, A. (2001). *Chronic Poverty: Meanings and Analytical Frameworks*. Institute of Development Policy and Management. University of Manchester, Crawford House, Oxford. United Kingdom International and Development Department. School of Public Policy, University of Birmingham. UK. Chronic Poverty Research Centre (CPRC) Working Paper 2.

Ibrahim, B.E.A. (2003). *Poverty Alleviation via Islamic Banking Finance to Micro-Enterprises (MEs) in Sudan*: Sudan Economy Research Group, Institute for World Economics and International Management (IWIM). University of Bremen, Germany, Discussion Paper No. 35.

IFAD (2004). *Enabling the Rural Poor to Overcome Poverty in Sudan*. Rural poverty in Sudan-Rome, Italy. www.ifad.org

IFAD (2007). *Enabling the Rural Poor to Overcome Poverty in Sudan*. Rome, Italy. www.ifad.org

Krishna, A.; Kristjanson, P.; Kuan, J.; Quilca, G.; Radeny, M. and Sanchez-Urrelo, A. (2006). Fixing the Hole in the Bucket: Household Poverty Dynamics in the Peruvian Andes. *Development and Change* 37(5). Institute of Social Studies Blackwell Publishing. Oxford, UK.

Kristjanson, P.; Krishna, A.; Radeny, M.; Kuan, J.; Quilca, G.; Sanchez-Urrelo, A. and Leon-Velarde, C. (2006). *Houshold Poverty Dynamics and the Role of Livestock in the Peruvian Andes*. Q-Squared Working Paper No. 24. Q-squared • Centre for International Studies University of Toronto Canada.

Kyereme, S.S. and Thorbecke, E. (1991). Factors Affecting Poverty in Ghana. *Journal of Development Studies*; 28(1).

Lanjouw, P. and Ravallion, M. (1994). *Poverty and Household Size*, Policy Research Working Paper 1332, the World Bank, Washington, USA.

Lipton, M. and Litchfield, J. (2001). *Successes in Anti-Poverty: National-Level Poverty Performance*. Employment Paper 2001/22, International Labour Office, Geneva.

Lofgren, H. and Richards A. (2003). *Food Security, Poverty, and Economic Policy in the Middle East and North Africa*. Trade and Macroeconomics Division. International Food Policy Research Institute. Washington, U.S.A.

Maxwell, S. (1999). *The Meaning and Measurement of Poverty*. ODI Poverty Briefing 3. Overseas Development Institute, London, U.K.

Mellor, J.W. (1985). *Determinants of Rural Poverty: The Dynamics of Production*, Technology and Price. International Food Policy Research Institute. The Johns Hopkins, University Press, London.

Miguel, E. (2003). *Poverty and Witch Killing*. University of California, Berkeley and NBER.

Nyoro, J.K. (2002). *Agriculture and Rural Growth in Kenya*. Tegemeo Institute. Egerton University. Kenya. Nairobi.

Peden, D.; Freeman, A.; Astatke A and Notenbaert A. (2005). *Investment Options for Integrated Water-Livestock-Crop Production in Sub-Saharan Africa*. International Livestock Research Institute (ILRI), Ethiopia.

Ravallion, M., (1994), *Poverty Comparisons: A Guide to Concepts and Methods*; Harwood Academic Publishers, Chur, Switzerland.

Regehr, S. (2006). *Poverty Profile*. National Council of Welfare. Ontario K1A 0J9, Canada.

Rodriguez, A.G. and Smith, S.M.A. (1994). *Comparison of Determinants of Urban, Rural and Farm Poverty in Costa Rica*. World Development; 22(3).

Roushdy, R. (2004). *Intra-household Resource Allocation in Egypt*: *Does Women's Empowerment Lead to Greater Investments in Children*? Population Council. West Asia and North Africa Region. Cairo, Egypt.

Satterthwaite, D. (2005). The Under-Estimation of Urban Poverty in Low and Middle-Income Nations. Human Settlements Programme. London WC1H ODD, UK. www.iied.org/urban/downloads.html

Streeten, P.; Burki, S.J.; ul Haq, M.; Hicks, N.; and Stewart, F. (1981). *First Things First: Meeting Basic Needs in Developing Countries*. New York, University Press.

Sullivan, T. (2006). *The Current Status of World Hunger*—Web Articles—http://www.webarticles.com

Székely, M. (1998). *The Economics of Poverty, Inequality and Wealth Accumulation in Mexico*. St. Antony's Series. New York: St. Martin's Press; London: Macmillan Press; in association with St. Antony's College.

Thornton, P.; Kruska R.; Henninger N; Kristjanson P.; Reid R.; Atieno F.; Odero A.; Ndegwa T. (2002). *Mapping Poverty and Livestock in the Developing World*, ILRI, Nairobi, Kenya.

Williams, T. (1994). *Energy Supply Options for Low Income Urban Households*, Energy for Development Research Centre, University of Cape Town.

WHO (2003). *World Health Organization*. Khartoum Office, Sudan.

World Bank (1991). *Assistance Strategies to Reduce Poverty*. A policy paper, Washington, D.C.

9

Globalization and Farmers: Crisis in Maharashtra

R.B. PATIL

Introduction

Maharashtra is one of the agriculturally advanced States of India. In the recent years there has been increase in the number of farmers' suicides in Maharashtra. The agricultural produce is not getting appropriate rates. Due to the free market policy, there is no safety net for the farmers. There is no improvement in disbursement of loans to poor and marginalized farmers. Due to increase in loans and uncertainty of crops the farmers are committing suicide. The general trend emerges that farmers from Vidarbha region have committed more suicides than other regions.

The studies on suicide of farmers in Maharashtra have been conducted at Gokhale Institute of Politics and Economics, Pune, Tata Institute of Social Sciences, Mumbai and Indira Gandhi Institute of Development Studies, Mumbai. The criterion set by Government of Maharashtra for giving financial assistance to the families of the deceased. Taking a serious note of farmers' suicides in Vidarbha, the Prime Minister made a visit to Vidarbha area and declared package for the farmers. Even then the incidences of suicide have not stopped.

In the Maharashtra State Assembly it has been reported on 16th March, 2006 that during January 2004 to February 2006 due to different reasons 1100 farmers have committed suicides. This chapter is entirely based on secondary sources and puts forth some observations on Globalization and farmers' suicide with reference to background factors, statistics, concentration of suicides in certain districts, and government assistance etc.

Globalization, Subsidies and Farmers

Agriculture is being considered as a backbone of Indian economy. The liberalization of economy, globalization of international market, and implication of various clauses under World Trade Organization has far-reaching influence on the agricultural system.

Agriculture is an area where there are serious inequalities and imbalances in the World Trade Organization agreement. It has been observed that "under WTO, there is an Agreement on Agriculture (AOA), which is based mainly on three principles: free market, subsidy for export and assistance from government. WTO recommends that the member countries should open their markets for agricultural produce to all members. The agricultural policies of developed countries are opposite to free market. The farmers from the developing countries are unable to compete because of the subsidies given by the developed countries. In Europe the farmers receive subsidy of 40 crore Euro per year. The declaration of America in 2002 indicates that subsidy of $ 48 lakh be given to farmers which should be continued for ten years. The developing countries are demanding to remove these subsidies.

The farmers from the developing countries are unable to compete because of the subsidies given by the developed countries. In India, a mango is sold @ Rs. 5, but if mango is produced in America and if it has more subsidy of Rs. 2, then it will be available @ Rs. 3. So it will be cheaper than Indian mango. On the one hand America advocates for free market but on the other hand by giving higher subsidies it closes market for agricultural produce and this is being practiced by the developed countries.

In the developed countries, agriculture is an issue of commerce whereas in countries like India it is a means of livelihood. The rich developed countries are industrial countries and their policy is to gain profits through industrial productions. These countries have the same principle for 'Agreement on Agriculture'. Without reducing the subsidies on agriculture, these countries try to send 'Genetically Modified' food to developing countries[1]. Thus the issue of subsidies in agriculture is affecting to a larger extent.

A more serious problem is that the developed countries (the OECD estimates the producer support estimate at $ 279.5 billion in 2004) that encourages their farmers to continue with unviable agricultural production. This is like an export subsidy but a much larger extent harms the farmers of the developing countries in two ways. They face unfair competition in their home market from such highly subsidized imports and at the same time their prospect for export to third world countries is severely constrained[2].

The industrial countries like America, Japan and Germany gives subsidies to farmers, they have government transportation. The production expenditure is less as a farmer cultivates thousands of hectares of land under mechanization. In India cotton is produced which is needed for India. But the cotton from America, Sudan, Egypt, Pakistan is imported under free trade policy. This import cannot be stopped due to free trade.

Report of British NGO on Farmers in Developing Countries

The London based NGO "Christian Aid"[3] conducted study in India, Ghana and Jamaica. Dalip Mukherjee, Director of the Organization, observes that the British Government policy and development programmes carried out of British tax-payers have led to the farmers suicides. In Andhra Pradesh under Chandrababu Nayadu's regime the schemes of British International Development Department of Rs. 84 crore was implemented. These schemes expected as blessings were turned into curse in reality. The report notes that since 1998 nearly 4400 framers have committed suicides. The farmers have been greatly influenced as the State Corporations were transferred into private firms operated by Adam Smith Institute.

In 1991 International Monetary Fund and the World Bank while giving assistance have asked Indian Government to devalue Rupee to increase export. The farmers were encouraged to cultivate cash crops like cotton and sugarcane. On the one hand the farmer became indebted for the expenditure on the items like seeds, fertilizers, pesticides, irrigation and electricity. On the other hand the subsidies were reduced on fertilizers and other items. As a result, the farmers became indebted and ultimately led to suicide.

Farmers' Suicides in Maharashtra

In the recent years there has been increase in the number of farmers' suicides in Maharashtra. The details of these are presented in Table 9.1.

Table 9.1: No. of Farmers' Suicides in Maharashtra (2001-2006)

Year	*Suicides*
2001	49
2002	105
2003	143
2004	441
2005	429
2006	973 Sept. 30
Total	**2150**

Table 9.1 shows that farmers' suicide have increased during the recent years.

The data regarding region of farmers' suicide since June 2005 are presented in Table 9.2.

Table 9.2: Farmers' Suicides in Vidarbha (Since June 2005)

Region	*Since June 2005*
Akola	113
Amravati	186
Buldhana	28
Vashim	112
Yavatmal	57
Chandrapur	35
Gadachiroli	10
Gondia	15
Nagpur	32
Wardha	80
Total	**261**

Source: *The Times of India*, October 25th, 2006.

Table 9.2 indicates that in Vidarbha, District Yavatmal had the highest number of suicides. The general trend is that farmers from Vidarbha region have committed more suicides than other regions like Marathawada, Western Maharashtra, North Maharashtra and Konkan.

Even Prime Minister Manmohan Singh's July 1, 2006 package of Rs. 3750 crore has not slowed down suicide rate as the numbers were: July 90, August 111, and September 125.

Studies on Farmers' Suicides

Tata Institute of Social Sciences, Mumbai

The team (1) found that the root problems were the soaring debts taken by the farmers to purchase the high-cost fertilizers and high-yielding seeds. The report suggested that the courts should intervene and direct the State and Union Governments to create insurance safety net for farmers. The Government should design policies that focus on farmer rather than seed and fertilizer corporations who enhance their profits at the cost of farmers.

Indira Gandhi Institute of Development and Research, Mumbai

The Report (2) notes that 'the Suicide Mortality Rate for Maharashtra was 15.1 as against 10.6 in 2001. SMR for male has trebled to 53 in 2004 as against 17 in 1995. The skewed global trade tariff are as much to blame for the problem as absence of affordable agricultural financing and technology.

Daily Sakal, Pune

The study (3) reported following causes of farmers' suicides. 1. Indebtedness. 2. Dry land, 3. No agro-related business, 4. No due price for agricultural produce, 5. Use of agricultural loan for other purposes. The study has suggested the following measures to curb suicides: 1. Change in mechanism bank loan distribution and actions on private money-lenders, 2. Implementation of irrigation projects, 3. Study of markets of industrial background, 4. Availability of loan for other than agricultural purposes.

Gokhale Institute of Politics and Economics, Pune

The study[4] notes that high caste farmers saw those from lower castes as potential economic competitors who had already gained advantages as a result of State intervention. In the absence of any assistance from higher castes, small farmers were compelled to rely on local dealers and private agencies for information about new methods of agricultural production. Most of the lower and medium caste farmers who committed suicide had followed the advice of local shopkeepers regarding doses, quality and timing of chemical inputs. These commercial enterprises recommended high quantities of the most expensive inputs that were not of the best quality. This resulted into indebtedness to shopkeepers spiralled and agriculture suffered from poor quality inputs.

Swami Ramanand Teerth Research Institute, Aurangabad

The study[5] covered eight districts of Marathawada and families of the 77 farmers who committed suicides. The study revealed that 51 per cent farmers would like to join any Government job, while 25 per cent want to work as agricultural workers. Just 5 per cent want to continue with farming, the remaining would like to do business or trade. Majority of the farmers were small or marginal farmers 57.50 per cent holding up to 2.5 hectares of land.74 per cent belonged to Open Category and out of them 90 per cent were from Maratha Community, followed by STs (9%), OBC (5.2%), SCs (5.2%) and NTs (5.2%). R.P. Kurulkar, former Head, Dept. of Economics, Dr. Babasaheb Ambedkar Marathwada University, Aurangabad and Director of the Institute reported that 68 per cent of farmers, with an average family size of 4.5 per cent committed suicide, due to huge indebtedness to institutional lenders (54%) and money-lenders (14.5%) while others killed themselves for family reasons like ill-health, alcoholism, loss of status and crop failure.

NSSO Survey 2002-03

The survey[6] reports that 40 per cent Indian farmers want to quit agriculture.

Farmers' Suicides and Assistance by Government of Maharashtra

The helping hand by the Central and State Government is as follows: The Central Government Rs. 3873 crore: Three-year relief package September 2006 Original PM's package was Rs. 3750 cr. The

Centre's package will help reschedule debts, waive over-due interest, and allow fresh bank loans and additional credit flow. Over Rs. 2100 crore earmarked for construction of irrigation facilities, Rs. 3 crore for direct distribution.

State Government Rs. 1075 crores (December 2005): A Rs. 150 crores package offers assistance worth Rs. 25,000 each to 60,000 farmers over three years.

Mr. D.K. Sankaran, Chief Secretary, Government of Maharashtra, discussed the steps taken by the Government to curb the rising number of farmer suicide[7]. All outstanding crop loans upto a limit Rs. 25,000 are being rescheduled in Vidarbha. The interest on these loans is being written off. The principal amount of Rs. 203 crore is being rescheduled over a period of next five years which will have 9 per cent interest. The other steps include arrangement for fresh crop loan, distribution of loan through Self-Help Groups and subsidy on crop insurance on premium.

The assistance is provided to the families of deceased farmer. The details in this regard are presented in Table 9.3.

Table 9.3: No. of Farmers' Suicides in Maharashtra (2001-2005)

Year	*Suicides*	*Eligible for Govt. Assistance*	*Not Eligible for Govt. Assistance*	*Assistance (Rs. In Lakh)*
2001	64	07	57	07
2002	131	39	92	39
2003	180	23	157	23
2004	524	109	415	109
2005	134	40	94	28
Total	**1033**	**218**	**815**	**206**

Source: *Daily Sakal*, December 3, 2005.

The figures of farmers' suicide are not matching in particular years as the sources are different and the higher side figures are from experts who are studying this issue. Table 9.3 indicates that the number of suicides has increased from the year 2001 and reached highest in 2004 and declined in 2005. Out of 1033 suicide cases only 218 *i.e.* 26.74 per cent were eligible for Government assistance. The eligibility criterion includes failure of crop, indebtedness and the pressure exercised by the concerned parties for repayment. The Government of Maharashtra gives assistance of Rs. 1 lakh from

Chief Minister's Assistance Fund. The Government has given assistance of Rs. 2 crore 6 lakhs.

There are certain criterions set by Government of Maharashtra for giving financial assistance to the families of the deceased. These include: 1. Name on 7/12 report, 2. Reason of death cause is verified, 3. Loan from credit societies and banks eligible, 4. No compensation if loan from private money-lenders or private creditors, 5. If the 7/12 has name of father and if there is no bifurcation in the name of children, then no compensation, 6. Surety of no impact of family members, widow and sons. 7. Justification by Divisional Commissioner.

The survey of TISS indicates that the Government agencies have not recorded 80 per cent of suicides. It has been reported that in Nanded district, 18 such families are requesting for financial assistance to the offices of Talathi to Zila Adhikari. The similar situation prevails in Beed, Parabhani, Aurangabad and Vidarbha.

The provision of funds has been made for awareness and Prabodhan of farmers to stop suicides. Mr. Narendra Lanjewar, Freelance Journalist obtained the details from Vasatrao Sheti Swambalan Mission which implements Chief Minister's Package.[8] The provision of Rs. 6 lakh was made out of which Rs. 5 lakh were received in six districts of Yawatmal, Buladhana, Akola, Washim, Amravati and Wardha. The funds of Rs. 50,000 were fully spent in Akola, Washim and Wardha. Out of 2.50 lakh fund for Amravati district, Rs. 1.13 lakh were spent. But though Yawatmal and Buladhana districts received Rs. 50 thousand each, not a single Rupee was spent on awareness and prabodhan in these districts.

Hiraman Patil committed suicide due to failure of crops and indebtedness. But the Government authorities marked suicide due to death of wife and the case was made ineligible. This case was referred to Mumbai High Court as Hiraman's wife was expired 14 years earlier. This truth was revealed and the Court ordered to pay assistance to the deceased family. The High Court also ordered State Government to produce details of the farmers who were ineligible for the assistance.[9]

Vidarbha Jan Andolan Samiti

The Samiti is an NGO working for the cause of farmers. The Nagpur Bench of Bombay High Court passed order on PIL by VJAS. The contention was that farmers in Vidarbha were dying because of wrong Government policies. It also alleged that the State Chief Secretary and the bureaucrats of agriculture, finance and home departments were totally apathetic to the farmers' woes and had taken no effective measures to control farmers' suicide. Taking a serious view on the failure of top officials of the State Government to respond to Court's notice on the issue of farmer suicide, the Court slapped a cost of Rs. 1000 each on State's Chief Secretary and 12 other high officials[10].

Kishor Tiwari, President of Samiti blamed the flawed policies of the Central and State Governments for surging suicides. The help if any reaching distressed farmers was too late and too little to make any difference. The Samiti knocked the doors of High Court seeking urgent intervention and action against the Government and the bureaucrats for their alleged failure to stop the farmers suicide. The Nagpur bench asked the State Government to post details of implementation of the relief package on a Website[11].

Kishor Tiwari says that these suicides have a pattern. It is happening primarily among debt-ridden small and marginal farmers facing one or more of these problems: someone sick in the family for a long time, a daughter of marriageable age or just married off, an unemployed son pushing the farmer to get out of agriculture, the shock of sudden crop failure due to floods or a product price drop that dramatically alters his life for the worse. Sujay Patil, Akola based psychiatrist indicates that such situation injects a feeling of hopelessness, helplessness and worthlessness driving many to take the extreme step[12].

Tiwari estimates that one acre of cotton cultivation costs Rs. 10,000. With every acre producing an average six quintals, the cost barely matches the produce as minimum support price averages Rs. 1750 per quintal[13].

Art of Living

Mohse Tehsil in Amravati district topped in the number of farmer's suicides in Vidarbha. The villagers were reeling under debt, drought and the effects of a poor crop pattern. The members of the Art of Living Foundation began Samagra Arogya Shibir courses in 19 viilages of the district. Since then there has not been a single suicide. The five day camp focusing on trauma relief, stress management, yoga and meditation instills hope in depressed farmers who may have lost the will to live. The camp is just beginning. The basic aim is to make farmers self-reliant. The farmers have already formed a Kisan Cooperative Society for marketing of organic products[14].

Social Aspects

The fact that the element of self-respect (*maan-apmaan*) is very strong in Vidarbha leading farmers to take drastic step to maintain their dignity also accounts for the high number of suicides in this region[15].

Prof. Prakash Bobade, former Head, Department of Sociology, Sant Tukadoji Maharaj University, Nagpur observes that broken both financially and psychologically, the farmer needs an emotional anchor. But the new rural society offers little support or succour. The chawri (chaupal in north India) where villagers informally shared problems is gone. The joint family system too, is breaking down. There are no social cushions left[16].

The study conducted by Sakal had shown that out of 348 farmers who committed suicides, apart from the main reasons related to agriculture, 19 per cent farmers took loan for marriages of their sons and daughters. It has now become inevitable to take loan for the marriages to nearly all classes of people. When there is sure income, taking loan is practical. But when income is not guaranteed for them borrowing loan is a gambling. The situation of loan taker becomes similar to the person who constantly loses the gamble. The farmers take heavy loan for marriages of their children for performing these functions to improve his prestige. This loan is not repaid on time which leads him to indebtedness. The farmers will have to follow the ways to have these functions in least expenditure, marriage under Registration, Common Marriages, etc.

The 18.18 per cent farmers took loan for education of their children. The farmers expect that after completion of education, the children will get employment. The employment chances are very limited and if one gets it, the donation is demanded. In this situation, the son wants to sell the land and the clashes begin between father and son which may lead to suicide of farmers. So the way out is to keep transparency in employment, priority to children of farmers/agricultural labourers and financial provision in medical and engineering education[17].

The farmers spend large amounts on marriages, festivals and become indebted due to the social prestige. But there is a need to spread the message that it is dangerous to celebrate with loan amounts. The Health Services in rural area are poor. So the illness in a family leads the farmer to the loan trap. The exploitation of farmers in rural area is one of the serious issues. If these social issues are not given attention, the economic package will not be successful. Drought and failure of crops are seen in Maharashtra. But in such situations, there is increase in the number who work on Employment Guarantee Scheme (EGS). Vidarbha does not show this trend as it is considered of low social prestige to work on these schemes. These false ideas and notions must be removed[18].

The Union Government took the State's EGS programme as a role model while devising the National Rural Employment Guarantee Scheme (NREGS). The scheme provides needy families employment for 200 days per year and guarantees job for every adult with a minimum daily wage of Rs. 60. The programme was initiated in February 2006. The Union Government, sanctioned Rs. 412 crore but the State could utilize only Rs. 130 crore. The State Government implements EGS in all the districts. The Union Government has selected 12 districts in Maharashtra of Dhule, Nandurbar, Ahmednagar, Aurangabad, Nanded, Hingoli, Amravati, Yavatmal, Gondia, Bhandara, Chandrapur and Gadachiroli. The last six districts are from Vidarbha which counts to 50 per cent. There has been no response to the EGS in Vidarbha. Unlike in Western Maharashtra and Marathawada there is stigma attached in Vidarbha to work on EGS—one of the many reasons why funds have remained unutilized. This attitude needs to be changed[19].

Some Observations

Globalization in general and the subsidy policies of the developed nations in particular have adversely affected the farmers in Maharashtra. The cases of farmers' suicide are more in Vidarbha region and the trend is continuing. The Government of India and Government of Maharashtra have given financial assistance to the deceased families of the farmers. The NGOs are doing their work in the area. The farmers suicide is not only the economic issue, it is also a socio-psychological issue. So there is a need to take into consideration of these issues while tackling issue of farmers suicide in Maharashtra.

NOTES

1. "Debt trap drives farmers to suicide" Report by Tata Institute of Social Sciences, Mumbai, *The Times of India*, 25th June 2005.
2. Times News Network: "Why State ranks high in Suicides?: Deaths in Vidarbha make the suicide rate higher than the national average", *The Times of India*, 28th January, 2006.
3. *Daily Sakal*, Kolhapur, 29th March, 2006.
4. Mohanty B.B. "We are like the Living Dead": Farmer Suicides in Maharashtra, Western India, *The Journal of Peasant Studies*, Vol. 32, No. 2, April 2005. pp. 243-276.
5. Syed Rizwanullah "Marathwada Farmers want to opt out" *The Times of India*, Pune November 25th, 2006.
6. Avijit Ghosh. "Kiss of Debt" *The Times of India*, Pune, October 8th, 2006.
7. News Item: "Interest on farmers' loan to be written off" *The Times of India*, 2nd September, 2006.
8. News Item: *Daily Sakal,* November 12th, 2006.
9. *Daily Sakal*: Editorial, 20th Jan., 2006.
10. Ramu Bhagwat. "HC slaps Rs. 1000 cost on state bureaucrats, *The Times of India*, Pune, 15th June, 2006.
11. Ramu Bhagwat. "105 Vidarbha suicides in August alone" *The Times of India*, Pune, 31st August, 2006.
12. Avijit Ghosh. "Kiss of Debt", *The Times of India*, Pune, October 8th, 2006.
13. Avijit Ghosh. "Kiss of Debt", *The Times of India,* October 8th, 2006.
14. "Art of Living instills hope in Farmers", *The Times of India*, November 21st, 2006.
15. Abhay Vaidya. "Vidarbha farmers more prone to suicide: study", *The Times of India*, Pune, 13th April 2006.
16. Avijit Ghosh. "Kiss of Debt", *The Times of India*, Pune, October 8th, 2006.
17. R.R. Borade. "Whether Farmers will Change?" *Daily Sakal,* 7th April, 2006.
18. Padmbhushan Deshpande. "Social Package is also important for Farmers", *Daily Sakal*, 28th October, 2006.
19. Prakash Joshi. "No response to EGS in Vidarbha", *The Times of India*, Pune, 23rd October, 2006.

10

Methodology of Grassroots Planning for Rural Employment

R. CHINNADURAI

Introduction

The concept of grassroot level planning is a recent addition to the strategies of micro-planning for development. It might be considered as a logical extension of the national planning scheme promoted by most countries. An alternative explanation of its emergence, however, might be traced to the failure of both the national and regional plans to adequately respond to the needs of the people at the grassroot level. By bringing planning to a smaller spatial unit, it is envisaged that the inadequacy of national planning might be remedied (Mishra, 1980).

In India grassroot planning has received much attention after effective enforcement of 73rd and 74th constitutional amendments of the Indian Constitution in relation to empowering of local bodies. But for various reasons, there have been very little efforts and initiatives taken for planning at the local or grassroot level in many States in India. Frequently, the conditions necessary for the success of such planning are not well understood as can be seen from several attempts made in this respect in our country. The local self government institutions and individual planning organizations are looking for an effective strategy for preparing micro-planning in a systematic manner. Therefore, this chapter gives a detailed methodology, with focus on mobilization target people for effective participation in the process of planning at the grassroot level, to attain greater success in the field of rural development. Any strategy of planning should rely on the availability of local resources to attain sustainable development. This chapter at the beginning gives details on conceptualization of the new approach called Resource Based Grassroot Planning Approach.

Resource Based Grassroot Planning Approach

It implies that the "planning for a smaller region like for a village, block or district, for optimum utilization of locally available resources, by the local people, priority in order to satisfy their own needs, by adopting appropriate technologies without disturbing environment".

Merits of the Approach

Proper implementation of this approach will yield the following results:

(a) Optimum utilization of locally available resources.
(b) The locally available resources will be used in the local area itself on priority basis.
(c) Guaranteed people's participation in all aspects of planning and implementation.
(d) Minimization of cost especially in production and transportation of input and output and also related services.
(e) Possibility of satisfying local needs.
(f) Employment generation on perennial way.

Methodology for Resource Based Grassroot Planning Approach

This approach needs a separate methodology in order to develop a realistic plan for any particular region. The data required for planning have to be collected through suitable participatory method by involving stake-holders and line departments for better results. The new methodology has been discussed in the subsequent sections.

Preparation of General Profile of the Area

The first and foremost step in the formulation of any plan is the collection of statistical data regarding the general profile of the area through social mapping and observation. The characteristics and conditions prevailing in various parts of India are not homogeneous and has its own endowments of climate, resource base, manpower, infrastructure, etc., it is always better to prefer to plan for smaller units like a group of villages constituting village Panchayat or at block level. For example, plan of a village Panchayat in the State of Punjab may not be suitable for a village of the State of Rajasthan, because Punjab is having surplus water for irrigation, whereas Rajasthan is a drought prone State. Similarly, plan of a village in Tamil Nadu may not be suitable to villages of Manipur and Megalaya States which differ in socio-economic and agro-climatic conditions. The planner should be very well aware of the profile of the region. Therefore, region specific micro plans are inevitable for the successful and sustainable development. The data required to prepare profile of the areas are discussed below:

Topography: It is much essential to understand the nature of topography, major physical divisions, drainage system, soil type and texture in order to quantify the resource base of a region.

Climatic Conditions: Rainfall rate over a period of time, temperature variations and weather conditions are to be properly assessed.

Technology Adoption: Level of technology adopted in agriculture and allied sectors are also to be ascertained. Technology status on infrastructure such as road network, communication facilities, power supply, financial institutions are to be identified.

Agriculture: In order to understand the agricultural status in the region, the data relating to area under cultivation, land use pattern, cropping pattern, crop cycle, nature and quality of soil, sources and adequacy of irrigation, types of farming, ownership of land, size of land-holdings and the system of tenure, production and productivity are to be collected at village level.

Resource Inventory: Identification of various resources available in the region like physical and natural resources to be carried out in a proper way. Data on quantum and quality availability of local resources, their utilization level and possibility of usage for various purposes have to be collected and verification to be done through different sources.

Social System: Data regarding demography of the region like male-female ratio, child population, education, employment status, caste system, land-holdings, land-man ratio, wage rate, size of agricultural labourers and their migration, etc; to be collected to understand the sociological aspects while formulating a plan.

Identification of Problems and Needs of the People

The next important step in planning process is identification of problems and needs of the local people. For this purpose, the planning region has to be surveyed and the data must be collected from all households and discussion to be carried with resource persons and general public. Planner should also understand the nature and acuteness of various problems through observation in that particular region. Particulars on educational status, income and expenditure, level of poverty, consumption pattern of people, living standard and life styles have to be collected. The proposed plan should be given focus on solving the identified problems through satisfying the needs of the people.

Availability of Infrastructural Facilities

In India, still some of the remote areas and villages are not provided with adequate infrastructural facilities to enable faster development and growth. Facilities like roads, communication, power supply, marketing channels, etc., are inadequate or low standard in the rural areas. Hence, the planning team has to collect information about the availability and requirement of infrastructural facilities. It will help the planner to prepare a suitable plan to fill up the gap before initiating implementation of any programme.

Identification of Skills, Opportunities and Technological Options

Developmental opportunities in the planning area have to be identified. If an area is facing acute unemployment problem, it has to be tackled by generating adequate employment opportunities in that area. But, where employment can be created? whether in agriculture and allied sector? or in industrial sector? or in services sector?. Answers to these questions will help the planner to create a suitable plan. Then, it is essential to find out the availability of skilled persons in that particular region. Technology is another important factor in planning. Technologies adopted in agriculture and allied sector and also in industrial sector have to be identified in order to avoid overlapping of technologies. Therefore, better understanding of available opportunities, skills and technological gap is essential and linking them in a systematic way to utilize these three factors at an optimum level for better development.

Review of Earlier and Current Programmes and Projects

Another important task of a planning is, before starting into the planning process, it is necessary to review earlier and current programmes and projects implemented by the governmental and non-governmental organizations in the region. This will help the planner to prepare a suitable and useful plan. Information regarding what kind of programmes were implemented, targets, achievements and failures, level of people's participation, suitability, feasibility, type of organization, staffing pattern and source of finance have to be analyzed. Further, this information will help the planner to avoid repetition of programmes and get away from the failures. Study of ongoing programmes and strategies will help to set the targets of the proposed plan in achievable manner.

Understanding of Attitudes and Aptitudes of the Local People

The next important step in the present planning exercise is survey of attitudes and aptitudes of the people. Certain social taboos, customs and religious beliefs of the people will not recognize certain kinds of business activities and professions. For example, the areas which have orthodox Hindu culture will never allow and accept to start any animal flesh processing oriented industry. Similarly, the people in the upper layer of the caste hierarchy and highly educated society will not accept the lower level labour jobs even they are in deprived condition. Therefore, attitude of the people may not accept certain programmes. It is also essential that the prepared plan should suit the aptitude of the local people. Same way high technology oriented employment will not suit the non-technical people. This kind of mismatching can be avoided by studying their attitude and aptitude.

Availability of Funds and Flow

Finance is the first and foremost criteria for putting any plan into action. Success of a plan depends on the financial provisions and its timely flow, whether a short term or long term plan; it is shaped by the fund availability. The decision regarding, when plan is to be started and to be completed, the type of machineries to be used, personnel to be employed and other related matters can be finalized only on the basis of the financial availability. Hence, the planner should clearly understand the finance related aspects.

Level of Local Demand and Market Potential

The proposed plan for industrialization of villages, planner has to identify the location for different types of industrial units based on the availability of resources. In this situation, to find out local demand for a proposed industrial activity will give ideas to it sustainability. Whether it is a product which going to satisfy the basic needs of the local people? or a product for the outside market? all areas have to be checked. If a product or service is not satisfying the local needs, then, it has to find out the outside market potential. If a product has both local demand and outside market, it will flourish and achieve the desired results. In its absence, the plan will become a failure. In this situation, the planner has to clearly point out the plan for market and delivery system.

Environmental Sustainability

Planning at the grassroot or State or at the national level should aim at sustainability in development. Instead of planning for *ad hoc* solutions, striving towards arriving permanent solutions create much impact on the development scenario in the region. For example, if a region is having problems of unemployment and poverty, the plan should pave the ways and means to provide permanent employment opportunities, either farm or off-farm, in government or non-governmental organizations or by self-employment. Only then the plan will become full fledged. The programmes like providing wage employment through various government schemes may satisfy the immediate requirement but will not solve the problems of people permanently. Therefore, planners have to do maximum efforts to solve the problems through sustainable way by alternate mechanisms with suitable strategies. At the same time, the proposed industrial or business activities should not degrade the environment.

Formulation of Objectives

Formulation of objectives is one of the major tasks of project planning. The important points to be considered during formulation are: the objectives should correlate with the goals of national plans; it should be formulated towards solving the problems of the people and other creatures on the earth. The planner should concentrate on the peculiar problems for immediate solution. The objectives can be both general and specific. For example, agricultural development may be the general objective but it is broader. In order to achieve targets in quantitative terms, the planner has to specify the objectives as increasing production of grains in tonnes, generation of employment in mandays, etc.

Prioritization of Problems and Objectives

In rural areas, problems are multi-dimensional nature and prevail at various levels. These problems cannot be solved at one go. Certain problems may take a few years to solve and some other within a few days or months. Some problems like epidemics and other health related problems are very serious which would need the urgent attention by government. Whereas some others like provision of transport and communication facilities can be given second preference. Depending upon the urgency of problems, planner should prioritize and develop programmes accordingly.

Designing of Strategies and Programmes

After identification of the problems and finalizing the objectives and priorities, the planner should prepare proper strategies depending upon the problems encountered and objectives enunciated by involving people and acknowledging the people concerns. The strategies have to be prepared in order to deliver benefits to the local people within the stipulated time and to fulfil the objectives.

Target Setting

Setting of targets is an important function in development planning. To fulfil the objectives, the targets are to be fixed in specific terms with a time-frame and should be based on the availability of resources, ability of services, and capacity of the implementing mechanism and state policies.

Resource Allocation and Project Implementation

It is another important stage in the planning exercise. Resources in the form of men, material, money and energy, their proper distribution, timely delivery and steady flow of resources and finances are the vital factors contributing to the success of any plan. If any one of these resources is not available or scarcely available that will lead to delay in achieving the fixed targets. Therefore, the resources are to be properly distributed among various activities spelt out in the plan in such a way that their optimum utilization must pave the way for achieving the specified objectives. For example, organizing of a dairy unit in a particular place may be the plan. This plan has activities like, selection of place for a dairy unit, construction of a shed, purchasing of animals, purchasing of animal feed, medicines, arrangement of water, appointing labour for rearing, milking, sending milk to the market, etc. Each and every activity of this plan will incur certain amount of manpower, money, and material. The amount of men, material and energy needed for each and every activity is needed to be spell out before implementation of the programme.

Manpower Planning

Human resources are as important as physical resources. One of the reasons for the failure is under-utilization of the human resources. Therefore, the plan should clearly state the details of human resources that are available in a particular location. The planner should collect the demographical data like total population, sex, age, educational status, occupational status and skill availability. If the region has inadequate skilled labourers, then, the planner should suggest the ways to train the people to equip them with some suitable skills. If the local region has surplus labour, the planner should find ways to utilize the surplus labourers by providing suitable employment.

Identification of Location

Selection of the location is one of the most important steps in the planning process. The location should be selected in a place where resources and infrastructural facilities subject to requirement like road and transport, power, telephone, post office, school, market, health centres etc. are available. For this, the planner should prepare a resource map which will help the planner to select the right place to locate the project. The plan should also express the gaps in the infrastructural development and should also suggest for the establishment of certain infrastructural facilities which are not available in the planning area. Ultimately activities should consider the beneficiaries choices for location for better delivery and management of the provided services.

Conclusion

Thus, any planner who plans for a village or a block should follow the above steps carefully, sequentially and systematically so as to develop a suitable plan to generate adequate employment opportunities to improve the standard of living of the targeted people. Moreover, importance to be given in considering people views and involvement of target people at every stage of planning will yield fruitful results and the plan will get effective support from the beneficiaries in implementation and management after implementation. People's participation at all levels will create feeling and responsibility of ownership among the stakeholders which is an effective strategy for the success of any developmental project or programme. Local Government institutions efforts and line department's coordination, community organization's support and local non-governmental developmental organization's involvement are vital for chalking out a grassroot plan.

REFERENCES

Adiseshiah, M.; Mukherji, P.S.; Hegde, R.; Das Gupta, A. and Fernandes, G.; 1994. *Decentralized Planning and Panchayati Raj*. New Delhi, Institute of Social Sciences and Concept Pub. Company.

Aziz, A., 2000. Democratic decentralization: experience of Karnataka. *Economic and Political Weekly*, XXXV (39): 3521-6.

Bohra, O.P., 2000. Decentralization and devolution of powers and functions to Panchayats. *Journal of Rural Development*. 19(2):185-197.

Das, M.K., 2000. Kerala's decentralized planning: Floundering experiment, *Economic and Political Weekly*, XXXV (49): 4300-3.

Mukherjee, A. (ed.), 1995. *Participatory Rural Appraisal Methods and Applications in Rural Planning*. New Delhi, Vikas Pub. House Pvt. Ltd.

Ratha Raman Singh, Decentralised Planning in India—"Retrospect and Prospect", *Southern Economist*, January 1989, Vol. 27, No. 17.

Sathya Sundram I., Approaches to Poverty Alleviation, *Southern Economist*, July 1990, Vol. 29, No. 6.

11

Working of Rural Employment Guarantee Scheme: A Study in a Village Panchayat of Tamil Nadu

R. MANI and K. MANIKANDAN

Introduction

Employment generation, particularly in rural areas, appears to be most challenging task for planners and policy-makers in India. The unemployment situation has worsened over a period of time. One of the main objectives of various five year plans is to create employment avenues for over six million rural people every year. In addition to the number of unemployed in rural areas is reportedly increasing at the rate of one million in a year. The rural labour force is adversely affected due to meagre wage rates and rising unemployment. The Government sought to improve the plight of the rural labourers by implementing (1) special programmes for supplementing work opportunities; and (2) programmes for increasing labour absorption in agriculture. While the former provides temporary relief, the latter is crucial for long term employment growth. But, programmes so far implemented to enhance the labour absorption capacity of the agricultural sector have failed to reach the point of success. In this context, a new Act has been passed, National Rural Employment Guarantee Act (NREGA) 2005, by the Government of India to assure employment for 100 days in a year to rural households. The nucleus of the Act is discussed as follows:

The National Rural Employment Guarantee Act 2005

The National Rural Employment Guarantee Act 2005 (NREGA)

guarantees 100 days of employment in a year to any rural household whose adult members are willing to do unskilled manual work. The Act has come into force initially in 200 districts and will be extended gradually to other areas notified by the Central Government.

First, the Act was prepared through a wide range of consultation with people's organizations; second the Act addresses itself chiefly to working people and their fundamental right to life with dignity; third, the Act empowers ordinary people to play an active role to the implementation of employment guarantee schemes through Gram Sabhas, social audits, participatory planning and other means. More than any other law, NREGA is an Act of the people, by the people and for the people.

This act is an important set-up towards the realization of the right to work. It is also expected to enhance people's livelihood on a sustained basis, by developing the economic and social infrastructure in rural areas. The choice of works seeks to address the causes of chronic poverty such as drought, deforestation and soil erosion. Effectively implemented, the employment generated under the Act has the potential of transforming the geography of poverty.

The objectives of the Act are as follows :

- To enhance livelihood security in rural areas by providing at least 100 days of guaranteed wage employment in a financial year to household whose adult members volunteer to do unskilled manual work.
- To empower rural women, reducing rural urban migration and fostering social equity among others.

Rural Employment Guarantee Scheme (REGS)

The Act direct every State Government to prepare Rural Employment Guarantee Scheme in order to implement the work guarantee. Thus the Act provides the legal foundation of the work guarantee and the scheme is the means through which this guarantee comes into effect. Each REGS is supposed to follow the operational guidelines issued by the Ministry of Rural Development in January 2006.

The *modus operandi* for getting employment under the scheme is as follows:

- The Gram Panchayat will issue job cards to every registred household,

- ❖ The timely issue of well designed job card is essential,
- ❖ This is a critical legal document, which also helps to ensure transparency and protect labourers,
- ❖ Job cards should be issued in the presence of the local community.

The works prescribed under the scheme include, Water Conservation, Water Harvesting, Drought Proofing including afforestation and tree plantation, Renovation of Traditional Water Bodies including silting of tanks, Land Development, Flood Control and protection work, rural connectivity to provide all-weather access and other such works.

As the scheme is new in all dimensions and being implemented currently, it attracts the interest of people from many quarters including policy-makers and academicians to know about the procedures and implementation of the scheme at the grassroot level. In view of this, the present study was carried out in an REGS implemented village Panchayat, Malvarpatty in Dindigul district of Tamil Nadu.

Objectives of the Study

The following are the objectives of the study:

- ❖ To assess the nature of works and employment provided to the people,
- ❖ To ascertain role of key agencies in the scheme and working of the scheme, and
- ❖ To suggest measures for improvement.

Methodology

The study is based both on primary and secondary data. Primary data were collected from those who were registered and got employment in the scheme. The secondary sources include guide book and documents on the scheme and reports with the Panchayat office. Random sampling method was adopted for investigation. The total number of households registered with the village Panchayat is 432. But, the number of households availed employment opportunities is 272. Of which 60 households were interviewed and data were collected from them using pre-tested interview schedule.

Findings of the Study

The major findings of the study are given below:

- Out of those who availed employment opportunity, the female form a majority (57%).
- Among the beneficiaries (respondents) under the scheme, the percentage of female is more (55%) than that of male.
- Eighty three per cent are Hindus and rest are Christians. Most of the respondents belong to scheduled caste (52%) and rest belong to backward class.
- Most of the respondents (96%) fall in the age group of below 55.
- Half of the respondents are educated at primary level and another half are educated at middle level and above.
- A vast majority of the respondents (73%) are basically landless agricultural labourers and the rest are marginal farmers and non-farm labourers.
- Each respondent received uniformly Rs. 80 per day for his/her work as stipulated by the State Government without any deviation.
- Only 26 per cent of the respondents have completed 100 days of employment and the rest lie between 50 days to 70 days.
- Most of the beneficiaries are not fully aware of the Act and the scheme.
- The opportunity cost of the respondents has increased to Rs. 80 per day due to the wage rate followed in the scheme.
- The Panchayat Officials maintain clear records and books of accounts related to Registration, attendance and wage etc.
- The activities under the scheme undertaken in the village are renovation of tank, repairing of drainage, clearing of bushes and thorns, laying village roads which fall very much in the line of scheme activities envisaged in the document.
- Social audit has been done during the Gram Sabha meeting by the community members verifying the documents and appraising beneficiaries.

Suggestions

The respondents during the study suggested a few practical measures based on their need which would help them and also help implementation of the scheme. They are:

- Most of the agricultural labourers suggested providing employment throughout the year excluding busy agricultural seasons.
- The payment may be made in cash instead of cheque as most of them are not acquainted with bank transaction. The payment in cash may be in the presence of committee consisting of Panchayat body members, the beneficiaries and social activist.
- Awareness may be generated among those registered for employment on the contents of NREGA and REGS.

Conclusion

The study reveals that no discrimination was seen while selecting the beneficiaries, gender-wise and caste-wise. The village Panchayat appears to have selected the right type of beneficiaries that is the downtrodden and the needy ones. The scheme has really contributed in terms of a hike in general wage rate in the study area. The opportunity cost of labourers has increased. The study further reveals that no corruption was involved in the scheme. The scheme enlisted the participation of people in various decision-making process. As far as the study village Panchayat is concerned the scheme has really contributed (1) to increase employment opportunity and income, (2) in creating facilities and assets for the community as a whole, and (3) in promoting people's participation in decision-making through bottom-up plan.

REFERENCES

Government of India, (2006) *The National Rural Employment Guarantee Act 2005-Operational Guidelines*, Ministry of Rural Development.

Nikhil Dey, *et al.*, (2006) *Employment Guarantee Act: A Primer*, New Delhi, National Book Trust, India.

12

Reforms of Rural Local Government in Bangladesh: The Politics Within

SADIK HASAN

Introduction

The history of Local Government in Bangladesh is replete with instances of Central Governments jealously retaining their control over local bodies. There were periodic announcements in favour of decentralization, but they turned out to be mere rhetoric, intended to appease the native population. The actual steps taken by the Governments resulted in stronger centralization (Huque,1988: 20).

Local Government has been a colonial legacy in Bangladesh, inherited by her as a member state of the Himalayan sub-continent, which was ruled by the British up to August 14, 1947. Most of the Local Government bodies of Bangladesh, therefore, had their origin during the British days (Faizullah, 1985: 263). When the British came to India, hereditary noblemen ruled the area consisting of East Bengal as semi-independent chiefs paying only a small tribute to the British Government. There was no emigration and agriculture was the only way of earning a livelihood. In Bengal, lack of communication facilities and inaccessibility of the Central Government compelled the villagers to organize themselves into administrative units (Huque,1988: 27-28).

It was not until the takeover of Indian administration by the British Crown from the British East India Company that the development of Local Government institutions could be said to have begun on the Indian subcontinent (Huque, 1988: 28).

The rebellion of Indian soldiers in the British Army in 1857 against the ruling British East India Company gave British Empire a new conclusion about the subcontinent that a close relationship should be developed between the executive arms of the Government and the people and accordingly, Government enacted the *Bengal Village Chowkidari Act of 1870* (Thompson and Garratt, 1934: 476). This Act empowered the District Magistrate to form a five-member *Panchayat* in each union comprising ten to twelve square miles according to his choice. Thus, the first institution of rural Local Government in British India was introduced headed by nominated members (leaders). This ensured the inclusion of people close to the rulers in local bodies to control the activities politically. Therefore, this chapter is an attempt to make a succinct study of the reform initiatives in Local Government bodies introduced at different political periods in Bangladesh. This chapter tries to illustrate these initiatives in the context of the political reality of that time and makes an effort to explain the modifications taking the political motive in account and concludes identifying some characteristics of the initiatives.

Local Government System: Historical Background

Historians have traced the existence of village councils during the *Vedic* period (1500 B.C.—1000 B.C.). These councils, through a number of committees, managed and controlled the villages and were self-governing entities, which combined in themselves the functions of an assembly as well as that of a club. There is also reference to self-governing village administration in Kautilya's *Arthashastra*. The village government in ancient and medieval Bengal was autonomous body with little external interference (Begum, 1984: 3).

The institution of village self-government bodies often called *Village Panchayat* existed during ancient times and Mughal period in India. Most scholars tend to agree on the fact that these *Village Panchayats* were locally constituted bodies which looked after different aspects of village life such as enforcement of law and order, resolving legal and social disputes and maintenance of tanks, arrangements of village education. The villagers led a corporate life and the *Village Panchayats* played an effective role in managing village community affairs exercising a high degree of social control based on the age old traditions, customs, and religious sanctions. The *Panchayats* were self-financed and used to generate their own resources to fulfil their functions (Choudhury, 1987: 5-6). Thus, tradition and local customs contributed to the formation of laws and village bodies consisting of the elderly and respected villagers looked after their implementation (Huque, 1988: 27-28).

The British Period (1757-1947)

But the British rulers in India did not adopt the indigenous institutions of Local Government. The institutions nurtured by them were modelled on their own (Siddiqui, 1984: 33). The British took nominal efforts to make local government institutions democratic and delegate authority to the lowest levels. The tendency to withhold control was evident in the various schemes of reforming Local Government that were undertaken by the British. They announced plans to make local government institutions autonomous, and to encourage participation by the natives. But these plans were never implemented in full. Withholding control of local bodies and looking after the interests of the traditionally dominant groups continued on the excuse that there was an inadequate supply of qualified leaders and resources to run Local Government efficiently (Huque, 1988: 20-21).

During the East India Company rule there was nothing called local government. Company's activities in the rural areas exclusively confined to work of revenue settlement. After the revolt of Indian soldiers in the British East India Company army in 1857, power was transferred from the East India Company to the Crown and Parliament marked the beginning for instituting local government as a matter of financial necessity especially in the context of imperial financial strains and stresses due to mutiny. This has also led to the idea of making a distinction between local and imperial services (Muttalib and Khan, 1983: 68). Since 1858, the British rulers made every efforts to bring their subjects under the bureaucratic control of the Government (Choudhury, 1987: 7).

The first step in streamlining local administration was taken with the publication of Lord Mayo's resolution in 1870 as demands for responsible government started to be voiced. Lord Mayo—the Viceroy—recognized the ability of Indians to administer local affairs and in response the *Bengal Village Chowkidari Act of 1870* was passed. This Act empowered the District Magistrate to form a five-member *Panchayat* dividing the rural areas into unions, each covering approximately ten to twelve square miles according to his choice.

The *Panchayat* was given authority to appoint the *Village Chowkidars* and to assess and collect tax from the villagers to pay salaries of the *Chowkidars*. Noticeably, *Panchayats* lack of authority to take any development work.

But the *Panchayat* was not a representative body. The office of the *Panchayat* was not a voluntary one in the sense that no one could refuse to be a member of it. The District Magistrate could dismiss *Panchayat* member at his will. The *Panchayat* could not even remove the *Chowkidars* (Choudhury, 1987: 8). Consequently, the *Chowkidari Panchayats* established under the Act of 1870 "were popularly regarded not as the representatives of the village folk, but as servants of the government" (Tinker, 1954: 40).

The real landmark in the emergence of the concept of local self-government was Lord Ripon's historic resolution. It was to his credit that he realized that it was the infusion of new life rather than mere organizational reform that set out the future development of local representative institutions. The liberal policies pursued by Lord Ripon gradually brought the extension of the representative character of the local bodies by emphasizing the system of election and participation of non-official members in these bodies. Ripon's Resolution on Local Self-government of 1882 explicitly stated its objectives (Tepper, 1964):

> *It is not primarily with a view to improvement in administration that the measure is put forward and supported. It is chiefly designed as an instrument of political and popular education . . . the government should check the acts of the local bodies, but not dictate them.*

But Ripon failed to realize his plans as intended. The conservatives who were also prominent during the time looked for greater consolidation of their empire in order to control it more effectively so that economic gain could be maximized (Choudhury, 1987: 9). Ripon's resolution on local self-government with certain modifications was passed as *The Local Self-Government Act of 1885* creating three tiers of local bodies into operation—the *District Board* in the District, the *Local Board* in a sub-division, and the *Union Committee* in a group of villages. All these three tiers had the provision to be composed of elected members as well as nominated members by the Government. Only men who attained the age of 21 years and paid *Chowkidari* tax or cess tax or possessed certain educational qualifications had the right to vote.

The provision of the *Local Self Government Act of 1885* came into force in 16 districts with effect from October 1, 1886. The rural local bodies established under this Act did not prove to be effective owing to their limited funds and perpetuation of elaborate official

Table 12.1: Local Government under the Bengal Local Self Government Act of 1885

Tier	*Local Government Institution*	*Type of Selection*	*Elector/Selector*	*Person in Charge*
District	District Board	Election *(Two-third members)* and Nomination *(One-third members)*	Local Board Members Divisional Commissioner	District Magistrate as the Chairman
Sub-Division	Local Board	Direct Election *(Two-third members)* and Nomination *(One-third members)*	Only Male Voters *(Conditions apply)* Government	Chairman *(Subject to the approval of the Lt. Governor)*
Union	Union Committee	Direct Election	Only Male Voters *(conditions apply)*	Chairman *(After the amendment of 1908)*
	Panchayat	Nomination	District Magistrate	—

Sources: Ali Ahmed, *Administration of Local Self Government for Rural Areas in Bangladesh* (Dhaka: Local Government Institute, 1979); Lutful Hoq Choudhury, *Local Self Government and its Reorganization in Bangladesh* (Dhaka, National Institute of Local Government, 1987); Najmul Abedin, *Local Administration and Politics in Modernizing Societies: Bangladesh and Pakistan* (Dhaka: The National Institute of Public Administration, 1973).

control. The work of the District Board was particularly hampered by the paucity of resources. With such meagre resources they were unlikely to delegate any function and funds to the Local Boards and the Union Committees. Besides, with the practice of appointing officials as chairmen of local bodies, these bodies could not attain a truly representative character. Rather the system gave rise to an exploiter class in the rural areas.

Table 12.2: Local Government under the Bengal Village Self Government Act of 1919

Tier	*Local Government Institution*	*Type of Selection*	*Elector/Selector*	*Person in Charge*
District	District Board	Direct Election *(Two-third members)* and Nomination *(One-third members)*	Only Male Voters *(conditions apply)* Divisional Commissioner *(After 1932, Minister-in-Charge)*	Chairman *(From among the elected members)*
Union	Union Board	Direct Election *(Two-third members)* and Nomination *(One-third members)*	Only Male Voters *(conditions apply)* District Magistrate	President

Sources: Ali Ahmed, *Administration of Local Self Government for Rural Areas in Bangladesh* (Dhaka: Local Government Institute, 1979); Lutful Hoq Choudhury, *Local Self Government and its Reorganization in Bangladesh* (Dhaka, National Institute of Local Government, 1987); Najmul Abedin, *Local Administration and Politics in Modernizing Societies: Bangladesh and Pakistan* (Dhaka: The National Institute of Public Administration, 1973).

From 1885 to 1919 several commissions namely, Indian Police Commission (1902), the Decentralization Commission (1907), the Bengal District Administration Committee (1912), the Montagu-Chelmsford Report (1918) clearly pointed out the need for providing more opportunities for greater popular participation in the local bodies, which could serve as a platform for political training of the people and called for abolition of nominated members from local bodies.

But these recommendations were totally overlooked by the Government and consequently extensive bureaucratic control coupled with limited financial powers hampered the growth and operation of local self government bodies and thus the general principles laid down by Ripon in the famous resolution of 1882 did not largely materialize. The practice of appointing officials as Chairman of local bodies allowed official control and dominance over the local bodies that failed to attain their real representative character. Reform efforts in local self government from 1885 onwards were conceived more for administrative convenience and administration improvement rather than for meeting either national or local political aspirations (Roy 1937: 85). Therefore, local bodies with elected members failed to be the representatives of the commoners rather turned into an extended arm of the government.

The Montagu-Chelmsford Report ushered the *Bengal Village Self Government Act of 1919*. The *Panchayats* and Union Committees were merged and named the Union Boards. Only a third of the members of the Union Board were nominated, thus ensuring the control of the Government. The functions of the Board were extended to cover watch and ward, communication, education, sanitation and settling of petty disputes in civil and criminal cases. The Board was authorized to levy local rate to meet its expenditure (Ahmed, 1979: 16).

There was no doubt that the Act of 1919 contributed a lot towards the development of the village local body but it was not yet a fully representative body. The Government nominated one-third of its members and the element of nomination was a clear violation of the concept of local self government (Ahmed 1979: 17).

The Pakistan Period (1947-1971)

The most visible legacy of colonialism in India was its partition in 1947. The birth of Pakistan presented the challenge of organizing and building up the new state. Initially, there was no attempt to reorganize local government. The colonial system of local government continued in East Bengal (now Bangladesh). The euphoria of independence prevailed for some time and there were no demands from the people for reforming the local government system (Huque, 1988: 35).

In Pakistan years, the formal structure of local administration has operated in a considerably changed and still changing political, administrative, and social environment. As a result, the last two and a half decades have witnessed some very important developments in local areas: Firstly, one of the major developments has been the emergence of a powerful class of politically oriented local leaders. These leaders are very eager to increase their influence on the members of the local bureaucracy, who are officially and hierarchically responsible to the government at the central/provincial level. Secondly, the local officials and the members of the local bodies have been required to undertake responsibility for planning and implementing the fast expanding community development programmes. Thirdly, with the expansion of, and increase in the importance of the nation building departments, the officers of these departments have strengthened their position vis-à-vis the general administrative officers. Fourthly, the introduction of the four-tier system of local bodies-cum-electoral college (called "Basic Democracies") by the first Martial Law regimes in former Pakistan institutionalised the relationship between local politics and provincial and central politics, accelerated the process of politicisation of the local leadership and changed the nature of the relationship between the local bureaucracy and the non-official members of the local bodies during the period between 1958 and 1969 (Abedin, 1973: xvii-xviii).

In contrast with the provincial character of the earlier local government enactments, *the Basic Democracy Order (BDO) 1959* was a central legislation havingjurisdiction over the whole of Pakistan. Basic Democracy introduced a four-tier local government structure consisting of the Union Councils/Town Committee/Union Committee, *Thana/Tehsil* Council, District Council, and Divisional Council at the Union, *Thana/Tehsil*, district and divisional levels respectively (Abedin, 1973: 164). Pakistan was divided into 120,000 electoral units and the persons enlisted in the electoral roll for each electoral unit were required to elect from among themselves a person known as the electors for that unit. These members played the political role of electing the President of the country and members of the National and Provincial Assemblies (Siddiqui, 1984: 48). To provide a semblance of democracy, the Union Council was made a representative institution; the rest were all under the control of civil servants largely responsible for administrative coordination and supervision of the affairs of the respective councils below them (Zafarullah and Khan, 1994: 645).

Although the Government continued to shower praise on Basic Democracy which, it said, was achieving the goals of economic development, social equality and political democracy (Friedman, 1961: 9), it could not be considered democratic because it did not "represent control by the people over government power except in an extremely limited manner" (Friedman, 1961: 9). Gradually, the political role of the Basic Democrats assumed more importance than their administrative and local government functions. The system favoured big farmers, and resulted in a rise in the participation of new moneyed classes such as businessmen and contractors (Jahan, 1972: 113-122). The majority of village residents—small farmers and landless labourers—were still excluded from decision-making in local affairs (Huque, 1988: 40).

Table 12.3: Local Government System under Basic Democracy Order 1959 in East Pakistan

Tier	*Local Government Institution*	*Type of Selection*	*Elector/Selector*	*Person In charge*
District	District Councils	Election and Nomination	Chairmen of the Union Councils/Town Committees and Government	Deputy Commissioner as the Chairman
Thana	Thana Councils	Ex-officio Members	—	Sub-Divisional Officer as the Chairman
Union	Union Councils	Direct Election	Universal Adult Franchise	Chairman

Sources: Ali Ahmed, *Administration of Local Self Government for Rural Areas in Bangladesh* (Dhaka: Local Government Institute, 1979); Najmul Abedin, *Local Administration and Politics in Modernizing Societies: Bangladesh and Pakistan* (Dhaka: The National Institute of Public Administration, 1973).

Basic Democracy had corrupted the entire local government machinery, particularly the rural local bodies. It failed like other reform attempts mainly because the system was designed to serve the interests of a certain group that would support the regime (Quadir 1972:28-29). In course of time, rural people lost faith in these representatives, and ultimately they revolted against the system. Indeed, during the 1969 mass uprisings in the countryside, elected and official functionaries connected with the Basic Democracies system became the favourite targets of '*Gherao*' (siege) and '*Jalao*' (set fire) programmes (Siddiqui 1984:57).

Reforms in Local Government System in Bangladesh: 1971-2006

The emergence of Bangladesh as an independent nation state in 1971 was the first time that its people had been exposed to control over their own destiny since the Battle of Plassey in 1757. The people of Bangladesh have never before or since at least up to March 1971, had any expectations from their rulers. Till then whomsoever had exercised state power had derived authority through the capture of power rather from the people. Since it now exercised sovereign power it was expected as no other Government before it had been, to fulfil the long suppressed aspirations of the people of Bangladesh. It would have been difficult for any government to carry on its shoulders the unfulfilled aspirations of its people accumulated over so many years. The Awami League's regime was hardly prepared for this historic task. Never having exercised effective state power, they were expected to learn the rules of governance from its practice under the leadership of *Bangabandhu* Sheikh Mujib—the father of the nation (Sobhan 1993: 12).

The Awami League Period (1972-1975)

The liberation war had brought the Government virtually to a standstill, and local government institutions, too, were inoperative. However, in many areas, local affairs continued to be managed informally by existing local leaders. During the liberation movement, the nationalist leaders had put into discredit all the institutions designed by the Pakistanis as instruments of exploitation. The nation expected a major overhaul of the system, including local government institutions. But in its first year of rule, the AL faced the task of restoring order and setting up an administrative machinery in the country. As a result, little attention was paid to local government reform (Huque, 1988: 46).

Moreover, the AL had its support base among the rural middle farmers and did not want to antagonize this group ushering in major changes in rural local government that might favour poor villagers at the expense of the party's supporters (Huque, 1988: 46). Even though the first reorganization of local government took place in early 1972. *The Bangladesh Local Councils and Municipal Committees (Dissolution and Administration) (Amendment) Order, 1972* (The President's Order No. 7 of 1972) was proclaimed to dissolve local Government Councils constituted through BDO 1959 throughout the country. Under the Order, the Basic Democracies system was abolished in response to the popular will and a three-tier local government was introduced in line with the previous arrangement. This Order also changed the name of the local bodies—the name of

Table 12.4: Local Government System in the Awami League Regime

Tier	*Local Government Institution*	*Type of Selection*	*Elector/ Selector*	*Person in Charge*	*Prescribed Authority*
District	Zila Board	Ex-officio Represen-tation	—	Deputy Commissi-oner as the Chief Adminis-trator	Deputy Commi-ssioner
Thana	Thana Develop-ment Committee	Ex-officio Represen-tation	—	Circle Officer (Develop-ment) as the Chief Adminis-trator	Sub-Divisional Officer
Union	Union Parishad	Election	Universal Adult Franchise	Chairman	Sub-Divisional Officer

Sources: Ali Ahmed, *Administration of Local Self Government for Rural Areas in Bangladesh* (Dhaka: Local Government Institute, 1979); Abul Maal Abdul Muhith, *Government for Districts* (Dhaka: The University Press Limited, 2002).

the Union Council was changed to *Union Panchayat*, the *Thana* Council to *Thana Unnayan Committee* (Thana Development Committee) and the District Council to *Zila Board*. On March 22, 1973, "*The Bangladesh Local Government (Union Parishad and Pourashava) Order 1973* (The President's Order No. 22 of 1973) was promulgated and the name of *Union Panchayat* was changed to *Union Parishad* (Hasan, 2004:126).

According to the P.O. No. 22, each union was divided into three wards. Three members were directly elected from each ward. The total number of members for the *Union Parishad* (UP) was thus nine. Besides, there were one Chairman, and one Vice-Chairman for each UP who were directly elected by voters of the entire Union. Each UP operated its business and activities through general meetings of its committee meetings (Ahmed, 1979:110-144). The Circle Officer (Development) under the overall supervision and control of Sub-Divisional Officer (SDO) managed the functions and administration of the *Thana* Development Committee. Neither elected nor nominated members were in the *Zila Board*. The Deputy Commissioner of the district assumed the post of chief administrator as per Government circular (GOB 1972).

Gradually it appeared that the powers exercised by elected representatives in the local councils upto this point were being transferred to Government officials (Huque, 1988: 47). What emerged was a reincarnated basic democracy system with only slight modifications in composition and functions of the lowest rung of the local government structure (Zafarullah and Khan, 1994: 645). Thus the rare chance to build a people-oriented local government system in Bangladesh embraced the fate of being controlled and used as political weapon by the Government officials *i.e.,* by the political leadership.

The beginning of 1975 witnessed major changes in the political scenario of Bangladesh. Prime Minister Sheikh Mujib unilaterally and capriciously replaced the Parliamentary form of Government by a strong Presidential type that would ensure his hold over the entire political and administrative structure. An offshoot of this changeover was to redesign the local government structure; all sub-divisions were converted into *Zilas* (districts) and placed under powerful governors who were to take order from the President and remain responsible to him. A web of strong Central control was woven with this "reform". However, before it could be implemented, the regime itself was liquidated by a military coup (Zafarullah and Khan, 1994: 646).

General Zia Period (1975-1981)

Politics in Bangladesh entered a new phase in August 15, 1975. The undisputed leader of the liberation movement, Bangabandhu Sheikh Mujib and his family were killed by a group of junior and former army officers and Martial Law was declared for the first time in the history of Bangladesh. The Military Government continued amid a series of coups and counter coups and finally General Ziaur Rahman emerged as *de facto* ruler of the armed forces and, as well, of Bangladesh.

But many problems plagued Zia as he tried to rule the country under Martial Law. It became evident that Zia had to have a power base outside the armed forces to establish the legitimacy of his regime. This could only be achieved by organizing a political party, which would be able to secure a majority of seats in the Parliament. Since the rural areas would elect most of the legislators, Zia had to start wooing the rural voters to accomplish this objective (Huque, 1988: 67).

Therefore, a new *Local Government Ordinance* in November 1976 was made retaining the *Union Parishads* with some changes in their composition. The office of the Vice-Chairman was abolished. The term of office of the *Parishad* was five years and consisted of fourteen members including two women and two peasants members, and the Chairman was vested with all executive powers (GOB 1976: Article 8 and 40). According to the Ordinance, the Government could exercise supervision and control over the *Union Parishads* to ensure that their activities conformed to the purposes stated in the order. It also provided the Sub-Divisional Officer with the authority to direct, suspend, or otherwise control UP. In short, Central control was visible in all the parts of the *Union Parishad* (Ahmed, 1979:174).

The other two bodies—*Thana Parishad* and *Zila Parishad* were to remain under the direct control of the national Government. No system of election was provided for the two tiers (Khan, 1991: 3-4). However, in 1979, a body called the *Thana* Development Committee (TDC) consisting of all UP Chairmen was allowed to operate in addition to the existing *Thana Parishad*. In 1980, a fourth tier, called the *Swanirvar Gram Sarkar* (Self-reliant Village Government) was introduced at the village level (Hasan, 2004: 127).

Table 12.5: Local Government System in General Zia Regime

Tier	*Local Government Institution*	*Type of Selection*	*Elector/ Selector*	*Person in Charge*	*Prescribed Authority*
District	Zila Parishad	Election and Nomination	Adult Franchise and Deputy Commissioner	Chairman *(From among the elected or women members)*	Deputy Commissioner
Thana	Thana Parishad	Ex-officio Representation and Nomination	Government	Sub-Divisional Officer as the Chairman	Sub-Divisional Officer
	Thana Development Committee	Ex-officio Representation	—	Chairman	—
Union	Union Parishad	Election and Nomination	Adult Franchise and Sub-Divisional Officer	Chairman	Sub-Divisional Officer
Village	Swanirvar Gram Sarkar	Consensus of the Villagers	–	*Gram Pradhan* (Village Chief)	Circle Officer (Development)

Sources: *The Local Government Ordinance 1976*; *The Local Government (Amendment) Act 1980*; Ali Ahmed, *Administration of Local Self-Government for Rural Areas in Bangladesh* (Dhaka: Local Government Institute, 1979); Abul Maal Abdul Muhith, *Government for Districts* (Dhaka: The University Press Limited, 2002).

Not being sure of their political power and support, the new military rulers of Bangladesh decided to postpone the national elections, which were scheduled for 1977. Instead, elections to the local councils were held. As political parties were not permitted to operate at the time, candidates for *Union Parishad* membership contested the election as independents though the electorates knew the political affiliations of the candidates. The military recognized the potential threat to their position in the political arena and sought to win over these local leaders. Programmes were implemented to train members of local bodies to perform their duties better, attempts were made to bring the village leaders closer to the Government through meetings and conferences, and members were sent abroad for training (Huque, 1988: 59).

In the mean time, being the President of the country, Zia formed Bangladesh Nationalists Party (BNP) with the help of his military aides bringing splinter groups of different political parties representing different—sometimes even exactly opposite—ideologies together to legitimise the civilianization of the military rule (Khan, Islam and Haque, 1996: 22). The BNP needed a rural support base, and the creation of new local government institutions provided the party with an opportunity to win over local leaders. Thus, while all attempts at reforms in local government were ostensibly aimed at satisfying the aspirations of the people to participate in local affairs, and at improving conditions in the localities through rural development, they were primarily intended as a network of support for the central rulers (Huque, 1988: 172).

Zia depended more on civilian-military bureaucratic institutions than on political ones (Chowdhury, 1995: 217) and continued the control of Government officials over the local bodies and at the same time introduced the provision of election (which never took place) to pick elected members at the *Zila Parishad*. Just to please the public representatives he introduced parallel body (*Thana* Development Committee) with ex-officio representation at the *Thana* level with authority to take developmental activities. To further concentrate its power at the grassroots, Zia introduced the *Swanirvar Gram Sarkar* in 1980 as the fourth tier of the local government system. This micro-governmental system actually amalgamated two programmes—the *Swanirvar Bangladesh Andolan* (Movement for a Self-reliant Bangladesh) and *Gram Sarkar* (village Government), which had been successfully experimented with by private initiatives and sans initial support of the Government (Zafarullah and Khan, 1994: 647). General Zia was impressed by the progress and convinced the leaders of the ruling BNP, members of his Cabinet and Government officials of the need for having village-based organizations. The political benefits that would accrue to the BNP made Zia and followers persist in their endeavours (Huque, 1988: 46-58).

The SGS died rather prematurely without being allowed to work for any considerable length of time. They were abolished by the succeeding regime, which came to power through another *coup d'ētat* in early 1982. But, even during their existence, these grassroots 'governments' were influenced and controlled by the bureaucracy and used for narrow partisan purposes. In effect they were used to serve as the underpinning for the BNP—the political party launched by General Zia (Zafarullah and Khan, 1994: 647).

General Ershad Period (1982-1990)

Like Sheikh Mujib, General Zia was also assassinated by a group of army officers on May 30, 1981 and Lieutenant General H.M. Ershad, the then Chief of Army Staff, proclaimed Martial Law throughout the country for the second time in the history of Bangladesh on March 24, 1982. Justice Abdus Sattar, elected President of the country, was forced to resign and Ershad became the Chief Martial Law Administrator (CMLA).

Keeping in mind the realities of politics in Bangladesh, the rulers were keen to build up a support base for themselves not only in the capital, but in the outlying areas as well. Following the example of the previous regime, they eyed the local government system, and saw that there was scope for reorganization at the lower levels (Huque 1988: 180).

The Military Government introduced a three-tier local government structure and the middle tier (renamed as *Upazila Parishad*—UZP) was made the focal point. Responsibility for all developmental activities at the local level was transferred to the *Upazila Parishad*. The National Government retained direct responsibility for regulatory functions and major developmental activities of national and regional importance. In order to give effect to the Government Resolution the *Local Government (Thana Parishad and Thana Administration Reorganization) Ordinance 1982* was promulgated on December 23, 1982. The only change compared to the Zia regime was the renaming of *Thana* to *Upazila* (Sub-District) (Hasan 2004: 128).

Table 12.6: Local Government System in General Ershad Regime

Tier	*Local Govern-ment Institution*	*Type of Selection*	*Elector/ Selector*	*Person in Charge*	*Prescri-bed Authority*
District	Zila Parishad	Ex-officio Represen-tation and Nomina-tion	Govern-ment	Chairman	Divisional Commi-ssioner
Upazila (Sub-District)	Upazila Parishad	Election, Nomina-tion and Ex-officio Represent-ation	Adult Franchise and Deputy Commi-ssioner	Chairman	Deputy Commi-ssioner
Union	Union Parishad	Election and Nomina-tion	Adult Franchise and Upazila Parishad	Chairman	Deputy Commissi -oner
Village	Palli Parishad	Election	Adult Franchise	*Gram Prodhan* (Village Chief)	—

Sources: *The Local Government (Union Parishads) Ordinance 1983; The Local Government (Thana Parishad and Thana Administration Reorganization) Ordinance 1982; The Palli Parishad Act 1989; The Local Government (Zila Parishad) Act 1988;* M. Mahbubur Rahman Morshed, *Bureaucratic Response to Administrative Decentralization: A Study of Bangladesh Civil Service* (Dhaka: The University Press Limited, 1997).

The UZP consists of a directly elected Chairman, all elected Chairmen of UP within the *Upazila*, four nominated members including three women, Chairman of the *Upazila* Central Co-operative Association, and National Government officials working at the *Upazilas* in different nation-building departments. The UZP Chairman was given the status of a Deputy Secretary to the Government and most importantly the civil servants located at *Upazila* were now made accountable to the UZP. UZP Chairman was also held responsible for writing the Annual Confidential Report of the civil servants located at *Upazila* level (Morshed, 1997: 147). But the National Government retained the right to direct, control, and interfere in the affairs of the *Parishad*, if and when the Government so desired. The elected body has very little to do in Planning, Programming and Project Design (PPPD). In fact, in performing their functions in the arena of PPPD they are directed, guided, controlled, monitored and evaluated by the designated officials of the National Government. It can, therefore, be argued that the democratic and autonomous appearance of the UZP was an attempt to camouflage the fact that was controlled by the National Government persisted as ever before. The political interest of Ershad was the primary motive behind the creation of the institution of *Upazila Parishad* (Hakim, 1993: 17-18).

Besides, *Zila Parishad* was totally changed to a nominated body of the Government consisting of public officials. Its only function worth mentioning was coordination of developmental activities in *Upazilas* under its territorial jurisdiction and in doing so it was under the total domination of bureaucrats (Zafarullah and Khan, 1994: 647). Except some cosmetic changes rules and regulations relating to UP were remained the same.

Therefore, from the policies of previous regimes with regard to local government and decentralization it becomes apparent that the governments efforts perhaps were not primarily for decentralization, development or nation-building. The system was just casually changed by the Government perhaps to create a new image of local Government and widen their support base (Hoque, 1986: 6). Since the two major political parties, the AL and the BNP were leading the opposition to the government, the regime could not extend its support base among the masses and beyond the personnel of the armed forces. At the end of 1982, the regime managed to organize pro-government students, youths and labour fronts. The various fronts were brought under a common banner of an 18-point programme announced by Ershad. The programmes sought to solve the socio-economic problems of Bangladesh. And at the local levels, the leaders were ready to take advantage of the opportunities opened up by the changes in the system of local Government. By late February 1984, a quarter of the candidates of *Upazila Parishad* election declared their loyalty to Ershad (Huque, 1988: 179) and helped him to stay in power till December 6, 1990.

The Bangladesh Nationalist Party Period I (1991-1996)

After the mass upsurge in December 4, 1990 against the military dictator H.M. Ershad, Bangladesh Nationalists Party (BNP) headed by widow of General Zia—Begum Khaleda Zia—won the election and formed Government on March 20, 1991. On November 24, 1991, the *Upazila Parishad* system was declared null and void by promulgating the *Local Government (Upazila Parishad and Upazila Administration Reorganization) (Repeal) Ordinance 1991*. It was replaced by *Thana* Development Coordination Committee (TDCC) consisting of all UP chairpersons with the local Member of the Parliament (MP) acting as advisor. Except this everything was as before till 1997 (Hasan, 2004: 129).

Table 12.7: Local Government System in BNP Regime I

Tier	*Local Govern-ment Body*	*Type of Selection*	*Elector/ Selector*	*Person in-Charge*	*Prescri-bed Authority*
District	Zila Parishad	Ex-officio Represent-ation and Nomina-tion	Govern-ment	Chairman	Divisional Commi-ssioner
Thana	Thana Develop-ment Coordina-tion Commi-ttee	Ex-officio Represen-tation		Member of the Parlia-ment as Advisor	
Union	Union Parishad	Election	Adult Franchise	Chairman	Deputy Commi-ssioner

Sources: M. Mahbubur Rahman Morshed, *Bureaucratic Response to Administrative Decentralization: A Study of Bangladesh Civil Service* (Dhaka: The University Press Limited, 1997); Abul Maal Abdul Muhith, *Government for Districts* (Dhaka: The University Press Limited, 2002).

The abolition of *Upazila* system was prompted not by any rational administrative or economic reason but by political factors; the new leadership, which was instrumental in leading the movement against the previous regime, was determined to get rid of almost everything done by its adversary. The Prime Minister and other key Ministers minced no words in censuring the existing system lock, stock, and barrel. They were unwilling to let the system continue even with modifications; indeed, they were keen to see it replaced by a system of their own making (Zafarullah and Khan, 1994: 647-648).

The Government decision, therefore; can be described as vengeance against Ershad and his regime. The reasons probably: Firstly, from the very beginning, Begum Khaleda Zia was accusing Ershad of being involved in the murder of General Zia. Secondly, Ershad seized power through a bloodless *coup d'ētat*, which was unconstitutional and illegal while BNP was in power. Thirdly, after assuming power Ershad cancelled the activities of *Swanirvar Gram Sarkar*—the last contribution that Zia brought into local government system. Fourthly, the *Upazila* system was introduced in an autocratic era and everything of that era should be voided. Fifthly, the UZP and its chair persons played a key role in promoting Ershad and his autocratic rule. Finally, the term '*Upazila*' was coined for the first time by Ershad Government and for that if *Upazila* system survives so would Ershad.

The Awami League Period II (1996-2001)

The Awami League came back to power after 21 years in 1996 after the assassination of the then President *Bangabandhu* Sheikh Mujib. Therefore, the new leadership of the AL was very much cautious about the political programmes and initiatives. So, the Government constituted a seven-member Local Government Commission to give report on the strengthening of Local Government Institutions in September 1996 and the Commission submitted its report in May 1997.

The Commission was asked to act under the Article 9, 11, 59 and 60 of the Constitution of Bangladesh (GOB 1997a: i). Besides, the Commission strongly considered the verdict and directions given by the Supreme Court in a case regarding local government in the previous regime of the BNP.[1] So, the guiding philosophy for the Commission was to establish local government body at each level of administration with elected representatives.

The Commission proposed a four-tier local government system

for Bangladesh (GOB 1997a: 24). According to the recommendations of the Commission the Parliament enacted *The Local Government (Gram Parishad) Act 1997* (Act No. 21 of 1997) by repealing the *Palli Parishad Act 1989*. This act was enacted bearing article 59 of the Constitution in mind and declared the *Gram Parishad* as an administrative unit of the republic according to the article 152(1) of the Constitution (GOB 1997b: Clause 3). Besides, the AL Government made some changes in the composition of *Union Parishad* like dividing the Union into nine wards and direct election of women members in reserved seats, reinstated the *Upazila Parishad* system by renaming *Thana* to *Upazila* in December 1998 (Hasan 2004: 130), had passed the *Zila Parishad Act 2000* on July 2000 consisting of 21 indirectly elected members (Muhith, 2002: 49).

The UP election held in December 1997 under the amended UP Ordinance. But the AL Government failed to hold election of other local bodies—*Gram Parishad*, *Upazila Parishad*, and *Zila Parishad*. However, a writ petition challenging the *Gram Parishad* Act and political hesitancy about the functions and composition of UZP compelled the AL Government to take any attempt to implement *Gram Parishad* and to hold UZP election in its tenure.

The Bangladesh Nationalist Party Period II (2001-2006)

Clinching the victory in the eighth Parliament election of 2001, the BNP led Four Party Alliance took initiative to introduce *Gram Sarkar*—the programme of late President Ziaur Rahman—at the ward level amid the opposition of other political parties. The Government enacted *the Gram Sarkar Act 2003* and gave priority to form the proposed *Gram Sarkar* (GS) (Hasan, 2004: 130). The Ministry of Local Government and Rural Development and Cooperatives supervised the formation in forty-five days starting from August 2, 2003 to September 15, 2003 and formed 39,768 GSs out of 40,392 (Star, 2003a: 3).

Right from the beginning, the formation process invited criticisms from various quarters due to a lack of people's spontaneous participation. The Government formed many GS without quorum and some without appropriate members while the formation has triggered feuds among rival groups in places. The ruling BNP or BNP-leaning activists dominate all these GSs (Ahsan, 2003b: 1). A survey based on the reports of formation of 1150 GSs published in

Table 12.8: Local Government System in the Awami League Regime II

Tier	*Local Govern-ment Body*	*Type of Selection*	*Elector/ Selector*	*Person in-Charge*	*Prescri-bed Authority*
District	Zila Parishad	Indirect Election	People's Represen-tatives of City Corpora-tions/ Upazila Parishad/ Poura-shava/ Union Parishad	Chairman	
Upazila	Upazila Parishad	Election and Ex-officio Represen-tation	Adult Franchise	Chairman	Deputy Commi-ssioner
Union	Union Parishad	Election	Adult Franchise	Chairman	Deputy Commi-ssioner
Village	Gram Parishad	Election	Adult Franchise	Chairman	Any Person Empo-wered by Govern-ment

Sources: *The Zila Parishad Act 2000* (Act No. 19 of 2000); *The Upazila Parishad Act 1998* (Act No. 24 of 1998); *The Local Government (Union Parishads) Ordinance 1983* (Amendment of 1997); *The Local Government (Gram Parishad) Act 1997*.

leading newspapers, found that the rules and procedures were not followed in majority (53%) of the cases and there was no quorum in 60 per cent of the places. Satisfactory and enthusiastic participation was observed in only 3.39 per cent of the cases. The *Upazila Nirbahi Officers* (Chief Executive officer at *Upazila*) ignored the rules and procedures in 54.96 per cent of the cases. The administration was found to be neutral in only 10.87 per cent instances. Evidence of the nomination of opposition party members was found in less than 1 per cent cases (Gupta 2003: 5). At the end, *Gram Sarkar* has become the ward-based extension of the Bangladesh Nationalists Party (BNP) and is a parallel institution threatening the very existence of the UP, which is a time-tested 135-year old institution (Majumdar 2005: 10).

Table 12.9: Local Government System in BNP Regime II

Tier	*Local Government Body*	*Type of Selection*	*Elector/ Selector*	*Person in Charge*	*Prescribed Authority*
District	Zila Parishad	Indirect Election	People's Representatives of City Corporation/ Upazila Parishad/ Pourashava/ Union Parishad	Chairman	
Upazila	Upazila Parishad	Election and Ex-officio Representation	Adult Franchise	Chairman	Deputy Commissioner
Union	Union Parishad	Election	Adult Franchise	Chairman	Deputy Commissioner
Village	Gram Sarkar	Consensus of 10% of Total Electorates		*Gram Sarkar Pradhan* (Village Government Chief)	Upazila Nirbahi Officer/ Circle Officer (Development)

Sources: *The Zila Parishad Act 2000* (Act No. 19 of 2000); *The Upazila Parishad Act 1998* (Act No. 24 of 1998); *The Local Government (Union Parishads) Ordinance 1983* (Amendment of 1997); *The Gram Sarkar Act 2003*.

Moreover, the BNP-led Government failed to take any decision regarding the UZP and *Zila Parishad*, rather the high up of the Government was divided into two opposite opinions over the issues like implementation process, the role of MPs, etc. (Begum, 2002: 228).

Concluding Remarks

The history of local government in Bangladesh shows that changes in levels of local bodies with the change of Government have created confusion in the minds of people while making it difficult for local bodies concerned to play any effective role in the absence of stability. Similar to the changes in levels, on the issue of representation also continuity has not been maintained. Emphasis on elected members has alternated with the system of nomination at various times (GOB, 1997a: 2).

This colonial legacy was not only the factor that led to the failure of local government reforms in Bangladesh. The absence of tangible rewards to be won by participating in local affairs often resulted in apathy and a resignation to fate by the villagers. Sometimes, family feuds and social rivalry were accorded more importance than local public affairs. Since the creation of Pakistan, the initiation of major developmental projects suddenly increased the importance of local bodies. Local leaders started to compete for the control of these institutions. Factionalism became prominent, and in many cases, obstructed the growth of local government. Uneven political mobilization affected all these factors, and villages were not adequately prepared to respond to reforms (Huque, 1988: 41).

The initiatives in various periods were sometimes conflicting and sometimes confusing. There is no rational basis or satisfactory explanation behind these changes. At the same time, the very broad nature of the responsibilities of the bodies has made it difficult to identify the specific activities that have been assigned to a particular level. But there are some similarities among these initiatives: firstly, governments at various times emphasized various levels as focal point of development and this measure left the other levels neglected in terms of responsibilities and fund allocation. In the name of block allocation for GS the Government has paved the way for plundering money by its men in rural areas. Previously allocations were made through institutions like UP, which is now being taking place through the leaders and activists of the ruling party. A news analysis in the *New Age*—a national daily—confirmed that in the 2005-2006 budget of $ 12 million was allocated for GSs as block allocation, which was distributed through the party-men of the ruling party keeping the next general election in mind.

Secondly, most of these initiatives were politically motivated. The first two military regimes used local government bodies to create their support base at grassroots levels. Local government bodies have undergone political vengeance at the second political regime and implementation of a 'dream' without judging its utility at the fourth political regime.

Thirdly, all of the governments used bureaucratic control over the local government bodies even though some were composed of elected representatives on the basis of adult franchise. To ensure control there was the provision of nominated members. The degree of control (direct or indirect) varied period to period only which have impinged on the autonomy of the local bodies.

Fourthly, all the governments were sceptical about the role of MPs in the local government bodies. In a country like Bangladesh, MPs not only play legislative role but also the developmental role. MPs are the main development agent. Therefore, MPs in their part want to have advisory role (which should be compulsory for the specific level to follow) at all levels of local government bodies. Since 1997, the advisory role has even extended to *Union Parishads* and hesitancy to ensure the effective role of MPs in the *Upazila* system is hindering the establishment of UZP system.

And finally, there is a visible conflict in the high commands of different governments regarding the establishment of decentralized and empowered local government system with devolution of key service functions and proper resource allocations. Local government bodies could never be made fully representative. Therefore, the low level of development and the limited franchise restricted popular participation.

NOTE

1. On July 30, 1992 in the Quadrat-e-Elahi Panir *vs.* Bangladesh, *44 DLR (AD) 319,* the Appellate Division ordered the Government of Bangladesh to modify the existing local government laws in accordance with the Articles 59 and 60 of the Constitution and at the same time the Appellate Division ordered the Government to hold the election of local government bodies within six months.

REFERENCES

Abedin, N. (1973). *Local Administration and Politics in Modernizing Societies: Bangladesh and Pakistan*. Dhaka: The National Institute of Public Administration.

Ahmed, A. (1979). *Administration of Local Self Government for Rural Areas in Bangladesh*. Dhaka: Local Government Institute.

Ahsan, Z. (2003). 'Gram Sarkar struggles to get people's zeal', *The Daily Star*, 19 August, p. 1.

Begum, R.A. (1984). 'Local Government in Ancient and Medieval Bengal', in Siddiqui, K., ed., *Local Government in Bangladesh*. Dhaka: National Institute of Local Government.

Begum, S. (2002). *Public Administration in Bangladesh*. Dhaka: Mallick Brothers.

Choudhury, L.H. (1987). *Local Self-Government and its Reorganization in Bangladesh*. Dhaka: National Institute of Local Government.

Chowdhury, D. (1995). *Constitutional Development in Bangladesh: Stresses and Strains*. Dhaka: University Press Limited.

Faizullah, M. (1985). 'Functioning of Local Government in Bangladesh', in Hye, H.A. (ed.), *Decentralization of Local Government Institutions and Resource Mobilization*. Comilla: Bangladesh Academy for Rural Development.

Friedman, H.J. (1960). 'Pakistan's Experiment in Basic Democracies', *Pacific Affairs*, 33.

Friedman, H.J. (1961). 'Notes on Pakistan's Basic Democracies', *Asian Survey*, 1.

GOB (Government of Bangladesh) (1972). Memorandum No. S-1/1U-7/72/103 dated the 28th April, 1972. Dhaka: Ministry of Local Government, Rural Development and Co-operatives, Local Government Division.

GOB (1976). *The Local Government Ordinance 1976*. Dhaka: Bangladesh Government Press.

GOB (1997a). *Report of The Local Government Commission*. Dhaka: Bangladesh Government Press.

GOB (1997b). *The Local Government (Gram Parishad) Act 1997*. Dhaka: Bangladesh Government Press.

Gupta, A.D. (2003). 'The Selection Process of Gram Sarkar: A Survey Based on Newspaper Reports', *The Daily Jugantor*, November 6, p. 5.

Hakim, M.A. (1993). *Bangladesh Politics: The Shahabuddin Interregnum*. Dhaka: University Press Limited.

Hasan, S. (2004). 'Local Government at Village Level: A Study of Gram Parishad Act 1997 and Gram Sarkar Act 2003', *The Chittagong University Journal of Law*, V.

Hoque, A.N.S. (1986). 'Local Government Institution-Building in Bangladesh and their Development Potentials', *Seminar Paper*. Dhaka.

Huque, A.S. (1988). *Politics and Administration in Bangladesh: Problems of Participation*. Dhaka: University Press Limited.

Jahan, R. (1972). *Pakistan: Failure in National Integration*. New York: Columbia University Press.

Khan, M.M. (1991). 'Critical Issues in the Selection Process of Local Leaders in Rural Bangladesh', *The Journal of Local Government*, 20(1).

Khan, S.I.; Islam, S.A. and Haque, M.I. (1996). *Political Culture, Political Parties and the Democratic Transition in Bangladesh*. Dhaka: Academic Publishers.

Majumdar, B.A. (2005). 'Gram Sarkar: A Problematic Initiative', *The Daily Star*, 5 October, p. 10.

Morshed, M.M.R. (1997). *Bureaucratic Response to Administrative Decentralization: A Study of Bangladesh Civil Service*. Dhaka: University Press Limited.

Muhith, A.M.A. (2002). *Government for Districts*. Dhaka: University Press Limited.

Muttalib, M.A. and Khan, M.A.A. (1983). *Theory of Local Government*. New Delhi: Sterling Publishers Private Limited.

Quadir, F. (1972). 'Local Government in Bangladesh: A Critical Review', *Local Government Quarterly*, I, 3.

Roy, N.C. (1937). *Rural Self-Government in Bengal*. Calcutta: Calcutta University.

Siddiqui, K. (1984). *Local Government in Bangladesh*. Dhaka: University Press Limited.

Sobhan, R. (1993). *Bangladesh: Problems of Governance*. Dhaka: University Press Limited.

Tepper, E. (1964). *Changing Patterns of Administration in Rural East Pakistan*. Michigan: Michigan State University.

Thompson, E. and Garatt, G.T. (1934). *Rise and Fulfillment of British Rule in India*. London.

Tinker, H. (1954). *Foundation of Local Self-Government in India, Pakistan and Burma*. London: Athlone Press.

Zafarullah, H.M. and Khan, M.M. (1994). 'Bureaucracy and Rural Development in Bangladesh', in Farazmand, A.(ed.), *Handbook of Bureaucracy*. New York: Marcel Dekker Inc.

13

Critiquing Sustainable Livelihood: An Experience from Rural (Tribal) Andhra

SASI KUMAR

Introduction

Sustainable livelihood is a new term in social sciences in general and anthropology in particular. It is necessarily related to the living strategies of the people. As defined by Robert Chambers and Gorden R. Conway, it comprises of people, their capabilities and their means of living, including food, income and assets. Assets consist of tangible assets and intangible assets. Tangible assets include resources and stores, and intangible assets are claims and access. Robert Chambers and Gorden R. Conway further argues that a livelihood is environmentally sustainable when it maintains or enhances the local and global assets on which livelihoods depend, and has net beneficial effects on other livelihoods. They have the view that a livelihood is socially sustainable which can cope with and recover from stress and shocks, and provide for future generations[1].

For Amartya Sen, sustainable livelihood is a core variable: the nature in which they have changed, transformed and diversified is a central, empirical question. He argues that in particular, we are interested in how rural poors secure entitlement, primarily through production and exchange, to the economic goods required for a means of living[2].

Robert Chambers and Gorden R. Conway noted that capabilities, equity and sustainability combine in the sustainable livelihoods. A livelihood in its simplest sense is a means of gaining a living. Capabilities are, they defined as, both an end and means of livelihood: a livelihood provides the support for the enhancement and exercise of capabilities (an end); and capabilities (a means) enable a livelihood to be gained. They defined equity as both an end and a means: any minimum definition of equity must include adequate and decent livelihoods for all (an end); and equity in assets and access are preconditions (means) for gaining adequate and decent livelihoods. Lastly, sustainability, too, is both end and means: sustainable stewardship of resources is a value (or end) in itself; and provides conditions (a means) for livelihoods to be sustained for future generations[3].

Robert Chamber and Gorden R. Conway argue that as a concept sustainable livelihood was put forward in the report of an Advisory Panel of the World Commission on Environment and Development. It proposed sustainable livelihood security as an integrating concept, and made it central to its report (WCED, 1987). It defines livelihood as follows:

> *"Livelihood is defined as adequate stocks and flows of food and cash to meet basic needs. Security refers to secure ownership of, or access to, resources and income-earning activities, including reserves and assets to offset risk, ease shocks and meet contingencies. Sustainable refers to the maintenance or enhancement of resources productivity on a long-term basis. A household may be enabled to gain sustainable livelihood security in many ways—though ownership of land, livestock or trees; rights to grazing, fishing, hunting, or gathering; through stable employment with adequate remuneration; or through varied repertoires of activities"*[4].

In most of the studies, available to us, on sustainable livelihood contain arguments that reduction of poverty would bring sustainable livelihood. Diana Carney has prepared a document for the Department for International Department (DFID) which is considered as key document. This document gives the conceptual understanding of poverty and how it causes that underpins sustainable livelihood approaches has influenced theory and practice throughout the development world[5].

There are many other views expressed in favour and against the above arguments. However, it has to be noted that most of the development theoreticians say 'growth with development'. This view goes with the capitalist idea on development whether it is sustainable or not. Economic growth is seen as the only way to tackle poverty, and hence to achieve environment-development objectives. The Brundtland Report's vision of sustainable development is predicated on the need to maintain and revitalize the world economy. This means 'more rapid economic growth in both industrial and developing countries, freer market access for the products of developing countries, lower interests rates, greater technology transfer, and significantly larger capital flows, both concessional and commercial' (Brundtland, 1987: 89).[6] Bill Adams identifies the critical objectives for environment and development policies proposed in the Brundtland Report as:

1. Reviving growth,
2. Changing the quality of growth,
3. Meeting essential needs for jobs, food, energy, water and sanitation,
4. Ensuring a sustainable level of population,
5. Conserving and enhancing the resource base,
6. Reorienting technology and managing risk,
7. Merging environment and economics in decision-making.

His criticism is that mainstream thinking about sustainable development not only fails to challenge the capitalist growth paradigm; it is also remarkably resistant to eco-centrist or bio-centrist elements within environmentalism.

Just touching upon the discourse does mean that we want to bring or engage in the whole debate, which has been a part of the literature. Though, the debate is not fully our concern, we cannot negate the fact that there are ideological and political underpinnings related to the whole issue.

Liberalization, Privatization and Globalization (LPG) that started in 1990's was a watershed in India as far as the political economy was concerned. It brought about backtracking the entire idea of the role of State in developmental issues. Role of the State is reduced to be minimal in the economic affairs and state has to withdraw public spending. The marketing of food has become increasingly unsustainable in social, economic and environmental terms. The globalization of food systems and the increasing power and domination of transnational companies (TNCs) over food marketing are seeing small farmers' livelihoods undermined globally; increasing levels of food insecurity; declining farm incomes; loss of people from agriculture; and lost links between producers, community and land. Globalization and trade liberalization are causing food to be transported over longer distance between producers and consumers exacerbating environmental pollution and increasing resource use[7].

It is argued in the same report that the Vision 2020 plan for transforming agriculture in Andhra Pradesh, from subsistence production to farm consolidation and mechanization is expected to cause the displacement of 20 million small farmers from the land (a reduction from 70 per cent to 40 per cent of the population working on the land). This Vision 2020 is being supported by a grant of $ 65 million from the British money[8].

This transformation, however, as we know, would not only directly affect the livelihood of the people of this country but would also harm the food security system of this country. However, specialists in this area argue that the transformation of Indian agriculture did not start with LPG but with the inception of India's "new agricultural strategy" from 1961 onwards. Under the new strategy the Intensive Agricultural Development Programme (IADP) was started in 15 districts selected from the availability of irrigation and absence of acute tenurial problems. High-yielding cereal seed varieties already developed in Mexico and Taiwan, along with fertilizers, pesticides and credit to farmers, were made available at subsidized rates. The high-yielding varieties programme was subsequently extended to all 324 districts in the country[9].

It is interesting to note here that sustainable development of people is a complex web of affairs, which needs a lot of attention. K.N. Reddy and N.S. Balaji Rao argues that modern civilization is like a tempest and today the traditional maintenance of interdependence among the tribes is put to cease and is thrown to individualistic living, thus they are eking out their life and livelihood in an uneasy situation putting their future at stake. They struggle between traditionalism and modernism and are caught between change and resistance and live amidst confusion over changing context of livelihood matters.[10]

Whatever may have been the mainstream arguments, which directly or indirectly supported the LPG, which, in turn, quite convincingly propagated that LPG would have more or less improved the livelihoods of the people. This view would be examined with the support of fieldwork data (mainly livelihood schedules and other methods) collected by the researcher from Mankapur Village in Adilabad district of Andhra Pradesh.

We would be examining the natural resources available to the community as a whole and how they are distributed among the households under five major heads: (1) Natural Capital, (2) Physical Capital, (3) Human Capital, (4) Social Capital, and (5) Financial Capital. The resources can be divided into tangible assets as well as non-tangible assets. Tangible assets include natural and physical capital and non-tangible assets include human, social and financial capital. Secondly, it is important to see how these assets are managed by the community as well as by the individual households.

Natural Capital

Land is considered as the main source of income for each household in the community. Land is not divided equally among households in the community. This unequal division has many implications for community in terms of their income and livelihood. Most of the people are marginal farmers who have to also work on others' lands for eking out their livelihoods. Much of the land available to cultivate is plain, dry and pasture land. Over the years, they have changed the cropping pattern.

Extent of Land

Land Details	*No. of Households*	*Percentage*
Landless	21	31.8%
1-5 acres	21	31.8%
6-10 acres	15	22.7%
11-15 acres	4	6.1%
16-20 acres	4	6.1%
21-25 acres	1	1.5%
		100.0%

The fertility of most of the land they cultivate is remarkably low and this again keeps their income level low and livelihoods unsustainable. There is high land in the area, which is not cultivable at all. The people use this land to graze their cattle, sheep, etc. These high lands were previously forested area but now they are completely deforested.

Forests and Water

Forests of the surrounding areas have been completely destroyed. Villagers get timber, firewood and other resources like Mahua flower from the forest, which is more than 5-7 km. away. All the households in the village have access to the forest. For firewood and timber they are completely dependent on the forest. This area is known for shortage of water. There are a few streams, springs, rivulets and other sources of running water but the location of the settlement in relation to the available water is such that both the access to irrigation and to clean drinking water is a problem. Irrigation system does not exist even nominally. Even though the resources exist in the area, they are poorly managed.

Livestock

Most of the households possess livestock in the form of 2-3 cows, bullocks, buffaloes, sheep and a few poultry. Bullocks are used to plough the soil for sowing seeds. It is found that villagers use bullock-carts as a mode of transportation for goods from the village to the market and *vice versa*. Bullock carts are also used to bring firewood and timber from the forest. The raising of cows, buffaloes and sheep is to be seen in the context of the villagers obtaining enough milk products for household consumption; products, which help them to maintain physical strength by giving them some nutrition. They do not sell the milk products. The raising of poultry is also to be seen in the same way. However, they are increasingly finding it difficult to get enough fodder for their livestock in the current situation.

Livestock

Category	*Total Number*
Oxen	69
Cows	56
Buffaloes	46
Sheep	48
Goats	60
Poultry	40

Flora and Fauna

With the increase in population, when the villagers fail to meet their increasing energy as well as other requirements they opt to depend mostly on the flora and fauna. This part of temporary solution already had adversely affected the environment and the diversity of flora and fauna in this area.

Physical Capital

Basic Living Space and Shelter

The houses where villagers live can be classified under three categories: *kutcha*, semi *pucca* and *pucca*. *Kutcha*, houses are made of bamboo, mud and other natural materials. The floor is levelled and cow dung is used to plaster the floor. Most of the semi-*pucca* houses are made of bamboo, mud and other items. However, in most cases, the walls are either made of bricks or the roof is reinforced with concrete or the floor is cemented. *Pucca* houses are made of bricks and roof is reinforced with concrete and the floor is cemented. It is important to note here that there are toilets attached to all the *pucca* houses. However the toilets are usually found to be completely neglected. All the *kutcha*, semi-*pucca* and *pucca* houses are not very spacious, with no windows and air circulation. The Government under various housing schemes has sanctioned the *pucca* houses, but most of the *pucca* houses have been converted into 'store houses' as it is difficult for them to stay in these houses in summer.

Types of Houses

House Type	*No. of Houses*	*Percentage*
Pucca	8	12.2%
Kutcha	36	54.5%
Semi-pucca	22	33.3%
	66	**100%**

Agricultural Machinery and Equipments

There is no modern agricultural machinery or equipment found in the village Only few peasants have these machineries and equipments and others completely depend on those farmers who have these machineries and equipments. This sometimes affects the cultivation and subsequently the production process itself. There is little hope of the communities acquiring new machinery and at best, the majority is likely to be dependent on the few individuals who are able to purchase or acquire the machinery or equipments. Groups formed for the purpose of sharing machinery do exist in the village and often work best if they comprise of close relatives or members of a particular clan.

Food and Clothing

Generally speaking, the rural poors have one advantage over the urban poors, that they usually possess assets in the form of land, even if it is only 2-3 acres of land from which they feed themselves, albeit at a rather basic level. Extended family networks and the social responsibilities existing in village communities and between close neighbours also mean that even the destitute are seldom allowed starving. But, it is found that the poverty is on the increase, particularly among the poorest, and that people are reduced to living on the bare minimum for most of the year. The local doctor speaks of the increasing number of cases of malnutrition among the village poors, especially among children and pregnant and nursing mothers.

Changes in the agricultural pattern due to commercialization of agriculture brought about a consequent change in the food pattern. It is found that significant changes have occurred in the food pattern in the last 10-15 years among 70-80 per cent of the households. Subsequently, the intake of rice has been on the rise. They cultivate their traditional *jowar* at their minimum disposal and few households depend on the market for foodgrains completely. The introduction of soya and cotton cultivation for the market and the cash economy has jeopardized the food pattern in an extreme way to such an extent that they have given up the cultivation of pulses and grams completely. The adoption of rice intake and commercial agriculture complement each other and this has significantly affected the livelihoods of the people in the village.

Most people use old clothes, most of which are already torn because of prolonged use. In fact, it demands lot of expenditure on the part of the households. Older people wear old fashioned clothes but the young have started wearing western style clothes.

Hospitals and Clinics

Village people have to depend on one Government Primary Health Centre (PHC), which is situated 2 km. away. It has five sub-centres in and around the area. One sub-centre is actually meant for twelve habitations. It has been found that the condition of the PHC is very pathetic and it has only one doctor and a staff nurse. The others are OPANM 1, MPHS 1 (the post reserved for women is vacant) PHN 1, Pharmacist 1 and Lab Technician 1. This PHC, which is meant for treating 22,000 people, has nothing to offer to the people. There are no beds in the PHC and no X-ray facility or other equipment to treat the people who approach the PHC. Usually, 50-100 people suffering from diarrhoea, malaria, upper respiratory throat infection, typhoid, gastro-enteritis, etc., approach the PHC.

Schools

There is a primary school (from 1st to 5th standard) in the village, which is in a dilapidated stage. There are only two rooms where the teachers run five classes at a time. There are 3 teachers to teach these five classes. The total number of students is 82 but the usual attendance is only around 70. Midday meals are served to the students regularly.

Literacy Figures of the Gond Community

	Illiterate	*(1-7) Primary*	*(8-10) Secondary*	*Intermediate*	*College*	*Total*
Male	66	29	27	10	03	161
Female	80	40	39	02	—	195
Total	**146**	**69**	**66**	**12**	**03**	**356**

There is another Ashram school close to the village, which was built in 1974. The students who get admitted here (from 6th to 10th standard) have to travel 8 kilometres from the village and the separate schools are for both boys and girls students. It is because of this reason that the school has no significant impact on people of the village even though it runs well.

Drinking Water Supply in the Village

Water tanks have been built in the village under Rural Water Supply (RWS) since 2001. At present, there are four water tanks that supply water to the villagers. Before these tanks were built, villagers used to fetch water from the wells that were far away. Even after the water tanks have been built, fetching water is a tiresome job for women and children. Even now, in summer, they are forced to fetch water from far away places. This seriously affects the health and education of children and women.

Rural Roads and Electricity

Roads to the village are partially concreted and are in a bad state. According to the villagers, these roads almost become ponds in the rainy season and are difficult to access. These roads that are built under different schemes thus serve no purpose.

Almost all the houses in the village were electrified way back in 1970s. Those whose houses are not electrified steal electricity from the lines that come to the village.

Communication and Newspapers

Tele-communication facilities are completely absent. Villagers who have to make call to any one staying outside have to go to Narnoor, almost 2 km. away from the village. One post office is working in the village in a small hut. There is only one newspaper *i.e., Andhra Bhoomi*, is bought, by the shop owner, which some of the villagers come to the shop and read.

Human Capital

Education and Literacy

Education and literacy are completely neglected as far as the villagers are concerned. The utter poverty of the villagers prevents them from sending their children to the school. The awareness of what education means for the future generation is also lacking in them. Secondly, for them, a 6-7 years old child looks after the house, their younger ones and aged people in the household. Girl children are completely deprived of schooling. Dropouts in the primary classes are more than those in the higher classes. It is also found that medium of teaching being Telugu creates many problems for the children in understanding subjects at the primary level and medium of teaching in their own mother tongue (Gondi) would have to be adopted which can solve the discord or disjuncture so far as the language is concerned.

Literacy Figures of Tribal Community

	Illiterate	*(1-7) Primary*	*(8-10) Secondary*	*Intermediate*	*Degree*
Gond	146	69	66	12	03

The syllabus adopted in the schools in the village is the Andhra Pradesh (A.P.). State Government syllabus. The teaching medium is Telugu and the children from the villages are taught only in this medium. The dominant view of the villagers is that the introduction of Gondi as a medium of teaching in at least in the primary section would have reduced the dropouts. Till now authorities have not paid any attention in this regard.

Marketing

Due to illiteracy and the lack of a communication system the villagers are unaware of the demand, prices and quality of their products and of market facilities. They also lack of technical or marketing information, which is a determining factor when the product should be sold in the market and, at which prices, etc., Girijan Co-operative Corporation (GCC) only purchases Minor Forest Products (MFP) from the farmers in the month of March every year. They only collect the Mahua flower from the villagers. If the GCC could purchase their entire produce of a particular season, this would provide a greater impetus for the farmers and they can be saved, to a large extent, from the exploitation by the money-lenders and other agents.

Health

There are an increasing number of health problems in the village. Diseases such as brucellosis, tuberculosis, diarrhoea, malaria, upper respiratory throat infection, typhoid and gastro enteritis are on the increase. Due to malnutrition many people, particularly women and children, become anaemic. Illness is one of the main reasons that lead most the people in the community to depend on private health care centres. The cost of health care and loss of family labour can reduce a reasonably well off family to poverty.

Social Capital

Traditional vs. Modern System

Market economy brought its despair and fluctuation not only in the economic life but also in social life. The say of traditional head in the affairs of community life is getting narrowed down due to the impact of modern political system. After adoption of modern political system, it is found that the evils of it crept into the entire affairs of the community. Disbelief and corruption have been affecting all the projects, which are basically intended to improve the life of the people. Traditional head here becomes a contractor and his brother becomes Sarpanch of the Panchayat.

Financial Capital

Gonds lack of financial capital. Cash economy plays a significant role in every exchange they make now-a-day in payment of land revenue, purchasing schoolbooks and whatever they buy in the market.

Savings

The villagers have no substantial savings in banks or any cash in hand so far as the households are concerned. The rural banking system is neither properly established nor well connected; institutional credit is not available to the villagers and this has led to the villagers becoming completely dependent on money-lenders for agricultural loans. This is a serious concern. Only 20 odd households have meagre amount of savings in the post office in which they deposit Rs. 20 per month.

Wages

The wages are very low during non-agricultural season. The lowest wage is Rs. 40 per day. It varies from Rs. 40 to 80 per day in accordance with the season and during the agricultural season they get around Rs. 80. There is a high disparity in wages between male and female labourers. Females get around Rs. 25 if it is a non-agricultural season and they are paid Rs. 50 during season. There are only two households who completely depend upon the salaries in the village.

Crop Sales

The paradox is that even though the villagers produce cash crops like soya and cotton for the market they would not get any thing in cash. It only serves to pay back the loan that they took in the beginning of the period from the money-lender. All the buyers in a way are money-lender who provide loans and buy the produce at lower price than the market price.

Food for Work Programme

Under this scheme small construction works are carried out in summer when villagers do not find any agricultural job. Wage labourers and the landless poor work in the construction of small roads, canals, percolation tank, mud roads and repairing roads. Wages are given in kind as well as in cash. They are given Rs. 80 worth of rice and Rs. 20 in cash. It is found that there is a lot of mismanagement of funds and corruption (See the case study of Kotnag Pawan in the vulnerability context).

National Old Age Pension Scheme and Benefits

Under the scheme, the Government provides a pension of Rs. 100 per month to the aged (65 years above), widows, and disabled people. But under this scheme deserved people are not getting the benefits.

Credit Facility

Credit availability through the bank is crucial for the villagers. The reasons are many. One is low rate of interest; the bank only takes 2 per cent interest for crop loan. It is meant for purchasing seeds, pesticides, livestock and amenities. In the initial period the bank only provides Rs. 2,000 subsequently if the loan is paid back, it would increase the amount. One problem villagers found in the whole system is that the amount is quite less than their actual need and the time taken in sanctioning of the loan. The loan is sanctioned long after they apply for a loan and this many times does not serve the purpose.

The Government had been providing loans through DWCRA groups since many years. (This programme has now become the Velugu Project, after getting a loan from the World Bank). In the year 2000-01 Velugu started giving loans to the members who had taken membership in the groups. The membership to the group is Rs. 30 and the account is maintained in the group name. There are 6 self-help groups working in the village. Each group has 10-15 members and has a President and Secretary. After 6 months of savings they can apply for a loan at the rate of 2 per cent interest. It is found that even the purpose of giving loans is to empower women in the village and help in the reduction of poverty. However these groups utilize the funds for fulfilling their immediate needs in life. It is nothing to do with the empowerment of women but to increase the purchasing power by distributing meagre amount of money.

Mutually Aided Co-operative Society (MACS) is an NGO, which also provides crop loan. Only in June 2001 it was established in the village and it takes 2 per cent interest. In the initial days it provided loans for land reclamation and development. Three Self-Help Groups (SHG's) are working under it. (i) Ganesh, (ii) Radhalaxmi, and (iii) Saibaba. To get membership in the MACS, each member has to give Rs. 510. Out of this Rs. 100 goes to share capital, Rs. 10 goes to membership, Rs. 300 goes to saving and Rs. 100 death insurance relief fund. The SHGs under MACS are doing better than the ones under Velugu Project.

The vulnerability context and the coping mechanisms have a major effects on the sustainable livelihoods of the people. It could be seen that the villagers are highly vulnerable to the shocks and stresses and the coping mechanism of the people are important while discussing the problems they face in this area. The study shows that there are at least four vulnerability contexts (*i.e.* shocks and stresses) existing in the village: (a) Environmental vulnerability, (b) Economic and Social vulnerability, (c) Political vulnerability, (d) Policies, Institutions and Processes.

Environmental Vulnerability and Coping Mechanism

Floods and draughts in consecutive years affected agricultural production. In the month of June-July if the amount of rainfall is more than expected, large scale damage to crops occurs. This is the time when villagers start their cultivation process. Due to rain everything may get washed away including the seeds. The seedlings will dry out if the rainfall is less than adequate. These two kinds of vagaries of weather wreck havoc on the life of the people. The summer is too long and temperature shoots up to 48° C, which makes life unbearable for the villagers. In the summer season, scarcity of water and scarcity of fodder for the livestock also leads to an alarming situation.

Illness due to environmental vulnerability combined with malnutrition appeared to be an important feature of rural life. Human health is more vulnerable to the environment when they do not have access to clean water, food and cloth. The dependence of villagers on private doctors is a serious concern because the resources of the family are spent on the health of the member leading to a worsening of the poverty of the family. Animals are also often struck by the diseases. It has been found that among the livestock Foot and Mouth Diseases (FMD), pneumonia, black water and Haemorrhage Septic (HS) and decline in the cattle population in the village. The veterinary doctor or his assistant visits the villagers once in 3-4 months only. Among the poultry it is found that Fowl Pox and the Ranikhet Diseases (RD) are common. In Narnoor Mandal only one hospital and one sub-centre are working which is inadequate to the needs of the villagers. The diseases that strike both men and animals ultimately affect the sustainable livelihood strategies of villagers.

Economic and Social Vulnerability and Coping Mechanism

Our study revealed that money-lenders have been exploiting the tribals leading to their pauperisation and it has a serious impact on the sustainable livelihood of the tribals. Money-lenders are allowed freely to exploit the villagers without any hindrance. Institutional rural credit facilities (except a branch of Bank of Hyderabad) are very minimal. Unlike the private money-lenders, bank needs *Patta* (Record of Land Rights) to extend the loan, which for the small and marginal farmers is an intriguing question. Most of them do not possess *Pattas* and are thus not qualified for bank loan. Not only that bank gives meagre amount of loan which is not even partially satisfying their need at the beginning of the agricultural season. Bank would not give loan to defaulting. It starts giving loan with Rs. 1000 as the initial amount and in later years it increases the amount to Rs. 5000 to those farmers who do not default in paying back the loan. The Cooperative banking system has not at all developed in these areas due to which farmers are increasingly dependent on the credit facilities extended by the money-lenders. This has led to exploitation of villagers to a great extent.

Our study shows that there is a money-lender-trader-input supplier nexus leading to the total dependence of the villagers on the money-lenders and once this dependence begins it is difficult to come out of that vicious circle. This nexus, which is a vicious circle, needs to be elaborated a little more here. When a farmer needs loan and goes to money-lender he does not provide money directly to the farmer. Instead he asks him go to specified shops and buy the seeds, chemical, fertilizers and pesticides he requires and the farmer has to sell his crops to the money-lender. Money-lenders never give the actual market price to the farmer; it has always been less than the market price. There are two rates of interest at which money-lenders provides loan to the villagers but the predominant one is *Dedi* (for Rs. 100 Rs. 50 has to be paid after six months), and the other one is *savai* (for Rs. 100 Rs. 25 has to be paid after six months) in which villagers avail of only the '*Dedi*'. This happens, as the villagers have no other option left except to approach the money-lenders. Besides the agricultural season is crucial to them and if they do not get money from money-lenders their livelihood is under threat. The following case study illustrates the case better: Kotnag Pawan used to cultivate around 8 acres of land, which at the height of the rainy season was washed away by water. It is not merely a natural disaster to him but a man-made one (See discussion in policies, institutions and processes). His land is actually situated near the percolation tank, which has been built to store some water to irrigate land. (This percolation tank collapsed two consecutive years, *i.e.,* 2004 August and 2005 July}. He lost his entire investment made for cultivating cotton. Each year, he had spent around Rs. 1600 for cottonseeds, Rs. 2,500 for chemical fertilizers, Rs. 5000 for weeding for which he also employed 25 persons. Borrowing from the money-lender compensated this loss of Rs. 20,000. The only option left to him was to work as wage labourer and earn and pay back the money he had already borrowed from the money-lender. As a wage labourer he would not get more than Rs. 1800 per month. Along with working as a wage labourer, he leased out his land for Rs. 3,500 per annum. When he lost his entire investment Government sanctioned Rs. 500 per acre, which he has not received so far. This case study revealed that it was difficult for a favour to come out of the shock he experienced. His only option seemed to be greater and greater dependence on money-lenders.

The second important factor is that the marriages that are held in an extravagant manner greatly affect the sustainable livelihoods. Among the villagers, marriages are held for five days as a part of tradition. This tradition continues significantly even today. It is found that their resources, mainly financial and human capital, are utilized to conduct these marriages. Villagers, in order to meet marriage expenses, approach money-lenders and borrow huge amounts. It has also been found that villagers are increasingly unable to get help from their kinsmen because all the houses in the village are in the same poverty-stricken situation.

Political Vulnerability

The decision of the Government to implement the green revolution in the village directly or indirectly through various agencies like ITDA has had severe consequences. The Government, did not, at any point of time, examine the peculiar situation existing in the village by conducting a survey or by other methods to analyse the after-effects of implementing green revolution. The villagers lost their subsistence economy and are today highly integrated into the global market. Subsequently, the sustainable livelihood of the people has been affected because of unequal way of integrating the villagers into the world market. The villagers are not aware of the prices in the market due to lack of communication facilities and credit facilities. This has eroded their bargaining power in the market substantially. The Liberalization, Privatization and Globalization (LPG) that led to cut down the subsidies and withdrawal of the State from the welfare policies has done a greater damage to the sustainable livelihood of the villagers. The villagers are now the victims of market fluctuations and governmental policies.

Policies, Institutions and Processes—Formal Government Institutions and Local Participation

All the policy decisions regarding the policies to be implemented in the village are taken at the higher bureaucratic levels and people have no say in it. People's participation in the implementation of any project does not mean that they are consulted at any point of time during the decision-making or implementation of the projects. The participation of people, merely as an instrument in implementing or carrying out some developmental work does not bring empowerment of the people in the village. A case study of the percolation tank, which has collapsed two times during 2004-05, would give us an idea as to how far MPLAD funds have been utilized in the food for work programme. Under this scheme three percolation tanks were built with the intention of creating employment opportunity during the summer season when the farmers carry out no agricultural work. They are devoid of any income during this period, which basically affect the sustainable livelihood of the people. As per the norms prescribed by the food for work programme, the workers should be paid Rs. 80 worth of rice and Rs. 20 cash for their work. But, when it was implemented in the village, it is learnt that it has been implemented in a farcical way. The traditional village head took the contract and built the tanks with machines and people who were only nominally involved were given Rs. 60 per day. All the foodgrains that were stored in the Panchayat office disappeared to some secret place, without even a single kilogram being distributed. It has also been found that this is the routine way in which every work (tanks, cc roads and other irrigation projects) has been completed. Peoples' participation, which is necessary for the success of every programme and also for the democratization of the society, becomes a mockery in the case of this village. This, in turn, affects the sustainable livelihood of the people and should be a serious concern for the development planners.

It is now important to see how globalization has influenced the sustainable livelihood. Many scholars in various ways have defined globalization. The study mainly intended not to look into the whole debate on the whole processes of the term 'globalization'. For our understanding, it can be defined that the globalization, is a process, which started in the historical past, but the intensification of the process of it has great impact on the Indian economy since 1990's. Globalization has some important logical sequence; it has some unique characteristics attached to it. In his article, 'Global Capitalism and the State' Jan Aart Scholte argues that 'the dynamics of surplus accumulation have been a major force behind contemporary globalization and on the other, globalization has considerably reshaped the workings of capitalism, including in particular the activities of the state'. He elaborates this idea 'To be sure, globalization cannot be reduced to a question of capitalism alone. Thus, when taken as whole, my study of globalization has not espoused a narrow materialist political economy; it has also accorded causal significance to structures of, for example, identity, community, knowledge, and ecology. Yet no account of globalization and the state is adequate without extended attention to capitalism either, and it is regrettable that so much analysis of globalization has neglected even to consider the importance of surplus accumulation'[11]

This study would examine mainly three aspects of globalization: One is that what are the challenges of globalization on the sustainable livelihood of the people; secondly, how the mediating role of the state in between global capital and the poors would directly affect and destroy the sustainable livelihood of the people and, thirdly, how the market has brought in the unequal power relations between the capital and the poors, which, in turn, destroy the sustainable livelihood of the people. From the above analysis it is clear that the globalization is not only mean economic globalization, which has far reaching consequences of it on the sustainable livelihood of the poors and marginal people.

The globalization brought about significant changes in the agriculture. Utsa Patnaik says that 'India, a signatory to GATT 1994, removed all quantitative restrictions on trade and converted to tariffs by April 2001, lowering the average tariff rate at the same time to 35 per cent or well below the bound rates which were 100 per cent for crops and 150 per cent for agricultural processed products. This thrust for trade liberalization could not have been worse timed, since advanced country markets were in recession and global primary product prices went into steep tailspin with 40-50 per cent decline in unit dollar prices of all crops–cereals, cotton, jute sugar, tea, coffee—and up to 80 per cent decline in some oil crops between 1995 and 2001. With a brief spike in 2002 prices have continued to fall and some prices are today lower than as far back as 1986. The prices to *jowar* is even lower than world price as State marketing boards' activities have been replaced by private transactional companies (2006:11-12)[12]. She continued that 'More than five thousand indebted farmers, mainly cotton farmers, have committed suicide in Andhra Pradesh alone since 1998 as its Government which had entered into a State-level Structural Adjustment Programme with the World Bank, raised power tariff five times even as cotton price fell by half'[13] (2006:12). The very nature of changes in agricultural pattern due to commercialization of agriculture affects the sustainable livelihoods of the people. Utsa Patnaik argues that changes in agricultural production pattern bring about large scale changes in the pattern of food consumption also. This is an all-India phenomenon and the changes give us bleak picture that the entire community runs the risk of market fluctuation because they are producing for the market.

Green revolution came about in the village through the direct interference of the Government, which again led to the destruction of food security (*See* the discussion in the introduction of the dissertation).

In the context of the commercialization of agriculture it is interesting to examine how the introduction of crops such as soya and cotton has affected the agricultural situation in the village. In the year 1982-83, through ITDA, the villagers have been given cottonseeds, chemical fertilizers and pesticides with subsidy. In the same year hybrid jowar seeds, chemical fertilizers and pesticides were distributed with subsidy. Soya was also introduced the same way in the year 1993-94.

In the case of cottonseeds the subsidy was 50 per cent, *i.e.,* one packet of cottonseeds, chemical fertilizers and pesticides were given to the villagers at almost half the market price. Cottonseeds, chemical fertilizers and pesticides were distributed for two consecutive years.

In the case of Soya, ITDA has given packets of seeds with each packet containing 25 kilograms of seeds. It has also given chemical fertilizers and pesticides to the villagers completely free of cost. In case of hybrid jowar, 25 kg. packets of seeds were distributed only for Rs. 12 along with chemical fertilizers and pesticides. Introduction of *jowar* has many implications on the sustainability and the indigenous knowledge of the community and also has significant implications on their health.

Most (80-90%) of the people in Mankapur have switched over

to the production of cotton, Soya and the hybrid jowar. It has been found that almost 90 per cent of the peasants are already engaged in cultivating either one of the above described crops. It has also been found that land they possess is a major factor in determining the extent of their cultivation of these crops.

It has been found that in the year 1982, the then Chief Minister of Andhra Pradesh, N.T. Rama Rao, announced that 1 kg. of rice would be distributed to the poor people at the rate of only Rs. 2. At present, around 80 per cent of the people are taking rice twice a day and the interesting fact is that the younger generation has totally discarded *jowar* intake. It is important to note here that there is a direct correlation between the changes in the agricultural production pattern and the pattern of the food consumption. With the cutting down of subsidies and the withdrawal of the State from the role of public caretaker, the villagers had no option left but to depend on the market for not only seeds, chemical fertilizers and pesticides but also for food items (like, jowar, pulses, grams and rice). This again shows that the villagers are completely thrown at the mercy of market, which destroys the sustainable livelihood of the people at large, which more or less existed in the earlier periods. G.V. Ramanjaneyulu in his paper 'Modern agriculture, Technology and alienated Farmer' argues that 'Modern agricultural science has developed technologies which promised a deeper understanding of the nature and indeed has few impressive achievements–making the country produce food enough to feed its people. At the same time there are dramatic failures. The chemicalisation has increased pest problems and dumped loads of poison in our habitat. Modern hi-tech agronomy watches our soils disappearing. The green revolution did not eliminate hunger but increased the polarization between rich and poor. It made small and marginal farmers lose their resource base and depend more and more on external inputs for production and the developing nations lose their self-reliance and depend on developed countries for food and other commodities. At the same time the damages done to the environment in the name of development are enormous which many a time are irrevocable. The trade, research and support policies governing agricultural development were always favouring industry and business than farmers. This asymmetry has completely alienated the Indian farmer' (2006: 136).[14] It has also been found that the indigenous knowledge at all the levels, especially medicinal knowledge, went astray. The use of chemical fertilizers and pesticides on a massive scale has affected the soil (See discussion Chapter III) badly. These chemicals have actually entered the bodies of villagers through various other crops like pulses and grams. G.V. Ramanjaneyulu argues that 'Green revolution based on external technological forces completely eroded the farmer's knowledge on one hand and made them dependent on the external industrial inputs on the other. For example, on seed the entire traditional knowledge of making selections, storing of seed, maintaining diversity to meet the local conditions and requirements is lost. Today the knowledge on seed is only about which packet of seed to be bought. Similarly on pest management and soil productivity management, it is about which bottle of pesticide to be used or how many bags of fertilizers to be used. Only few crops like rice, wheat were focused which led to monoculture and monocropping. This technological development rather than being need-based became market oriented' (*ibid.*, 137).[15] This, villagers say, resulted in their medicinal knowledge becoming redundant because their traditional medicinal plants or mixtures and other mixtures did not cure them when diseases struck them, as their traditional medicinal systems could not cure diseases caused by these chemicals. This again led to the complete dependence on allopathic doctors and medicines which, again, in turn, led to the complete dependence on medicines produced by multinational companies.

G.V. Ramanjaneyulu in his paper gives us an unfolding of some complex inter-linkages of State and the market forces, how the latter was brought into the scene. He argues that 'As long as the technological evolution was in the hands of farmers, the agricultural development was in tune with the nature, which means the newer plant types, crop growing and protection technologies were from their resources and never created any harm to the environment. The advent of modern science and technology coupled with growth of commercialization has changed this situation. The technological developments went initially into public sector research organizations and later to the hands of private companies making the farmer a passive receiver of the technology. This separation of the two groups those who develop the technology and those who use it have wider implications. The technological development rather being need based became market oriented. As the other trade policies have changed, even the production and produce have become market oriented. Only those technologies, which can be effectively marketed, were developed by the researchers in both public and private sectors. This make the resources poor farmers depend more and more on the markets for their inputs and external markets for their outputs and were deceived at both the ends. As the market dependency has increased agriculture has become more capital intensive. To cover up the costs and to meet their other needs the farmers started growing only those crops and varieties, which market demands. Thus farmers have lost control both over inputs and outputs' (2006:136).[16]

What was the State's role through various agencies like ITDA and how was it mediating between global multinational capital and the poor people in the villagers? Here, it has to be noted that all the seeds that were distributed by the Government through various agencies could not be set aside for another year as they could not be preserved. However, it was useless to keep the seeds for another year because it would give no produce the next time. Hence, villagers have to buy the seeds from the market every time they cultivated the land. In this way their dependence on market is complete. Besides, these seeds would not give any high yield without the use of fertilizers and chemicals. All these processes have highly integrated the villagers to the external world through which the exploitation of the villagers continues repeatedly.

Another interesting factor is that once they started using a particular brand of pesticide (a particular product of a company), it could not be changed and the villagers could not opt for a low price product because it would not be useful to destroy the pests. The pesticides distributed by the Government were highly costly and the peasants were forced to buy the same products again and again.

Another important fact that has been found in the course of whole process of integration of these villagers into the external forces is that they become powerless and their sustainable livelihoods have been eroded. They are being thrown to vagaries of unequal market relations. The villagers are unaware of the market price of their produce because of lack of communication (See discussion Chapter II). The integration process, which has become a one-way process, has led to the dominance and adoption of capitalist agricultural techniques in a way that has caused the collapse of village economy and the food security completely.

The withdrawal of subsidy and the lack of credit facility led the villagers to succumb to the pressures of the money-lenders. Money-lenders never pay the market price for their produce and charge high rates of interest. The villagers could get only *Dedi* (it has been found that 50 per cent named *Dedi* and 25 per cent *Savai*), which has again led them to continuously depend on the money-lenders for the future loans because they cannot completely come out of the vicious circle woven by the money-lenders and the other credit agencies of the same kind.

The villagers, due to the high price of fuel and their poverty, are unable to buy any form of fuel. This forces them to depend on firewood from the nearby forest for fuel. As a result, there has been severe environmental degradation with a marked decrease in forest cover. This environmental destruction, in turn, affects the finding of fodder for their livestock and grazing, which again affects the economy and the sustainable livelihoods.

It is interesting to see what is there for the new situation to finally offer to the villagers in Mankapur and elsewhere in India. Ramanjaneyulu, trying to capture the new situation, argues that "Today when we are talking about 'second green revolution' the context has changed. India is no more food deficient. The agriculture based livelihoods—farmers and agricultural workers are in a crisis. This is reflected in the form of suicides and large scale migration. If this continues, soon agriculture is going to witness a large scale displacement of people that human kind has never witnessed. Added on to this, the public sector research system that was providing major technology backstopping is caught in the whims and fancies of the genetic engineering based technologies whether it is pest resistance, nutrient deficiency or quality improvement the failure of public sector to meet the technology or input needs of the farmers have given way for huge multinational corporations. All the regulatory systems, accountability systems in the country proved to be a failure in fixing the responsibilities of the corporations. While the Green Revolution was the result of the public research, supported by public funds, the emerging gene revolution, by contrast, is spearheaded by proprietary science and can come under monopolistic control" (2006: 139)[17]. Sumi Krishna examines the current practices of natural resources management and argues for a participatory community management system, which should provide not just access, but sustainable livelihood across a range of small scale sectors women, landless and *dalits*.[18]

Sumi Krishna strongly advocates the principle that deprivation of the means of living or the livelihood is tantamount to denial of life itself and condemns subversion of these rights by global forces as a challenge to achieving the right to livelihood for the poor people.[19] (2004: 11).

Conclusion

1. The sustainable livelihood is a myth in the era of globalization.
   (a) The very nature of changes in agricultural pattern is due to commercialization of agriculture, which in turn, affects the sustainable livelihoods of the people.
   (b) Changes in agricultural production pattern bring about large scale changes in the pattern of food consumption.
   (c) The entire community runs the risk of market fluctuation because they are producing for the market.
2. The Indian State has been increasingly mediating in between the global capital and the exploitation of the poor, which leads to the complete destruction of sustainable livelihoods of the people.
   (a) Green revolution came about in the village through the direct interference of the Government, which again led to the destruction of food security.
3. 'Growth with development' is the concept proposed by the ideologues of sustainable development. They stress only on the reduction of poverty through which they tried to narrow down the concept of sustainable development. Sustainable livelihoods are part and parcel of sustainable development. The concept of growth has been taken from the capitalist dictionary, which suits the capitalist paradigm, leads to inequality, determination of prices by demand and supply of the market and it finally hits back at the concept of sustainable livelihood itself.
4. Destruction of environment is directly connected to the magnitude and intensity of poverty, which is again directly related to economic situation of the people. This greatly affects the sustainable livelihoods of the people.

NOTES

1. *Introduction, Sustainable Rural Livelihoods: Practical Concepts for the 21st Century* by Robert Chambers and Gorden R. Conway (1991).
2. Sen Amartya, (1981) *Poverty and Famines: An Essay on Entitlement and Famines*, Oxford University Press, 1987. (Chapters 1, 2 and 10).
3. *Sustainable Rural Livelihoods: Practical Concepts for the 21st Century* by Robert Chambers and Gorden R. Conway (1991).
4. *Ibid.*
5. *Sustainable Livelihoods Approaches: Progress and Possibilities for Change* by Diana Carney. Document prepared for Department for International Department (DFID), Year is not mentioned.
6. Sustainable Development and the Greening of Development Theory by Bill Adams in *Beyond The Impasse: New Directions in Development Theory,* Edited by Frans J Schuurman (Zed Books, 2004).
7. *Local Food, Future Direction: A Report for Friends of the Earth* by Helen La Trobe, November 2002.
8. Hines, C. and Shiva V., 2002. *A Better Agriculture is Possible: Local Food, Global Solution*. A Report for the UN Food and Agriculture Organization, World Food Summit, Rome, Italy, June, 2002. A discussion paper prepared by International Forum on Globalization and the Research Foundation for Science, Technology and Ecology, Quoted in the above report.
9. Economic and Political Consequences of the Green Revolution in India by Utsa Patnaik in *The Earth Scan Reader in Sustainable Development* Edited by John KIrkby, Phil O'Keefe and Lloyd Timerlake, page 146.
10. *Technology, Life and Livelihood Strategies of Tribes of the Nilgiris: Past, Present and Continuum* by K.N. Reddy and N.S. Balaji Rao, Department of Anthropology, S.V. University, Tirupati. Paper presented at the interdisciplinary conference on "Livelihood strategies among forest-related tribal groups of South India" held at the Centre for Indian Studies, Mysore, during October, 17-19, 2003.
11. *Globalization and the State* by Jan Aart Scholte [International Affairs (Royal Institute of International Affairs, 1944)] Vol. 73 No. 3, Globalization and International Relations (July, 1997), 427-452.
12. Keynote Address *'Agrarian Crisis in the Era of the New Imperialism and the Role of Peasant Resistance'* by Utsa Patnaik at the National Seminar "Understanding Agrarian Change in India: Challenges for Theory and Method" held on 2-3 March, University of Hyderabad.
13. *Ibid.*, p. 12.
14. A paper presented on *Modern Agriculture, Technology and Alienated Farmer,* by G.V. Ramanjaneyulu in the National Seminar "Understanding Agrarian Change in India: Challenges for Theory and Method" held on 2-3 March, University of Hyderabad.
15. *Ibid.*, page 137.

16. A paper presented on *Modern Agriculture, Technology and Alienated Farmer,* by G.V. Ramanjaneyulu in the National Seminar "Understanding Agrarian Change in India: Challenges for Theory and Method" held on 2-3 March, University of Hyderabad, p. 136.
17. *Ibid.*, p. 139.
18. Gobalisation and Peoples' Development Choices, 2004.
19. *Ibid.*, p. 11.

REFERENCES

Anna Toner, (2001). *Exploring sustainable livelihoods: Approaches in relation to two interventions in Tanzania,* Bradford Centre for International Development, University of Bradford (*Journal of International Development*), 2001.

Bill Adams and Frans J. Schuurman, (2004). *Beyond the Impasse: New Directions in Development Theory*, Published by Zed Book, London and New Jersey (2004). (Chapter 10)

C. von Furer Haimendrof, (1979). *Tradition and Change in Indian Tribe,* Vikas Publishing House Pvt. Ltd. Delhi, 1979. (Chapter 8)

Diana Carney, (1998). *Sustainable Livelihoods Approaches: Progress and Possibilities for Change,* Diana Carney is a freelance consultant currently based in Toronto, Canada. She has been working with DFID (Department for International Development) on the development of sustainable livelihoods approaches since 1998.

Harry W. Pearson, and Karl Polanyi, (1977). *'The Economy Embedded in Society' in The Livelihood of Man,* Academic Press 1977. Chapter 4.

Helen La Trobe, (2002). *Local Food, Future Direction: A report for Friends of the Earth,* November 2002.

Jan Aart Scholte, (1997). *Globalization and the State,* [International Affairs (Royal Institute of International Affairs, 1944)] Vol. 73, No. 3, Globalization and International Relations (July, 1997), 427-452.

K.N. Reddy and N.S. Balaji Rao, (2003). *Technology, Life and Livelihood Strategies of Tribes of the Nilgiris: Past, Present and Continuum,* Department of Anthropology, S.V. University, Tirupati (2003).

Livelihood Options in South Asia: Diversification, Poverty and Public Policy, Project Aims and Methods, March 2001.

Pauline Kolenda, (1984). *Caste in Contemporary India: Beyond Organic Solidarity,* published by Rawat Publications (1984).

Per Pinstrup-Andersen and Rajul Pandya-Lorch, (2001). *The Unfinished Agenda: Perspectives on Overcoming Hunger, Poverty and Environmental Degradation,* published by International Food Policy Research Institute, 2001.

Priya Deshingkar, (2000). *Seasonal Migration for Livelihoods in India: Coping, Accumulation and Exclusion,* Priya Deshingkar is an ODI Research Associate and the Andhra Pradesh Research Director for the Livelihood Options

Project and Daniel Start is also Research Associate (formerly Research Officer) of the Overseas Development Institute and directed the Madhya Pradesh Component of the Livelihood Options study from 2000. (Working Paper, 220).

Robert Chambers and Gordon R. Conway, (1991). *Sustainable rural livelihoods: Practical Concepts for the 21st Century,* IDS Discussion Paper 296, (1991).

Robert Chambers, Richard Longhurst and Arnold Pacey, (1981).*Seasonal Dimensions to Rural Poverty*, published by IDS (1981).

Sen Amartya, (1981). *Poverty and Famines: An Essay on Entitlement and Famines*, Oxford University Press, 1987. (Chapters 1, 2 and 10).

Sumi Krishna, (2004). *Globalization and Peoples' Choices,* (2004).

Teodor Shanin, (1987). *Peasant and Peasant Societies: Selected Readings,*

The Livelihood Analysis: Sustainable Livelihoods for Livestock producing Communities in Kyrgyzstan (2001).

Utsa Patnaik (1995). *Economic and Political Consequences of the Green Revolution in India: Sustainable Development*, Edited by John Kirkby, Phil O'Keefe and Lloyd Timber Lake, Published by Earth Scan (1995).

Utsa Patnaik, and G.V. Ramanjaneyulu, (2006). Keynote Address '*Agrarian Crisis in the Era of the New Imperialism and the role of Peasant Resistance*', A seminar paper, 'Modern Agricultural Technology and Alienated Farmer' at the National Seminar "Understanding Agrarian Change in India: Challenges for Theory and Method" held on March 2-3, 2006, University of Hyderabad.

Uttam Kumar Deb, G.D. Nageswara Rao, Y. Mohan Rao, (2003). *Diversification and Livelihood Options: A Study of two villages in Andhra Pradesh, India 1975-2001,* Scientific Officers on Socio-economic and Policy Programme at the International Crop Research Institute for Semi-arid Tropics and Rachel Slater is Research Officer in the Rural Policy and Environment Crop at the Overseas Development Institute. (This report is based on research funded by the UK Department for International Development (DFID), 2003.

14

Poverty Alleviation through Micro-Credit: A Case Study from Eritrea

SHANKAR CHATTERJEE

Study Area

Eritrea is located in the northeastern corner of Africa. It became an independent country, through a UN supervised referendum, in April 1993. This followed a 30-year war for independence with Ethiopia which ended in 1991. The country consists of highlands, midlands and lowlands. Asmara, the Capital city, was developed in 1897 by the Italians and has almost a Mediterranean life style. Eritrea is situated in the horn of Africa and lies between 1-2 and 18 degrees north latitude and 36 and 44 degrees east longitude. With over one thousand kilometres of the Red Sea coastline, Eritrea is bordered to the north and west by Sudan and to the south by Djibouti and Ethiopia. Eritrea covers an area of 125,000 square kilometres, including over 350 Islands of the Dahlak Archipelago. Its geographical area is approximately 123,300 square kilometres (Eritrea Basic Education Statistics, 2002). On the other hand, the World Bank data reveal that its geographical area is 118,000 square kilometres. So there is little controversy about its area. In the absence of population census, its population has been estimated as 3.2 million with average density of population of 29 persons per square kilometre, in the year 2001 (*Eritrea Basic Education Statistics, 2002*). The country is having six provinces/regions, locally known as Zoba, 57 sub-Zobas/sub-regions and 2606 villages. Capital of Eritrea is known as Asmara, located at about 2500 metres high than the sea level. So throughout the year the climate is very pleasant. The currency of Eritrea is known as Nakfa which in terms of one U.S. dollar is approximately 15 that is 1 U.S. $ is equal to 15 Nakfa.

Poverty in Eritrea

Poverty is a great issue in the modern world, particularly in the developing countries. In the G8 Summit which was held in Scotland during July 6-8, 2005 was under severe pressure from several fronts, *inter alia*, of which include poverty. The slogan from world famous musicians was, "Make Poverty History". Now everywhere there is talk about poverty. The question is what is the concept of poverty? The first Director General of Food and Agriculture Organization (FAO) Lord Boyd-Orr is the first person to introduce calorie concept for determining of poverty in the year 1945. Calorie depends on consumption of food. Scientifically and medically, it has been proved that an adult person requires minimum 2300 calories of food value per day. Based on this, poverty is calculated. Since the process of determining calorie is cumbersome so income is the criterion for determining the same. In other words, income is the main criterion of determining poverty in any country. The people who are not having minimum income to get calorie and other basic necessities are termed as "Living Below the Poverty Line" (popularly known as BPL). According to a latest estimate more than 800 million people in the world don't have enough food to meet their basic nutritional needs.

Poverty is an issue in Eritrea also. In 2003, National Statistics and Evaluation Office (NSEO) of Eritrea defined poverty line as 240 Nakfa per person per month. In other words any person earning less than 240 Nakfa per month is considered as poor *i.e.* BPL. There is other category of poor persons in Eritrea, "Extreme Poverty" – any person earning less than 150 Nakfa per month is under "Extreme Poverty". Out of total population of Eritrea, 66.40 per cent (2.36 million in absolute number) are poor and again out of total poor, 36.97 per cent are in the category of extreme poor. The Government of Eritrea is aware about the gravity of the situation. In the year 1996, a Government department under the banner of Savings and Micro Credit Programme (popularly known as SMCP) was established. SMCP extends credit to the poor echelon of the society. The poor persons are provided credit for setting up of self-employment ventures. As a result of SMCP's credit thousands of poor families have been benefited. For example in 1996, the number of beneficiaries was 1,525 which went upto 22,509 in 2005.

For determination of poverty in Eritrea, National Statistics and Evaluation Office (NSEO) of Government of Eritrea conducted household Living Standards Measurement Survey (LSMS, hence LSMS will be used) in 2003. According to LSMS, 66 per cent of their total population was unable to get sufficient food (calorie terms) *vis-à-vis* other essential goods and services to lead healthy life.

Of the 66 per cent population, 37 per cent were in the category of extreme poor that is they live below the food poverty threshold. It is pertinent to mention here that the Report used the words—"Poor" and "Extreme Poor". Concentration of poors are more in urban areas than the rural areas—64.64 per cent poors in rural areas against 70.32 per cent in urban areas.

This may be attributed to the fact that poors have been migrating to urban areas for search of livelihood. Asmara, the capital city of Eritrea, is also not free from high poverty ratio as poverty ratio in Asmara is approximately 56 per cent.

One noteworthy point of the Report is that, "the proportion of the population that is poor and dependent on food assistance has increased because of the adverse effects of the recent border war and severe drought". Some important findings with respect to women issues (*Source*: LSMS and Dimensions of Poverty, NSEO, Eritrea, 2003) are as follows:

(a) Of the total households of Eritrea, the women-headed 30 per cent households. Of the 30 per cent of women-headed household 18 per cent were widows.
(b) On an average female worker earns less than half of the men.
(c) A majority of the poors rural women earn their income through manual labour particularly through construction works and agriculture.
(d) Women-headed households have comparatively less hold assets including livestock than non-women-headed household.

In the present age everyone believes that without the development of women, a nation cannot develop. Participation of women in all the sphere of life enhances their role in development process. Mention may be made here that Fourth World Conference of Women held in Beijing, China in the year 1995, declared that "develop the fullest potential of girls and women of all ages, ensure their full and equal participation in building a better world for all and enhance their role in the developmental process". It further stated that, "promote women's economic independence, including employment and eradicate the persistent and increasing burden of poverty on women . . . ." The women are as dynamics as men. In many respects their works in numerical term cannot be measured as all the household works they carry are without payment. It is estimated that in addition to work within the household women provide 60 to 80 per cent of agricultural labour in Africa and Asia and around 40 per cent in Latin America (Todaro, 2000).

The Government of Eritrea is serious to eradicate poverty from the country. Altogether four surveys have been conducted at the initiation of Government of Eritrea in recent years. The objectives of these surveys were to get a thorough idea about the nature, causes and extent of poverty in Eritrea. Apart from household Living Standards Measurement Survey (LSMS) by National Statistics and Evaluation Office in 2003 (as mentioned already), another survey was conducted in 2003 that is known as Rural Livelihood Security Assessment. The other two are – Participatory Poverty Assessment (PPA) and second Demographic and Health Survey (DHS).

After the independence of Eritrea in 1991, the Government has initiated from, Savings and Micro Credit Programme popularly known as SMCP (hence SMCP will be used). It is the first largest Eritrean micro-finance institution under government-owned in terms of both members and amount of credit for eradication of poverty. Economists believe that micro-finance is essentially a process to activate and involve people in the theme of self-help and mutual-help, so that they can manage their livelihoods on sustainable basis. SMCP extends credit to those persons who are basically poor and without access to formal financial services. SMCP extends credit to its beneficiaries (client in SMCP's language, however, as a common word beneficiary is used henceforth) under Two tiers – First-tier and Second-tier. First-tier credit is given to the beneficiaries forming groups. The groups, which are formed under First-tier, are known as Solidarity Groups. All the groups are under one umbrella that is known as Village Bank (VB). In one Village Bank minimum members should be 35 and maximum should be 105. If members exceed more than 105 then another Village Bank (VB-2) has to open in the same village, thus third one will be VB-3 etc. Again from all the members Solidarity Groups are formed. Thus under the umbrella of one Village Bank many Solidarity Groups are formed. Under First-tier a beneficiary can borrow money up to ten cycles that is ten times. After repayment of first loan, second loan may be sanctioned and so on. But all the group members have to repay. In other words no one can be defaulter. In case of First-tier if members of the group repay timely loan then after five cycles individually credit may be sanctioned to each member. Here also all the group members have to repay the loan. This is termed as First-tier *B*. Both First-tier *A* and *B* members are under the control of Village Bank. Three members' group—one chairperson (a Government official known as Village Administrator), one secretary and one treasurer (both are selected from the beneficiaries) control Village Bank. The secretary and treasurer get lump sum honorarium. The repayment is made in the village. The treasurer of the Village Bank immediately gives the receipt. On the other hand, Second-tier beneficiaries include individual person. The beneficiaries are under the direct control of SMCP, not under Village Bank. The beneficiaries are given loan only no subsidy is involved here. The Second-tier beneficiaries can borrow up to six times/six cycles.

Regarding interest payment, it may be mentioned that rate of interest under First-tier is 16 per cent per annum with simple rate of interest. Rate of interest is calculated on the basis of declining method. For example if a person borrows Nakfa 5000 (Interest rate is 16% for first installment) and repays Nakfa 4000 then rate of interest will be calculated on Nakfa 4000, etc. In case of Second-tier beneficiaries albeit rate of interest is 16 per cent but if it is repaid within stipulated time then 2 per cent is refunded to the beneficiary. Thus finally Second-tier beneficiary has to repay 14 per cent interest. The reason is that Second-tier beneficiary is extended much more higher loan amount than the First-tier beneficiary. The cases of beneficiaries studied are presented later on of this article. The Annual Report of SMCP reveals that maximum amount of loan is extended under First-tier (90.8 %) and Second-tier accounts only 9.2 per cent. This is a noteworthy point as group lending dominates than individual lending. The Annual Report of SMCP 2005 shows that for last several years' repayment rate was declining but in the year 2005 it went up to around 83 per cent, against 79 per cent. The noteworthy point is that from 1996 onwards more and more women beneficiaries are extended assistance from SMCP. For example, in 1996, under First-tier 30 per cent of women beneficiaries (clients) were extended credit, which went up to 40.60 per cent in 2005. Under Second-tier although in 1996 no one was extended credit, but in 1997 percentage of women beneficiaries assisted was 14.29 which went up to 37.52 per cent in 2004. That is within a span of eight years, it went up to several times. Percentage of women beneficiaries (clients) covered from 1996 to 2005 may be seen in Table 14.1.

Table 14.1: Percentage of Women Beneficiaries covered under SMCP Credit

Year	*Percentage of Women Beneficiaries*	
	I Tier	*II Tier*
1996	30.00	–
1997	30.26	14.29
1998	27.62	6.45
1999	29.60	14.29
2000	30.18	29.00
2001	37.00	36.00
2002	40.00	36.00
2003	40.00	39.00
2004	42.60	42.04
2005	40.60	37.52

Source: SMCP 2005, Annual Report, Asmara, Eritrea.

Table 14.1 reveals that less than a decade women beneficiaries have been greatly benefited by SMCP credit. During 1998 and 1999, due to war normal situation was disturbed so coverage was not high.

To get an idea about the impact of SMCP credit, a study was conducted at Anseba Zoba (province), headquarters of Anseba namely Keren is located at about 90 kilometres away from Asmara. SMCP has been functioning in this region since its inception. Number of beneficiaries in 2004 was 2,697, which was increased to 3839 in 2005. An increase of 42 per cent was observed over a period of one year. With regard to disbursement of credit, a sum of 6.44 million Nakfa was disbursed in 2004 that was increased to almost 100 per cent in 2005. Thus, it is evident that more and more poor persons have been benefited from SMCP credit. Regarding delivery of credit it may be mentioned that a team of officials consisting of banker, SMCP official and village administrator come to the village and deliver credit in presence of villagers. Thus villagers need not go to the bank or SMCP office to check up their case. This process also prevents corruption (as SMCP officials informed), because everything happens in the presence of villagers. For repayment of loan, beneficiaries need not go to bank. Locally a person is recruited to collect the money and immediately receipt is given to the beneficiary.

Analysis of economic activity-wise credit reveals that out of total loan disbursed (July 1, 1996 to December 31, 2004) under First tier trade and service got top priority as out of total disbursement 56.16 per cent share of trade and service was 56.16 per cent, followed by agriculture 42.95 per cent and manufacturing 0.88 per cent. On the other hand, under Second-tier share of trade and service was more than 70 per cent (72.74%) of total loan disbursed. Next to it was agriculture (20.47%) and manufacturing (6.79%). Data at the *prima facie* mean that poor persons are more interested in trade and service than any other activities. Inclination towards the tertiary activity is an indicator of development. Interestingly last eight and half years cost of loan amount has come down. The costs per Nakfa loaned were Nakfa 21, 5, 4.7, 4.5, 6, 5.4, 5.2, 8 and 9.6 starting from 1996 to 2004. This clearly indicates cost effectiveness and efficiency of the programme. To get an in-depth idea about the impact of micro-credit among poor women beneficiaries the study was carried out.

Study Area

To get an idea about the impact of SMCP's credit among the poor persons, the author did a number of studies in different parts of Eritrea—Himbirty village of Maakel region (study conducted in October 2005), Maiduma of Debub region in November 2006 and Hagaz and Keren of Anseba region in May 2006. The study has been carried out with the objective of assessing impact of micro-credit among poor women. Beneficiaries were randomly selected and in depth study was made. The results of the study reveal that poor women with the help of micro-credit could change their economic plight. Before the project they had to face economic hardship as a sequel children suffered. After the project the situation completely changed as poor women are not only earning income, but also economically they are self-sufficient, which has given them moral boost. The direct impact of the result is that children have been benefited. The women have proved that they are successful entrepreneurs also. The women are managing a computer centre to petty business. It was observed that psychologically they are prepared to face any eventuality. A detailed discussion is made in the following.

Findings of the Study

To get an idea about the impact of SMCP's credit among the poor persons, the author did a number of studies in different parts of Eritrea-Himbirty village of Maakel region (study conducted in October 2005), Maiduma of Debub region in November 2006 and Hagaz and Keren of Anseba region in May 2006. Altogether 31 beneficiaries comprising of both males and females were randomly studied. The beneficiaries were involved with various types of business activities *viz.* agriculture, animal husbandry, poultry, vegetables business, utensils business, cloth business, even one woman started computer typing business etc. A few cases are presented here.

Case-I

Mrs. Rumana (aged 26 years) belongs to Muslim community started her computer typing business in Keren town as she is the resident of Keren also. After completing her 12th grade examination, she had undergone computer training. She had a great desire to start computer typing works after her computer training. Problem is with the money as purchase of computers etc involves huge money. But there is a proverb, "where there is a will there is a way". So her problem was eased out when she came to know about SMCP's credit. Without wasting time, she completed all the formalities in SMCP's office. In the year 2003, she was provided with an amount of Nakfa 20,000 as loan. Within 2005 after thoroughly utilizing the loan she repaid. Again in 2005 she was extended an amount of Nakfa 40,000 as loan. She utilized the money and till the day of this study (May 2006) she was repaying loan. The author visited her computer centre and found that she purchased two computers with printers; both were in working conditions. She has also engaged one employee. She had a plan to expand her business in future as she can take further loan from SMCP after repayment of the same. To query about her net income, she informed that it ranges in between Nakfa 5000 and

Nakfa 5500 per month. As a mother of two children, a soft spoken person has proved that "women are not less than men".

Case-II

Mrs. Tsion of Hagaz village is a beneficiary of SMCP under Second tier. She is around 33 years old person having three children. Thus her total member of family is five. In the year 2005, she was extended an amount of 25,000 Nakfa with this she expanded her grocery business. The activity fetched her good income so within a year she repaid entire loan amount. She was enthusiastic to expand her business. On the day of study she informed that she had applied an amount of Nakfa 40,000 as second cycle loan to expand her business. To a query about earning of profit, she revealed that on an average a sum of Nakfa 5,000 was earned by her.

Case-III

Mrs. Amna of Hagaz village is around 39 years old is a member of self-help group. The group member consists of three women. All are the beneficiaries of First-tier. Amna is having only one child. Her husband is a freedom fighter. Along with the group members she was sanctioned an amount of Nakfa 3,000 in the year 2005. With this amount she started sheep and goat rearing business. She informed that within a couple of months she would be able to sell some sheep and goats. Thus she was expecting good return from her primary activity. She expressed her happiness for getting the loan from SMCP.

Case-IV

Mrs. Rumana of Keren is 26 years old educated woman. She is having two children, besides her husband. She is the beneficiary of Second tier. She had a desire to set up computer typing works etc. as she had undergone training on computer. In 2003, she was extended an amount of Nakfa 20,000 as loan from SMCP. With the amount she purchased computer and established her computer shop in Keren town. Motivated with the earning she applied for second cycle loan. She got an amount of Nakfa 40,000 in the year 2005. She expanded her business. On the day of interview she informed that she had two computers and one worker. After making all payments etc, she could able to earn Nakfa 5,000 per month. She spends the amount for the welfare of the family.

Case-V

Mrs. Zamila Nagash of Keren is 35 years old woman. She is having only one child, so with her husband, she has a small family of three. In the year 2005, she got a loan of Nakfa 15,000 as Second-tier beneficiary and with the amount she started hairdressing shop exclusively for ladies in Keren town. She hired a room at a cost of Nakfa 600 per month. She herself manages the shop. With all her efforts she could be able to earn an amount of Nakfa 15,00 per month even after repaying of loan. She is happy with her business and planning to expand it by borrowing second cycle loan immediately after repayment of first loan.

Case-VI

Mrs. Rigbe, of Himbirty village, Maakel region a middle-aged woman with nine members' family economically was suffering before getting SMCP. She was running a petty business to manage her family. In the year 2001, she was extended an amount of Nakfa 20,000 as loan by SMCP. With the amount she expanded her business and started readymade garments business. Return from the business was encouraging for her. By the end of 2003, she refunded the loan. Second dose of loan consisting of Nakfa 30,000 was extended to her in March 2004, from SMCP. This also greatly helped her as earning increased substantially. In her words, "My bad days are over".

Case-VII

Mrs. Rezan, an old woman of 64 years of age lives in Maiduma village of Debub region. Her family consists of three members. With five children only daughter and grand-son are staying with her but other four children stay separately. In view of this she managed herself. She decided to start grain business for which she had some knowledge. In 2001, she was given a sum of Nakfa 2,000 by SMCP. With the amount, she started the business and repaid the amount. Subsequently, she was given loans in different doses in different years as she was timely borrowing and repaying the loans. In 2002, loan amount was Nakfa 3,000; in 2003, it was Nakfa 5,000; and Nakfa 7,000 in 2004. By getting loans time to time, she could not only cross poverty line but no longer dependent on her children also.

Conclusion

The cases reveal that many poor persons have been greatly benefited by SMCP. Thus micro-credit has been helping the poor persons to eradicate poverty from the country. As we know, "Little drops of water, little grains of sand, makes a mighty ocean and a pleasant land". I have observed that whether in India or in Eritrea, poor persons including women have great potential in business. Their only problem is adequate resources. If resource is arranged to proper persons then earning will be greatly improved.

REFERENCES

Eritrea Basic Education Statistics 2001/02, Ministry of Education, Eritrea.
Living Standards Measurement Survey, 2003, Eritrea.
Savings and Micro Credit Programme 2005: Annual Report, Asmara, Eritrea.
Todaro P. Michael, (2000), *Economic Development*, Addison–Wesley, USA.

15

Using the Internet for E-Rural Development

TAPOMOY DEB

Introduction

India has attained independence since 60 years, but still 3/5th of the working population works in agricultural sector and lives in rural areas. Even at the threshold of twenty-first century, we still have a quarter of global poors here. Education, health, literacy, employment and social harmony are essential base for socio-economic development. At the same time we are world's largest English speaking country with a large highly educated people (we produce more Ph.Ds than UK does) yet in terms of overall international perspectives, we are far behind countries that have not done better than India in many other development aspects such as Ghana, Kenya, Zimbabwe, Zambia, Myanmar and the Philippines. In his forward to the Seventh Five Year Plan, late Prime Minister of India Shri Rajiv Gandhi observed: "In the final analysis development is not just about factories, dams and roads. Development is basically about people. The goal is the people's material, cultural and spiritual fulfilment. The human factor, the human context, is of supreme value. We must pay much greater attention to these questions in future." Hence development is key to national growth strategy of India.

Human Development

Looking at India's past, we find that change in Human Development Index (HDI) has considerably improved from 0.21 in 1960 to 0.56 in 1998. This implies that industrial growth has not resulted into comparative social development. This is critical to overall growth and progress of a poor country like India where around 75 per cent of the population still lives in rural areas, making for 750 million people distributed across 600,000 villages. Though 350 million of these people are poor and survive at subsistence level, the remaining 400 million are economically better off due to a combination of increased agricultural yield and rise in rural mini-industries. National Council of Applied Economic Research (NCAER) estimates that of these 400 million people, more than 200 million, a number roughly equal to India's urban population, are active participants in the modern economy. This implies that around 200 million people have enough disposable income to purchase a few modern goods and services such as bicycles, water pumps, motorbikes, TV, etc. Without adequate reference to development agenda of rural areas, seeking to achieve growth and prosperity of India is futile because even today agriculture is still the largest source of employment in India. Therefore, an agrarian economy like India will only develop once rural development is a key issue of the development agenda. Therefore, fostering and accelerating the pace of rural development is need of the hour.

Rural Development

Rural development programmes are an important integral part of national development strategy. Hence, increasing social responsiveness through rural development policies and programmes is crucial to promoting national goal of sustained economic and social development. All efforts should, therefore, be made to devise and implement rural development policies and programmes for effective education, awareness, information sharing and development of rural population which will enhance not only their quality of life but at the same time will help in sustaining rural development projects, schemes and programmes. Therefore, a valid question arises: how to do it? Scientific and technological progress is generating the knowledge and the tools to make strategy of sustainable rural development a possibility. The Green revolution in India and many developing countries has demonstrated how science and technology can contribute to the solution of social problems. Technology has been playing an important role in promoting agricultural and rural development during the last several decades. The role of radio and television in rural education and extension services has played a vital role in furthering rural development. In this globalized economy, growth is linked to information and knowledge. Knowledge includes technology which creates the capacity to generate knowledge, as well as the capacity to adapt to local circumstances for the benefit of rural population particularly farmers.

Interactions between humans and computers have greatly increased as we embark on the twenty-first century. The more recent technological revolution that is taking place is based on the emerging digital revolution. Information Technology (IT) and Internet growth observed during the last quarter of the twentieth century is often compared to technological revolutions brought about by invention of steam power, electricity or railroads. Information technology and the Internet have amplified brainpower in the same way that the technologies of the industrial revolution amplified mechanical power. Much of the growth in IT markets is attributed to the global information network—Internet. The average growth rate in number of Internet users around the world has been at the level of 50-55 per cent per year.

New Technology

With significant advancement in technology such as Internet can help realize 'knowledge for development'. The development of the inexpensive computers coupled with decreasing communication cost links is drastically changing the environment in which a person and a community live and interact. Ability to access computers and the internet has become increasingly important to completely immerse oneself in the economic, political and social aspects of the world. For those people who are unable to access Internet is increasingly becoming a disability.

Internet is a generic technology and its application to rural development is very extensive and pervasive. Internet can pave the way for interaction among rural population, research institutions and development agents on one hand, while at the same time being able to tap different information and knowledge sources. It can facilitate rural development by focusing on increased communication, accessing information resources, and deploying information for efficient development initiatives. Internet can provide agricultural information, distance learning, tele-pesticide management, environmental protection and natural disaster mitigation. Thus, Internet's contribution in rural development essentially revolves around sharing global knowledge and expertise to help support development initiatives against poverty and disease, better communication with trading partners through e-commerce and the ability to trade opportunities and to use across the globe. However, following factors puts impediment in the process of increasing use of Internet in rural areas:

- Lack of infrastructural facilities like tele-communication, computers, and availability of trained manpower/Instructors;
- Lack of general awareness on the benefits of Internet;
- Lack of computer skills and instructional support;
- Attitudinal barriers like cultural and behavioural attitudes towards Internet;
- Content lowly based on local language;
- Lack of governmental support; and
- Lack of motivation to use Internet for personal and community development activities.

Information Technology

Although e–chaupal is not a new concept, however, the penetration of Internet has been abysmally low due to lack of above cited reasons. Therefore, the role of corporate India, besides State Government and its agencies assume great significance. Government by itself has not been successful in increasing rural population's access to modern technology, therefore, business organizations also need to partner the process technological accessibility for sustained rural development. Many organizations particularly those in IT, computer hardware, and telecom sectors can play a pivotal role in digitizing rural development with their expertise, capital, equipment and trained manpower. Getting volunteers especially from corporate world for these activities can pose difficulty, but then this where NGOs can assume an important role for themselves. NGO volunteers can be trained on basic Internet operational techniques by personnel of software companies who shall in turn train the rural masses. Hardware suppliers can loan inexpensive desktops and telecom service provider's particularly mobile operators can also make their valuable contributions.

One may argue why should business organizations do this? The answer is not without an economic recourse. India currently has more than one million Internet subscribers and 3.2 million Internet users which are very low as compared to many countries including China. The numbers are expected to grow rapidly to 35 million internet subscribers and 100 million internet users by 2008. It is estimated that 90 per cent of the internet connections are concentrated in few large cities. This can be largely being attributed to poor telecom and power infrastructural facilities. Only 370,000 of 600,000 villages have phone lines though it is increasingly rapidly coupled with mobile phones. TARAhaat's research indicates that there is an increasing demand for Internet access and IT education exists among rural population, despite lack of prior exposure to computers or other aspects of the IT world. The expansion of Internet cafes in urban and rural areas is expected to play an important role in increasing the penetration of internet in India further. Thus, internet market in rural India remains largely untapped. By bringing internet to every village, one cannot image the volume of subscribers it is likely to add in the long term. In other words, the revenues are only going to multiply by many times. As regards, the rural population, they stand to gain immensely on the following account:

- *Education*: Although English remains one of the widely used language over internet, but information is also available in other languages including native Indian languages. It is rationale to assume that with rapid increase in internet usage from rural areas, language will not remain a barrier for long. Internet is basically a huge knowledge repertoire, only waiting to be leveraged as much as possible. This will help rural population to improve upon their existing education and knowledge. e-learning emerges as a critical resource for creating best practices in rural development. This will facilitate in improving local planning through enhanced participation of the rural population.
- *Skill Development*: Agriculture remains one of the pivotal means of livelihood in rural areas. Farmers typically require the following information: better crop management—growing crops, fertilizers, prices, benefits from use, quantities, mixes, pesticides, crop diseases, better farming methods, marketing of farm produce, how, where, and how

to get best prices, product storage, experiences in other countries, how to identify resources, community mobilization methods, etc. Farmers can access newer information on these areas and host of other relevant factors which can improve the quality of farming and allied activities. Therefore, with improvement in farming, quality of life of farmers is only going to improve given better crop cultivation and harvesting. This will reduce their dependency on money-lenders and help in containing out migration.

- *Networking*: Internet provides the possibility of connecting to various governmental research bodies, academic community, NGOs and rural product oriented organizations to pool their knowledge base and share for generating a cumulative and empowering process amongst practitioners of rural development.
- *Electronic Marketing*: Marketing of agricultural produce in India remains mostly unorganized and State controlled. Internet provides immense potential for networking of farmers and purchasers of agricultural produce across the globe at zero cost. Another significant source of savings comes from increase in communication speeds. Faster communication between agents allows taking better advantages of information and business opportunities that become open. Real-time access to information on commodity prices and proposition of goods allows rural population particularly farmers to take adequate decision without time lag and the problem of imperfect information becomes less evident. Internet allows the rural population to better approach the standard assumptions of perfect competition, based on full information access by farmers, large number of agents, zero transaction costs and free exit and entry. Therefore, farmers can network for marketing of their produce to a wider spectrum of customers and, therefore, can bargain harder for better prices. Thus, the dependency of farmers for support prices for their crop can be significantly reduced which will be beneficial for the overall economy (due to lesser subsidy) and the farmers themselves.
- *Corporate Partnership*: Corporate India has a crucial role to

play in attaining sustainable rural development through a combination of finance, technology and social performance initiatives. Given that organizations are no more mere economic institutions, converting some inputs in outputs; but they are social entities also at the same time and they have to give back to society what they take from it. Otherwise, then organizations will become agents of exploitation and soon will driven out of business by sheer power of people. Therefore, the role of corporate Inc. needs to extend beyond organization's human resources and embrace rural people in the wider network of human resource development. Needless to emphasize, rural populations are the people who need 'HRD' the most. It is amazing that rural development has not received much attention of corporates. Many of these organizations particularly MNCs have revenues in excess of economic size of many small and developing countries; yet they seldom choose to go beyond tickle of corporate social (CSR) responsibilities. According to Metcalfe's Law, attributed to Robert Metcalfe, a pioneer of computer networking, the value of a network grows roughly in line with the square of the number of users. As almost intuitively follows from the presence of network effects, each new internet user will increase the value of being online for all existing users and for the newcomers. By partnership with governmental and non-governmental agencies, corporates can generate increased business for them by helping to accelerate the penetration of internet infrastructure and usage in rural areas.

Conclusion

Using internet for sustained rural development remains a challenge not because of technological constraints but due to infrastructural, institutional and capital constraints. Hence, by improving infrastructural, institutional and capital constraints, internet usage among rural population can usher in new era of rural entrepreneurship at grassroot level and improve the socio-economic conditions of rural masses. Corporates also stand to gain by partnering the Internet access and increasing usage for enhanced market development and increased revenues. By doing so, corporate India and rural population can result in writing off a new chapter: e–rural development.

REFERENCES

Cullen, R. "Addressing The Digital Divide", *Online Information Review*, 2002, 25(5), pp. 311-320.

India: Infrastructure Economist Intelligence Unit's "Doing e-business", www.ebusinessforum.com

Klein, Lawrence R. and Palanivel, T., "Economic Reforms and Growth Prospects in India", *Working Paper*, August 2000, University of Pennsylvania.

Rao, S.S., "Information Systems in Indian Rural Communities", *Journal of Computer Information System*, 2003, 44, pp. 48-56.

16

Rural Development in Perspective: Theoretical Frameworks

MOHAMMAD TAGHI SHEYKHI

Globally speaking, currently above 51 per cent of world population live in rural areas (World Population: 2007), and Asia-wise rural inhabitants in 2007 have been recorded 59 per cent of the total population of the region. Such a great number of people in rural areas need its own planning and investment in order to be able to produce its own food and secure its other necessities of life. In the following chapter, various theories regarding rural development in developing world will be discussed.

Rural Development

By rural development it is meant to proceed through such schemes as to alleviate poverty in different sectors in rural areas. But, the fact remains that rural areas as a target group, and centre of activity for employment generation for all families has to be prioritized. In the process of rural development, various income-generating and employment-oriented schemes must be initiated in the rural areas. In achieving rural development schemes, glamourization and suitable family planning must be reached and achieved with special reference to the developing societies. In this process, reaching rural industries have to be ensured.

While talking about sustainable rural development, we may also briefly touch upon the concept of privatization (Taori:1995). This new phenomenon may be carried out, when a multi-disciplinary team takes up a holistic exercise of inducting rationale changes. The process also needs sustainable linkage-building between agriculture, rural development, and rural industrialization.

Rural development is a multi-dimensional process, and much broader than poverty alleviation. It is implemented through socio-economic programmes and transfers. A successful strategy will make it possible. Rural development needs changing environments — enabling poor people to earn more, invest in themselves, and their communities in order to reach their key goals, and maintain the necessary infrastructures.

As a global phenomenon, increasing developing countries are discovering that, if rural communities are properly empowered, they can and may manage their own local development efforts. However, the existence of rural poverty provides major challenges to the governments of, and the developmental agencies in many developing societies. The failure of any rural developmental project even negatively affects the urban development and industrial projects.

Rural areas throughout the world tend to have similar characteristics. That is, their populations are spatially dispersed, and under such conditions they cannot have access to many services. In such rural areas, agriculture is often the dominant activity, and often other opportunities for resource mobilization are limited. Such characteristics mean that people living in rural areas face a set of factors that pose challenges to development. However, the geographical dispersion of rural populations often increases the cost and difficulty of providing rural goods and services in a satisfactory manner. That results in fewer opportunities in rural areas than in non-rural locations. Therefore, rural areas are rarely able to mobilize sufficient resources to finance their own developmental programmes, leaving them dependent on transfers from external resources. Moreover, rural areas in the developing societies are often politically marginalized; leaving little opportunity for the rural poor to influence Government policies.

Developing countries are usually characterized by high levels of poverty within their rural areas (Chambers, 1983). In some cases such as South Africa, approximately 70 per cent of the country's poor people live in rural areas, and about 70 per cent of the rural residents are poors. In such cases incomes are constrained since the rural economy is not sufficiently vibrant to provide them with jobs or self-employment opportunities. However, rural areas in majority of developing countries are diverse with concentrations of poverty and relative prosperity. One of the features of the rural areas in such countries is that, rural housing is often substandard or non-existent, and many people are migrants; working in urban areas. As a result, the rural-urban continuum reflects as a way of life in such societies. That is to say, the population is often mobile in search of better living conditions and jobs.

Rural Population and their Problems

In most of the developing countries, because of the prevalent poverty and vulnerability, rural families almost commonly resort to a variety of different strategies to ensure their survival. Therefore, it has become more appropriate to describe their economic activities as livelihood strategies rather than jobs or employment. The deepest poverty in rural areas belong to women, and many children in such areas live in families/households with income below the minimum subsistence level. Such households usually have low levels of literacy and education, difficult and time-consuming access to water, fuel and other services. This results in high levels of under or malnutrition, morbidity and mortality of the children etc. Under such conditions, there is a permanent migration of people from rural to urban areas, and not *vice versa*. However, internal migration is a demographic process affecting rural poverty negatively in that, it has converted rural poverty to urban poverty (Goldstein, 1983).

Though many rural households in the developing world are totally marginalized, and have no income, they do not have pensions either to depend on. Wages in the agricultural sector fall well below the minimum living level, and the seasonal workers have the added disadvantage of earning approximately less than the permanent workers.

Governments in developing countries are required to contribute towards rural development through their programmes in the following broad areas:

- Economic development,
- Social investment (*i.e.* social infrastructure),
- Human resource development, and
- Natural resource-based programmes.

Such programmes lead to poverty alleviation through investment in infrastructure and provision of social services. However, various such elements of rural development are required to be addressed. As a whole, rural development is understood to be multi-dimensional, encompassing improved provision of services, enhanced opportunities for income generation, improved physical infrastructure, social cohesion and physical security within rural communities. The concept of rural development places emphasis on facilitating change in rural environments to enable poor people to earn more, invest in themselves and their communities, contribute towards maintenance of the infrastructure key to their livelihoods; in short, to identify opportunities, and to act on them. However, a successful strategy will thus make people less poor. Such specific measures assist the vulnerable, and relieve the burdens of poverty.

Social sustainability is an important dimension of a successful strategy towards rural development. However, rural communities hold a wealth of social capital in the from of extended networks of mutual solidarity, shared beliefs and traditions.

Dynamics of Growth

In rural areas, there is a dire need to revive the rural economies, and thereby to advance the engines of economic growth that would contribute towards development at national level in the developing countries. In case the direction is not so, functional and applicable strategies must be adopted. Although the specific processes vary over time and space, the general dynamics are understood in terms of sources of growth, and linkages that spread and multiply the initial impulse. Growth in agriculture, forestry, and other primary activities that bring incremental earnings into rural areas, generally generates additional incomes through linkage in expenditure and employment.

It is expected that rural communities in which agriculture, forestry, tourism and other activities are growing, such a process of growth would increase incomes, strengthen transport and communications, and thereby the "remoteness" of rural areas is reduced. This vision is realistically attainable for rural areas in which the natural resource base supports growth in agriculture, forestry and other such activities.

Dynamic growth will benefit many of the rural poors in the developing countries, *i.e.* even those who do not earn the initial incremental incomes. Moreover, as more active rural economies become less cut off, they are less prone to sickness and mortality. That is, with better roads and means of communications, the chance that a sick or injured person will get to the hospital in time increases for the prosperous and the poors, even though the chances may still not remain equal for both.

Although growth benefits many of the poors, it clearly does not benefit all. Safety nets are still needed, and the rural poors are greatly disadvantaged relative to their urban counterparts when it comes to social assistance. However, few developing countries include rural people in social security programmes, and the prevalence of self-employment means that unemployment compensation is largely irrelevant to those without work.

Human Resource Development

Rural areas in many developing countries generally suffer from capacity constraints linked to a low-skills base. What the developing countries need, is the development of a separate human resource strategy, so that the skills base in rural areas is increased. Through such master plan, rural development may be pursued. To achieve such goals, transfer of personnel to rural areas, to support both hard and soft skills, is quite necessary. Where appropriate, the goodwill of experienced citizens who seek to contribute on a voluntary basis, should also be utilized. However, over the intermediate to longer term, capacity constraints should be addressed through education and training. In such context, the rural development strategy must constitute deliberate and conscious choices and interventions usually through Government in all spheres, after and in consultation with different targeted personalities in rural areas.

Rural Development Paradigm

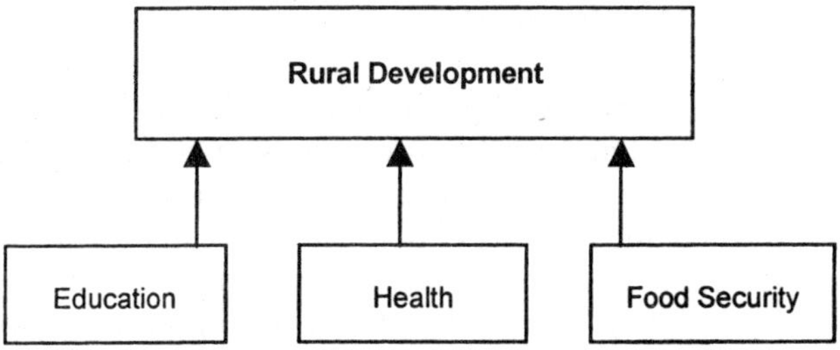

Rural Development Issues

One of the main problems of the Third World development is the struggle between the interests of the urban areas and those of the rural areas. The question is always one of either the urban areas must be developed for the best long lasting economic results, or the rural areas must receive more attention, because poverty is more visible there. First and foremost, poverty is severe in the rural areas, though it is also highly observed in urban areas.

Rural poverty is endemic among the poor households in the Third World, and manifests itself in a number of ways; among others malnutrition, hunger and disease. The groups which are affected include the landless, the near-landless, female-headed households and children. Harrison (1993) gives a good account of the extent and magnitude of the problem. Identifying a number of causes of the problem of poverty and tackling them with a view to possible solutions, will not eliminate poverty. The situation is extremely complex with many external and internal factors that exercise influences. Moreover, these factors are mutually influencing and strengthening to further complicate the situation.

A knowledging the complexity of causes of poverty, one can accept that rural poverty is created by a number of closely-linked processes that are mainly policy-induced. In many developing countries, national policies and institutions have built-in biases which exclude the poor from the benefits of development. The most important of these is urban bias which pre-empts resources from rural households (Lele & Adu-Nayko, 1992).

Institutional biases are a lack of access to productive assets such as land and water. Others are families in arrangements such as lack of access to credit and inputs, and lack of grassroots institutions to encourage people's participation.

Land Issues in Development

The crisis of poverty and food production has directed attention to the question of land and land tenure issues in some developing countries. Land is the source of livelihood for most people in the Third World where the majority of population live in the rural areas, and yet the land issues have remained unsolved in most of the region (Okoth-Ogendo:1993). In a study on world rural poverty, Jaizairy *et al*. (1992) found that access to land, particularly arable land for the poors, had declined. The path to sustainable growth for the poors is access to productive assets, the most important of which is land. A crucial determinant of income distribution and wealth is the distribution of land rights for the poorest of the poors in the Third World.

In many developing countries, landlessness has given rise to overcrowding and land degradation as people tried to make a living out of the meagre pieces on land on which they live, and this is one of the reasons land reform is about, how land is owned, and how patterns of ownership change. Land reform is said to be the only means of altering inequitable owner structures for effective development of participatory institutions, local and national (Doener:1972, Prosteman *et al*., 1990).

Integrated Rural Development

Rural problems are too many and diverse, and need more to be dealt with. That is to say, there are more that should form part of the framework for rural development in the developing world. At the same time, it is also important to identify the actors in rural development. What is often observed in the developing countries is that, the elite actors' actions are more cityward; they are more involved in urban projects which are more rewarding. However, integrated rural development is highly essential in multiple dimensions in these countries.

We can, therefore, state that rural development is not only to provide relief to the poors, but to eradicate poverty by *inter alia*, primarily addressing the following issues:

- *Equal Treatment*: This covers the problem of distribution, enrichment of the elite, corruption, and empowerment of the poors.
- *Land Tenure*: That includes rural development, access to land etc.
- *Migration and Population Pressure*: That means, rural-urban migration is closely related to both rural and urban development. There is also an integration between migration and rural production capacity.

Shift in development thinking from large scale economic development and self-sufficient development also requires adjustments in the implementation of rural development. This does not mean that industrialization and economic development are no longer acceptable. The difference lies in the fact of a shift in emphasis in which the knowledge, abilities, needs and interests of the poors are put first by means of a process of empowerment. This means that the people's basic needs as defined by themselves, are satisfied, and that social security is provided. However, in order to ensure sustainable development, and in particular rural development, each person and community must handle its own resources and environment with the necessary care.

Conclusion

While it is acknowledged that eradicating both rural and urban poverty is a phenomenal task, it is important to realize that it is impossible to give preference to one area to the detriment of the other. This approach has led to cityward migration, which has merely transferred rural poverty to even urban areas. Apart from the fact that certain key issues such as access to land needs specific attention, it is clear that a balanced approach is needed; and more, an all-out strategy is necessary where a clear policy will enumerate agenda items for specific actors to act on. Only in this way, can the problem of rural development be tackled successfully. Luckily, as our study has shown, the poors have shown their perseverance and enterprise. They just need the vehicle of a strategy and programme for them to play a major part in the rural development.

REFERENCES

Chambers, R., 1983, *Rural Development, Putting the Last First*, London, Longman.

Dorner, P., 1972, *Land Reform and Economic Development*, Hardmondsworth, Penguin.

Goldstein, S., 1983, Migration and Development in: Goldscheider, C. (ed), *Urban Migrants in Developing Nations: Pattern and Problems of Adjustment*, Boulder, Westview Press.

Harrison, P., 1993, *Inside the Third World: The Anatomy of Poverty*. Harmondsworth: Penguin.

Jaizairy, T., *et al.*, 1992, *The State of World Rural Poverty: An Inquiry into its Causes and Consequences*, New York, New York University Press.

Lele, U. and Adu-Nayko, K., 1992, *Approaches to Uprooting Poverty in Africa*, Food Policy 17(2).

Okoth-Ogendo, H.W.O., 1993, Agrarian Reform in Sub-Saharan Africa, Basset, T.J., and Crunmey, D.E. (eds.), *Land in Africa, Agrarian Systems*, Madison University of Wisconsin Press.

Prosterman, R.L., *et al.*, 1990, *Agrarian Reform and Grassroots Development*, Boulder, Lynne Reiner.

Taori, K., *et al.*, 1995, Rural Industrialization, New Delhi, Vikas Publishing House, Pvt. Ltd.

World Population Data Sheet, 2007, Population Reference Bureau, New York.

17

Does Social Capital Make Good Business Sense? Reflections on Rational Choice and Value Management

PRASENJIT MAITI

Introduction

Social Capital as an analytical tool can be used in the field of Business Management to facilitate different business practices from both an ethical angle and a utilitarian perspective. Business managers should try to entrench networks of trust, loyalty and cooperation within and without their organizations. This also makes good business sense in terms of rational choice theory.

Good business is also about establishing customer-friendly images in a manner that highlights values such as reliability, trustworthiness, quality, economy and durability. These values evolve over time and are underpinned by a sustained relationship of confidence. So specific products more often than not become identified with brand names either for niche or for broadbased markets. Brand equity and positioning so generally depend upon the successful merchandizing of products and their images.

Theoretical Underpinnings

The *problematique* of this chapter is structured around the polemic of civil societal institutions (networks and embeddedness) and democratic governance (inclusive growth and participatory development) among other critical areas of social scientific research. This line of theoretical research is expected to contribute new knowledge and facilitate innovative research to better understand the interactions and interplay between actors and their institutions.

The politics of everyday life and human development are generally informed by the dynamics of choice and the strategies of cooperation. This tension can be somewhat resolved by adopting the social capital approach, as inclusive growth can more often than not be ensured by empowered choices and delegated actions.

The above contention is supported by the World Bank's perception of social capital. The Bank tends to apply the lessons learnt from various projects funded under its auspices in the light of community fabric, collective trust and networks of cooperation sustained by the ethos of multi-stakeholder dialogues.

This highlights the importance of social capital in all our grand as well as small narratives today in a world where economic signifiers and their signified meanings are more or less in a state of constant flux provoked by the marketplace of politics and the social as well as cultural rhetoric of globalization.

The Bank has also championed the Think Globally Act Locally slogan while the Millennium Development Goals themselves are a construct of social capital that require meaningful negotiations with the perceptions of disengaged civil societies and panoptic state systems.

Ideas and Images

It may appear to be rather far-fetched to deploy a highly specialized social scientific theoretical category like Social Capital in the area of Business Management and Industrial Relations. The latter is a network of relationships that enter into professional dynamics with one another in the highly charged world of business informed by factors such as the profit motive, ethical applications, Corporate Social Responsibility, conflict resolution and a sense of accountability *vis-à-vis* the environment, sustainable development and inclusive growth.

So innovative ideas supported by creative images are required to streamline Industrial Relations in the post-globalized scenario that predicates upon both a breakdown of barriers as well as establishment of new and difficult barriers in the cyber world of netizens, their perceived expectations and their ever-increasing sense of achievements and complex role performances.

So we have to understand the *problematique* of the increasing hiatus between business managers and their employees in the context of relative deprivation that may be either incremental or else decremental in nature. The critical ploy that has to be strategized in this connection is the network of inter-dependence that depends upon the fluctuating degrees of trust and cooperation and overall organizational health of any given industry.

Role of Trust

A perspective analysis of the dynamics of trust in any business organization happens to be a most problematic exercise that has to be carried out over a period of time and that involves multiple stakeholders as well. Why should one trust his/her peers, superiors and subordinates? Is trust a construct of culture specifics? Can trust be equated with the given socio-politico-economic realities of any spatio-temporal context? Can trust be learnt or emulated? Can trust be analyzed in terms of cost-benefit calculations?

These are rather disquieting questions with no unilinear answers. Business leaders have to realize that the pedagogics of trust and resilience of professional relationships can only be tested against either hypothetical or real life situations where the actual motivations, aspirations, perceptions, preferences and culture root paradigms of individuals or groups are explicitly exposed in the given context of their informed self-interest.

Trust happens to be a matter of choices that is not altogether different from the various other choices we make during the course of an ordinary day. But choices are also inspired and conditioned by values that are established standards of social interactions and constantly relearnt during the life of organizations and the professionals who sustain such organizations.

But trust is also a societal resource that is limited by its very nature, as individuals more often than not put their own self-interest first rather than the interest of their respective organizations. The core challenge is to translate these small narratives of power into a grand narrative of preference that would ultimately facilitate a transition of business culture of given organizations.

So the game that is to be played by the different parties concerned would be to transcend the *actors and institutions* model to the *actors in institutions* prototype. This would be a game that requires a multiplicity of stakeholders and a plethora of their interests that would finally be integrated in an overarching design of motivations, aspirations and role performance.

When disjointed players start to commence upon the game upon a somewhat level playfield then emerges the ever-critical issues of entitlements and capabilities. Each and every player has got entitlements to improve upon his/her own material conditions of life, status of empowerment, value systems and catalyze the politics of everyday life. These entitlements have then to be qualitatively upgraded to the level of capabilities. So from professionals to stakeholders is a long journey of accomplishments that would institutionalize a culture of trust and cooperation in organizations for the mutual benefit of all the concerned stakeholders.

Reciprocity of Trust

Trust and cooperation happen to be dynamic aspects of human behaviour that are both acquired as well as achieved during the course of everyday interactive exercises. One has to appreciate that trust as an interface is perhaps more potentially real and tangible rather than trust as a construct, as the former is an arrangement of convenience, connivance and knowledge while the former is a living entity that comes across our daily social interactions as a concept that works in real time. In essence, therefore, reciprocation sustains trust while trust facilitates cooperation.

Why should one cooperate with another? Is it a learnt reflex or is it based on enlightened self-knowledge and self-interest? Would cooperation lead to intense creativity, new images, different ideas and better emotional and stress management? These questions and their answers have to be delved into and dwelled upon before we even try to garner an entire array of new knowledge on this subject.

Relationships can be built upon cooperation, competition and conflict. Each such mode will explore new models of interface and would finally lead to an inchoate world of new possibilities where men and women in the industry would steadily learn how best to unlearn past lessons and deschool themselves from the cultural baggage handed down the generations.

For one lesson is almost clear at this juncture of empirical findings *i.e.* actors will only cooperate if there are elements of confidence and potentialities of profit to be found in such bilateral or even multi-modal discourses. The architecture of social knowledge that fosters industrial relations and the microphysics of power that acts as a conducive ensemble in the background of labour welfare are, after all, situation-driven and culture-specific realities that need to be continuously re-examined against the context of changing politics and economics of the body social.

But what about the body corporate as a whole? This is an entity that can neither be enticed nor be allured into rash decisions and myopic strategies. If cost-cutting is the order of the day and free rider expenditures are on their way out, then it is also the duty of business managers to adequately sensitize their industrial work forces and integrate them in a culture of consensus without which the entire complicated domain of trust management would be severely disempowered.

Trust Management

From the management of human values to the management of corporate trust is a long, arduous and unenviable journey that requires out of the box thinking matched with the capacity to relate to the empathy of individuals. So rapport-building would appear to be a crucial requirement in this context of trust management when business leaders should be able to overcome the tedium of Human Resource Development overkill in order to efficaciously enter into revolutionary dialogues with both blue as well as white collar workers to make them chant the *mantra* of their respective organizations underpinned by their rational choices.

Rational Choice

It is somewhat difficult to estimate the rationality of a choice until the outcome of that choice is perceived either in material or else in psychological terms. Exactly *how rational a choice is* would have to be decided subsequently when the question *how utilitarian that choice was* would emerge in the future. The issue of Industrial Relations is all about the management of choices in the workplace. Why should workers obey the management? What are the concerns of the management that are reflected in its style of leadership? Is loyalty related to motivation? Or is loyalty a function of the chain of command? What are the effective outputs of hierarchy?

The entire discourse on *Discipline and Punish* is predicated upon the assumption that the State (in this case the Management) is always monitoring and evaluating the actions (and the consequences of such actions) of its Citizens (in this case the Workforce). This social scientific approach to conformity rests on the hypothesis that individuals as rational actors would intelligently choose between the options of conformity and non-conformity. While the former leads to the area of Reward Management the latter leads to theories of penology *i.e.* how to mete out punishment that would rectify and improve upon *i.e.* re-condition errant behaviour.

So the question of effective communications arises at this juncture. How effectively can managers communicate with their workers is a serious issue. Here emerge the concerns of dialogue versus pedagogue. What are the qualities of dialogue that distinguish the channels of communications from the aspects of the power-authority discourse.

Ownership/Trusteeship

The management and the workers have to mutually entrench an ethos of cooperation that would both create and sustain the values of Ownership/Trusteeship in their given organizations. One has to belong to and long for one's organization simply because organizations are the institutions of collective behaviour where people associate and interact to pursue certain set goals.

The very fact that these targets have to be achieved and new targets innovated point to the fact that the organizational health of any given industry is sound. The point of saturation has to be ably and creatively transformed into an arena of new possibilities that lead to new challenges and innovative gestures.

But achievement of targets is critically dependent on team performance, and so the team players have to share different degrees of responsibilities and have to be burdened with different measures of failures and successes. The most important consideration at this point is to determine who can shoulder what amount of burden. So the question of authoritative allocation of values has also to be pondered upon actively by the management concerned.

The issue of Ownership/Trusteeship is also almost organically related to the issue of institutions. Each business organization, in sociological terms, is an institution replete with a history of evolution, work culture, Trade Union ethics and typical management practices. So the study of business organizations as dynamic institutions of power, authority, repression, obedience, reward and punishment may lead to an ulterior understanding of Industrial Relations.

Actors and their interventions become criticalities that have to be objectively factored into the discourse of polemics that Centre on issues/concerns of Industrial Relations. The credo of loyalty is also another ponderable that may be studied or else addressed in order to appreciate the different dynamics of Social Capital, Rational Choice and Value Management.

Paradigm of Choice

The model of multiple preferences is rather complicated, as it entails different types of choices in different space, time, culture, knowledge and power discourses. The choices before a Trade Union may not always be uniform, and may be influenced by considerations like a global economic meltdown, local political tension, national emergency, social problems, regional discrepancies in development, bad economy of scale, retrenchment, cost-cutting etc.

But the critical central issue still remains the anatomy of choice: why do men and women ordinarily behave in one manner and why do they tend to behave otherwise under duress? This in itself constitutes an interesting universe of research where various factors such as values, beliefs, attitudes, inclinations, orientations, opinions etc. come into play in the wider area choice influenced by an inchoate regime of deterministic/indeterministic chaos.

Value Management

The question of moral values and business values may occasionally come across as a dichotomy, especially when the role of social values such as commitment, traditions and loyalty is concerned. The recent economic recession worldwide has prompted Big Business in India to retrench, cut costs, economize on operations, production, marketing and other strategic areas of their daily activities. But there have been instances where probationers given the pink slip were again brought back home, so to say.

This is perhaps a truly Indian phenomenon that has been also somewhat motivated by external political pressures. But this event is not to be identified with the somewhat out-of-vogue concept of Asian Values. The issue of Industrial Relations as sustained (hypothetically) by the arrangement of trust and cooperation in business is also perhaps a function of traditional Indian family values that happen to rely much more on loyalty and feudal ascriptions rather than the rational-legal structure of legitimacy and authority.

Culture as Capital

Culture is what we use while civilization is what we are. If we are to understand conflicts, stress and negotiations in business in a somewhat new light then we also have to appreciate the role of culture in the politics of everyday life of organizations where individuals engage themselves in pursuing different forms of economic activities.

Culture as capital can contribute effectively to the body corporate by defining the various role performances of the multiple stakeholders concerned in industry. Both the management and the workers can experiment successfully with different types of cultural modes relevant to their industry.

Senior business leaders in India occasionally make it a point to organize brainstorming sessions where even junior managers, worker representatives and Trade Union leaders can voice their own ideas about better productivity, new R&D, innovative marketing, revolutionary designs and improved economy of scale.

So it appears that both choices and voices have to be entrenched in the domain of better business sense boosted by motivation, inspiration, trust and cooperation. The more broadbased this industrial dialogue happens to be, the better would be the chances to experiment in a more creative manner with the changes that lead to overall better management of business organizations.

Change as Resource

Organizational change can be perceived as an industrial relational resource that can be utilized by different stakeholders to add value to their concerned industries. It is not always quite easy to address change in organizations, as multiple players find it more often than not difficult to cope with transformations and transitions. Organizational development, evolution and health depend upon targeting moving goals that are continuously in a state of flux.

But how really to use change as an organizational resource? Changes can take place in terms of qualities of output, levels of production, modernizing technologies, innovative methodologies, deschooled pedagogics and radically different marketing strategies. Such changes *vis-à-vis* organizations can even be studied in the context of the Guest-Host discourse where changes are not perceived as ghosts of spatio-temporal realities but rather as guests in the context of host organizations.

So change can also be sustained as a resource in the context of organizational change and metamorphosis. Whenever changes occur, there are sweeping as well as drastic effects on the levels of motivation, business strategies, styles of leadership performance, marketing techniques, economies of scale, interpersonal relationships, priority areas and preferential values. It is imperative that this phenomenon of change should be managed by professionals to yield better results and add enhanced value to the concerned organizations.

Change Management

The management of change is a critical discourse. It takes place at the levels of perception, motivation, attitude and leadership. How best to motivate both the management and the workers to coordinate business activities under a different regime of change is often a fascinating study that can lead to exciting new insights related to the organic realities of organizations. How people try to cope with stress and strain, conquer their anxieties and worries, battle with their learnt values against new values and finally emerge as either winners or else losers is a crucial exercise that impinges upon the working of processes, products and arrangement of realities both within and outside organizations.

Change Management is basically a function of strategized cultures pitted against fractured realities. The way in which the owners, managers and workers perceive reality/realities may be radically different from one another. Their perceptions are conditioned by their Culture Root Paradigms that constitute the overarching rhetoric of change of their organizations. Change can both create and destroy.

So Industrial Relations as a dynamic of Business Organizations can also serve as a metaphor of change against the overall backdrop of ethical applications in business. How objectively to wield any given technology, how to cohere and conjoin angularities in attitudes, how to add to the existing stock of Social Capital by sustaining working relationships in business etc. can arguably constitute the first step towards building what social scientists and field practitioners engaged in the Development Sector tend to address as Multi-Stakeholder Dialogues.

Multi-Stakeholder Dialogue

Such a dialogic mode of interaction involving multiple actors (and their roles) as well as different stakeholders (with their own typical interest/s in the organization concerned) is not always easy to institutionalize as a new credo of organizational reality. Tripartite talks between the Government, Management and labour may be cited here as a rudimentary example of such multi-level, multi-faceted and multi-functional dialogues. But Labour Laws and social welfare legislation apart, these dialogues are essential to understand in consensus the aims, aspirations and both long- and short-term business strategies of organizations.

One of the basic objectives of multi-sectoral stakeholder dialogues is to move away from the merely welfarist, altruistic and pluralistic orientation of organizations to a given mode of multi-culturalism that has to be learnt, lived with and assiduously practiced in order to transcend everyday realities to an aura of a changed way of business life. Post-postmodern societies have to desperately try and learn the post-global manner of existence where almost nothing is permanent, so to say. Markets change and clientele change while entire economies go through phases of radicalization that tend to impart new meanings to business strategies and ethical applications.

So the entire gamut of signifiers and signifieds also change and cater to further transitions in business organizations stylized and dictated by the polyphony of voices. These voices are supported by choices of change, regime of discourse and strategies of organizational development. The plethora of voices is an indicator of change in terms of both process and progress, although these are rather value-loaded expressions. So the more vibrant dialogues become the more adequate is their scope to include. Because if modern business today happens to stress increasingly upon Sustainable Development and Inclusive Growth, then it also becomes a necessary commitment to emphasize more on the broadbased nature of quality and multiple dialogues that encompass the small narratives of power and authority.

Business Sense

So it would appear that good or bad business sense impinges more upon the multiplicity of dialogues rather than decisions taken in isolation. So the analyses with regard to processes and progress necessarily indicate whether business decisions and/or solutions would be sustainable in the long or short run. An examination of perspective is important to both assess and understand the criticality of business sense in the context of improved Industrial Relations.

So how does one ensure better relations in business while at the same moment trying to make higher profits? This decision can only be made after a Knowledge Attitude Perception study is undertaken to evaluate the comparative benefits/estimates between better business relations and higher profits. Ethical applications in business activities should also be actively considered in this connection.

Ethical Applications

The combination of business sense with ethical sense is a utilitarian, altruistic as well profiteering strategy that is difficult to follow conscientiously in the real world. Individuals are not always driven by ethical aspirations. It is a given fact of life that we generally follow the predatory instincts of our personal profit motives. The challenge is to inculcate the best possible fit between profits and ethics, immediate gains and strategic alliances, present temptations and future goodwill. A modicum of balance has to be struck in this context so that the different types of extraneous and internal variables that tend to influence such a process of decision/policy-making can be balanced in an almost rational manner.

Our ethical selves may not always be our instinctive beings. It is a metaphysical question of existence versus sustenance, learnt values versus inherent proclivities and cost-benefit analyses between the self-satisfying self and the social satisfying other.

When such conflicts between the otherness of the other and the openness of the self tend to be reconciled in the context of specific industry and general society, then the other uncomfortable questions regarding globalized dichotomies, the Digital Divide and the inchoateness of the self versus the nascent sense of otherness emerge.

Sociability Discourse

So finally we are led to the direction of the sociability of business *i.e.* how social is business and how widespread and traumatic/therapeutic are the remedial effects of value applications to any given industry. Are workers now being consulted, are their priorities and preferences being listened to, are they more confident in the management, bolstered by the thought that retrenchment and lay-off would not be enforced until absolutely imperative? Power plays become operational at this juncture when not only the social and cultural aspects of business but also the political and economic facets of the industry have to be accounted for to study the art of resolution of conflicts at the workplace.

Conflict Resolution

Conflicts of interest that arise from clash of values, attitudes, perceptions, orientations and values are occasionally constructs of different cultures. The manner in which actors engage in conflicts and lock horns with each other over issues of preferences and priorities often emerge from skewed realities where the concerned parties are located at different levels and on different levels of cultural ensemble and trappings of power.

Because conflicts primarily begin at the level of knowledge where the mind is constantly busy weighing different options. The manner in which individuals approach conflicts is also rather culture specific. The issue of Industrial Relations can be better understood if the fragmented concerns of conflict are better appreciated. Conflicts at the higher echelons of power are more about abstract/ intangible realities such as power, authority, prestige, esteem, influence and access to the repository of high-end corporate values.

Insights and Enigmas

The insights dwelled upon in the course of this chapter and the enigmas studied tend to open up an entire new discourse of possibilities and politics that correlate Business Sense, Corporate Social Responsibility, Social Capital and Ethical Applications.

The more intricate and intrinsic happens to be the question of Industrial Relations, the more complicated becomes the entire debate of Social Capital. Because the specifics of trust, value and cooperation predicated by the realities of corporate networking and social embeddedness are inherently highlighted in the context of better performance, enhanced interactions and complex commitments of the industry to the market, clientele, quality, pricing and Corporate Social Responsibility.

Conclusion

While winding up this chapter it is important to retain the lessons that were learnt and the best practices identified during the theoretical discourse of drafting our original argument about Business Sense *vis-à-vis* Social Capital and Rational Choice Theory.

It lies in the rational interest of the concerned stakeholders to cooperate among themselves, make collective decisions and approach both the present and the future in a consolidated manner. This can be a viable way in which to sustain organizations in the face of the threats triggered by Globalization. But these threats can also be translated into potential opportunities.

The Market, Civil Society and State happen to interact in a dynamic manner that also tends to convert Weaknesses into Strengths in a post-globalized world. But the mode of inclusion of Social Capital Theory within the ambit of the discourse of Industrial Relations is a new benchmark that may lead to interesting new research in this area and collate new theories in the light of new facts and new possibilities.

REFERENCES

Bjørnskov, C. (2004), 'The economic use of social capital: The income relation', in M. Paldam, and G.T. Svendsen (eds.), *Trust, Social Capital and Economic Growth: An International Comparison*, Cheltenham, UK: Edward Elgar, Ch. 7 (forthcoming).

Beugelsdijk, S. Smulders, J.A. (2004), "Bridging and bonding social capital: Which type is good for growth?" In Arts, W. Hagenaars, J. and Halman, L. (Ed.), *The Cultural Diversity of European Unity: Findings, Explanations and Reflections from the European Values Study*, Brill European Values Studies, EVS 6. Koninklijke Brill N.V., Leiden, pp. 147-185.

Bjørnskov, C. (2004), 'The economic use of social capital: The income relation', in M. Paldam, and G.T. Svendsen (eds.), *Trust, Social Capital and Economic Growth: An International Comparison, Cheltenham*, UK: Edward Elgar, Ch. 7 (forthcoming).

Boix, C. and D.N. Posner (1998), 'Social capital: Explaining its origins and effects on Government performance', *British Journal of Political Science*, 28(4), 686-93.

Bourdieu, P. (1979a) 'Le capital social' [Social capital], Actes de la recherche en sciences sociales, 31, 2-3.

Bourdieu, P. (1986), 'The forms of capital', in J.G. Richardson (ed.) *Handbook of Theory and Research for the Sociology of Education*, New York, Westport, CT and London: Greenwood Press, pp. 241-58.

Burt, R.S. (2000). "The Network Structure of Social Capital". *Research in Organisational Behaviour*, Vol. 22, pp. 1-83.

Burt, R.S. (2007). *Brokerage and Closure: An Introduction to Social Capital*. Oxford University Press, Oxford. Forthcoming.

Chloupkova, J., G.L.H. Svendsen and G.T. Svendsen (2003), 'Building and destroying Social Capital: The case of cooperative movements in Denmark and Poland', *Agriculture and Human Values*, 20(3), 241-252.

Coleman, J.S. (1984) "Introducing social structure into economic analysis". *The American Economic Review*, 74 (2), 84-88.

Coleman, J.S. (1988a), 'Social capital in the creation of human capital', *American Journal of Sociology*, 94, 95-121.

Coleman, J.S. (1988b), 'The creation and destruction of social capital: Implications for the law', *Journal of Law, Ethics and Public Policy*, 3, 375-404.

Coleman, J.S. (1990), *Foundations of Social Theory*, Cambridge, MA: Harvard University Press.

Prasenjit Maiti, *Development Ethics* (New Delhi: Concept, 2008).

Prasenjit Maiti and Gunnar Lind Haase Svendsen *et al.* (eds.), *Social Capital*, Vols. 1 and 2 (New Delhi: Atlantic, 2008).

Social Capital Gateway (edited by Fabio Sabatini).

URL <http://www.socialcapitalgateway.org/>

Index